# A CASTE IN A CHANGING WORLD

# A Caste in a Changing World

## *The Chitrapur Saraswat Brahmans, 1700–1935*

FRANK F. CONLON

MANOHAR
2026

First published by University of California Press in 1977
Reprinted 2022, 2023, 2024, 2025, 2026



ISBN 978-81-944962-2-9

*Published by*
Ajay Kumar Jain *for*
Manohar Publishers & Distributors
4753/23 Ansari Road, Daryaganj
New Delhi 110 002

*Printed at*
Replika Press Pvt. Ltd.

TO MY PARENTS

*J. Edward Conlon and Helen Fowler Conlon*

# CONTENTS

# LIST OF MAPS AND TABLES

## MAPS



## TABLES

# PREFACE

THIS BOOK is an attempt to understand the historical development of an Indian caste from the eighteenth to twentieth centuries and thereby to illuminate both the workings of that institution and the effects upon it of British colonial rule. Originally the book was to have been entitled: "Amchi Gelé"—a Konkani expression meaning roughly "this of our own"—used by the Saraswat Brahmans when referring to themselves, their caste and that which belongs to their caste. Unfortunately the phrase, which symbolized very well the subject of the study, could not convey the book's content to a wider public, and thus the present title was chosen. Initial field work was undertaken in 1965–1967 under an N.D.E.A.-related Fulbright-Hayes Fellowship which permitted me a stay in India of eighteen months, and in England of seven. I was enabled to do further research in England in 1970 and India in 1971 by support from the Far Eastern and Russian Institute and Graduate School of the University of Washington and the American Institute of Indian Studies. Just as none of these organizations attempted to control or direct my research, so too they bear no responsibility for the content of the work.

Commencing in the Ames Library of South Asia at the University of Minnesota, I had the benefit of the services of many librarians and their staffs. I must particularly mention the great assistance I received at the India Office Library; the British Museum; the Library of the School of Oriental and African Studies, University of London; and the Centre for South Asian Studies, University of Cambridge, in Great Britain. In India, the Librarian and Deputy Librarian of the University of Bombay Library; the Librarians of the Asiatic Society of Bombay and the Mumbai Marathi Grañtha Sangrahalaya; the Directors of Archives, Maharashtra State; and the Secretariat Record Office and the Madras Record Office, all placed me greatly in their debt.

Many individuals directly or indirectly aided me in my work

in India. I must begin with a special acknowledgment of H.H. Shrimat Anandashram Swamiji and H.H. Shrimat Parijñanashram Swamiji of Shri Chitrapur *Maṭha*. So many Saraswats welcomed me into their homes and gave me assistance and encouragement that I fear mention of a few will do injustice to the rest. Nevertheless, I wish to thank the officers of the Kanara Saraswat Association and other caste organizations for granting me access to various materials. Others in Bombay, Bhanap and non-Bhanap, who must be mentioned include the late Mr. F. D. Nanavati and Mrs. Nanavati, Mr. and Mrs. Dara Sinor, Aman Momin, P. G. Sirur, Professor A. K. Priolkar, V. R. Bhende, S. G. Bhatkal, L. S. Dabholkar, G. L. Chandavarkar, C. S. Varde, N. B. Rangnekar, and Ramesh Nirody. Dr. Gopal S. Hattiangdi and his family, also in Bombay, must know that without them this book would not have been written. I cannot adequately express my debt to Dr. Hattiangdi.

Elsewhere in India, I am obligated to numerous individuals and institutions who welcomed and patiently assisted my efforts. In Poona, Dr. and Mrs. Y. B. Damle and R. V. Nadkarni were of great help. At Bangalore, R. G. Philar removed many obstacles from my path. There too I was aided by Kilpadi Guru Dutt, Mrs. Radha J. Sujir, and the late Kapnadak Guru Dutt. At Madras, G. R. Shirale and J. S. Prabhu inconvenienced themselves too often on my behalf. In North and South Kanara, special mention should be made of Sujir Sundarrao in Shirali, who patiently led me through the confusing documentation of Shri Chitrapur *Maṭha*; M. R. Karnad in Udipi; and at Mangalore, K. Shankar Rao, Y. Babu Rao, N. Rama Rao, A. R. Nadkarni, G. Somashekar Rao, and M. V. Bhandarkar. There I was also given access to materials relating to the Basel Mission by the Reverend B. Furtado of the Kanara Theological College. When I reflect upon the open, hospitable assistance and guidance given me during my work, I cannot but wonder what my reactions would have been if a young Indian scholar were to appear at my door in Seattle announcing that he was studying my family's history and the problems of the Irish-American community.

Several scholars in this country gave me the benefits of good teaching, guidance, and critical advice, particularly Professors Burton Stein, David Kopf, Morris D. Morris, Maureen L. P. Patterson, and D. R. Gustafson. Special mention must be made also of several persons who assisted me in problems of translation of Kannada materials: G. Gopinath Bhat and P. Prabhakar Rao at Mangalore, and later in America, Shankar Shetty and H. V. Nagaraja Rao. In the preparation of the manuscript, Mrs. Sylvia Wells-Henderson skillfully completed the typing, and Mrs. Alice Alden drafted the illustrative maps. All of these people have contributed to what merits this book may possess. All of its shortcomings are solely my responsibility.

Finally I owe much to my family. My wife, Joan Catoni Conlon, has been a thoughtful and gentle critic without whose support and encouragement this project might never have been completed. My aunt, Neva F. Fowler, generously provided moral and material support throughout my education. I am dedicating this book to my parents who, with their honesty, humanity, humor, enthusiasm for life, and interest in its beauties, first set me on the road to Bombay.

*Seattle, Washington* FRANK F. CONLON
*August 1975*

# ABBREVIATIONS USED IN NOTES

| | |
|---|---|
| B. E. M. | Basel German Evangelical Mission |
| *BHCR* | *Bombay High Court Reports* |
| *Bom. Gaz.* | *Gazetteer of the Bombay Presidency* |
| BRP | Bombay Revenue Proceedings |
| E. D. | Education Department (Consultations) |
| G. D. | General Department (Consultations) |
| IOL | India Office Library, London |
| IOR | India Office Records, London |
| *ISR* | *Indian Social Reformer* |
| *K. S.* | *Kanara Saraswat* |
| K. S. A. | Kanara Saraswat Association |
| MBRMR | Madras Board of Revenue: Miscellaneous Records |
| MBRP | Madras Board of Revenue Proceedings |
| MEP | Madras Education Proceedings |
| *Madras N. N. Rept.* | *Madras Native Newspaper Reports* |
| MRO | Madras Record Office |
| MRP | Madras Revenue Proceedings |
| M. S. A. | Maharashtra State Archives |
| R. D. | Revenue Department |
| R. S. C. M. | Records of Shri Chitrapur *Maṭha* |
| SRBG | Selections from the Records of Bombay Government |
| SRMG | Selections from the Records of Madras Government |
| SRSC | Selections from the Records of the Collector of South Canara |
| SRO | Secretariat Record Office, Bombay |
| S. V. C. Bank | Shamrao Vithal Co-operative Bank, Ltd. |

# PERSONS INTERVIEWED

His Holiness Shrimat Anandashram Swamiji, at Bangalore, June 4, 1966.

His Holiness Shrimat Parijñanashram Swamiji, at Bombay, Nov. 1, 1966, and Jan. 13, 1971.

Ved. Aldangadi Lakshman Bhat, at Ullal, S. K., Feb. 20, 1971.

Ved. Vasant A. Bhat, at Shirali, N. K., Feb. 15, 1971.

Shri Sadanand G. Bhatkal, at Bombay, May 18, 1966, and March 23, 1971.

*Shri V. R. Bhende, at Bombay, Feb. 26, 1967, and March 21, 1971.

Shri Ganesh L. Chandavarkar, at Bombay, June 17, 1966.

Shri Vinayak M. Chickermane, at Gokarn, N. K., Feb. 12 and 13, 1971.

Shri L. S. Dabholkar, at Bombay, Nov. 24, 1966, and Feb. 10, 1967.

Shri Anand V. Gangolli, at Seattle, Wash., Feb. 16, 1969; at Bombay, March 21, 1971.

Smt. Vatsala A. Gangolli, at Seattle, Wash., Feb. 16, 1969; at Bombay, March 21, 1971.

Shri G. Somashekar Rao, at Mangalore, March 24, 1967, and Feb. 21, 1971.

Shri Gulvadi Gopinath Bhat, at Mangalore, March 24, 1967.

*Dr. Gopal S. Hattiangdi, at Bombay, April 11, May 29, and Oct. 8, 1966, and March 16, 1967.

Shri Gourish V. Kaikini, at Gokarn, N. K., Feb. 12, 1971.

Shri Kapnadak Guru Dutt, at Bangalore, March 17, 1967.

Shri Mangesh R. Karnad, at Udipi, S. K., March 22, 1967, and Feb. 18, 1971.

Dr. Sumitra M. Katre, at Poona, April 25, 1966.
Shri Kilpadi Guru Dutt, at Bangalore, June 4, 1966; March 18, 1967; and Jan. 30, 1971.
Shri K. Shankar Rao, at Mangalore, March 24, 1967, and Feb. 21, 1971; at Vithal, March 25, 1967.
Shri S. D. Kombrabail, at Bantwal, S. K., March 25, 1967.
Shri Narayan R. Koppikar, at Dharwar, Feb. 11, 1971.
Dr. D. D. Kosambi, at Poona, Feb. 18, 1966.
Shri M. N. Kulkarni, at Bombay, Feb. 3 and June 14, 1966.
Shri R. A. Lajmi, at Bombay, March 18, 1971.
Shri Devadas G. Madiman, at Hubli, Feb. 9 and 10, 1971.
Dr. R. M. Masurkar, at Kumta, N. K., Feb. 14, 1971.
Dr. S. M. Masurkar, at Gokarn, N. K., Feb. 12, 1971.
Shri Molehalli Sanjiva Shivarao, at Madras, Jan. 26, 1971.
Shri A. R. Nadkarni, at Mangalore, March 25, 1967, and Feb. 21, 1971.
Shri Mangesh V. Nadkarni, at Madras, Jan. 27, 1971.
Shri Ramesh V. Nadkarni, at Poona, Dec. 7, 1966.
Shri Venkatrao S. Nadkarni, at Poona, Dec. 7, 1966.
Shri Nalkur Sripad Narsingrao, at Bombay, Feb. 28, 1971.
Shri Nayampalli Rama Rao, at Mangalore, Feb. 20., 1971.
Rao Bahadur R. N. Nayampalli, at Santa Cruz (Bombay), Feb. 5, 1971; at Bombay, Feb. 8, 1971.
Shri Padukone Prabhakar Rao, at Mangalore, Feb. 20, 1971.
Shri Ramesh Pai, at Manipal, S. K., March 22, 1967.
Shri R. R. Padbidri, at Bombay, March 18, and March 22, 1971.
Shri Pandit Shivarao, at Mangalore, Feb. 21, 1971.
*Shri Ramarao G. Philar, at Bangalore, June 4, 1966; March 11, 1967; and Jan. 30, 1971.
*Dr. Anant K. Priolkar, at Bombay, Sept. 30 and Oct. 31, 1966, and April 21, 1967.
Lady Dhanavati Ramarao, at Bombay, March 1, 1971.
Shri A. R. Savoor, at Bombay, March 22, 1971.
Shri D. G. Savoor, at Madras, Jan. 26, 1971.

Shri G. R. Shirale, at Madras, Jan. 27, 1971.

Shri N. M. Sirur, at Bangalore, Feb. 23, 1971.

*Shri P. G. Sirur, at Bombay, Sept. 14 and Dec. 4, 1966; Feb. 9, 1967; and Jan. 2, 1971.

Shri R. V. Sirur, at Hubli, Feb. 10, 1971.

*Shri Sujir Sundarrao, at Shirali, March 10, 1967, and Feb. 15 and 16, 1971.

Shri Ullal Sumitra Bhat, at Mangalore, Feb. 21, 1971.

Shri Yellur Babu Rao, at Mangalore, March 24, 1967.

Shri D. D. Yennemadi, at Bombay, Jan. 13, 1971.

*Persons thus indicated were frequently consulted; the dates and locations given in these cases are of formal, substantive interviews.

# INTRODUCTION

THIS IS a history of an Indian caste or *jāti*—the Chitrapur Saraswat Brahmans—from the eighteenth century to the twentieth. It represents an effort to better understand the institution of caste by looking at one caste and its corporate identity through an extended period of time. Historical reconstruction offers a fresh dimension for understanding the extent of transformations in Indian society brought on by colonial rule, urbanization, and industrialization. At the same time it calls into question easy assumptions concerning the changelessness of "traditional" India.

Who are the Chitrapur Saraswat Brahmans? What makes them worthy of study? Those who belong to the *jāti* number today about 21,000 persons, more than half of whom reside in the vast urban sprawl of Greater Bombay.[1] Organizations of the caste include at least 22 social and cultural associations, 11 educational institutions and scholarship funds, 4 religious associations, and 18 co-operative housing and service societies.[2] The initiative of Saraswat caste members in creating this array of institutions for the benefit of themselves and their kin has attracted comment by Indian and foreign observers interested in the place of caste in modern Indian society.[3] Some of those comments have garbled or distorted the place of such associations and organizations in the existence of the caste. The present purpose, however, is not to understand the phenomena of contemporary Saraswat activity, but to attempt to trace the history of the development of the caste itself from its "birth" in the early eighteenth century to the eve of its period of great corporate activity and prosperity in urban society, in the 1930s. The consider-

1. Kanara Saraswat Association, Census Working Committee, *Chitrapur Saraswat 1971 Census Report and Directory* (Bombay: Kanara Saraswat Association, 1972), p. 6.

2. *Ibid.*, Part 2, pp. 16–52.

3. Govind S. Ghurye, *Caste and Race in India*, 5th ed. (Bombay: Popular Prakashan, 1969), pp. 452–454, 446; Selig S. Harrison, *India: The Most Dangerous Decades* (Princeton: Princeton University Press, 1960), pp. 104–105.

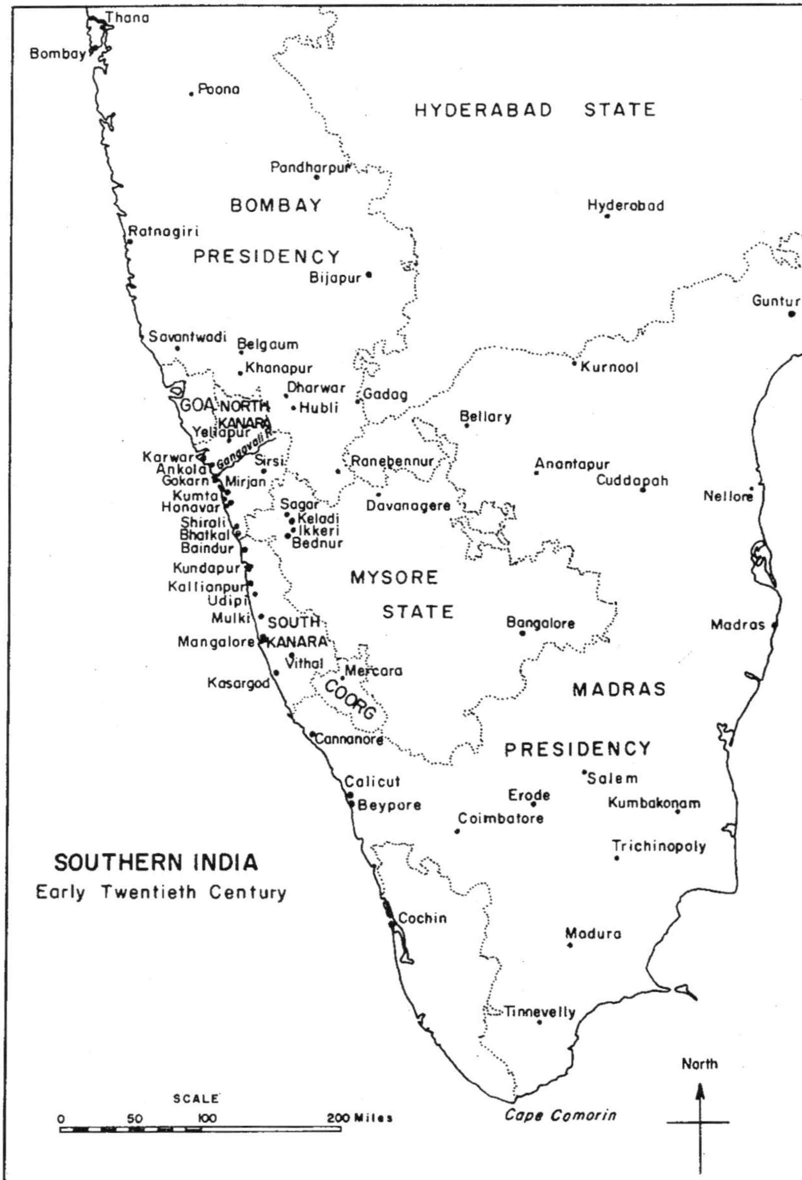


MAP 1. SOUTHERN INDIA IN THE EARLY TWENTIETH CENTURY.

able organizational achievements of the caste will be considered in the historical narrative, but a full and detailed study of Saraswat associational activity must be reserved for a later publication.

I began this work with the ideal of examining the history of a single, identifiable *jāti* to discover how the broad currents of political, economic, religious, and social change in modern India had altered or directed the development of that *jāti* and its members. On the other side of the coin, I wanted to discover whether *jāti* membership had influenced the patterns of change among its members. Put in simple form, I began asking "How has modernization affected caste, and how has caste affected modernization?" The historian's way is not smooth, and it became apparent as my research progressed that the history of the Saraswat Brahmans would not yield answers of commensurate simplicity. Nonetheless, this concern remains in the background of the narrative as it has been developed.

But why the Saraswat Brahmans? The choice has to be explained in two ways. When I began my study, I sought a *jāti* for which sufficient documentation seemed likely to exist. By virtue of previous training, I concentrated upon the Maharashtra region of western India. I had encountered references to Saraswat Brahmans, identified as a coastal elite that had played important roles in western Indian society during the past three centuries. As I began to explore the topic, I came to realize that the Saraswat Brahman label was often applied by others to any members of a large and widely dispersed cluster of castes known collectively as the Gaud Saraswat Brahmans. In exploring the multiple layers of identity I came to accept the assertion of Professor G. S. Ghurye that, while to outsiders the Saraswats were referred to as a single group, their subcastes were in fact the most important units, functioning as castes themselves.[4] It was in this belief that I settled upon examining the history of some subsection of the Gaud Saraswat universe. Chance and circumstance brought me into contact with one of these groups—the Chitrapur Saraswat Brahmans, or Saraswats, as they frequently call themselves. The availability of an extensive caste journal, historical documents, some genealogies, and other materials reinforced the choice.

A second explanation of the choice of subject is not of my construction, but merits the reader's attention. During my original

4. Ghurye, *Caste and Race*, pp. 182, 194–195.

fieldwork, I visited a number of places of Saraswat residence. At one of these the local gentlemen arranged a reception at which many kindly exaggerations were uttered about my research. The official host concluded his introduction by suggesting that in a previous existence I must surely have been a Saraswat! When I rose to return the compliments, I mentioned this point and remarked that if the law of *karma* still operated to condition rebirth in this *kaliyuga*, then, had I been a Saraswat in a previous birth, I must have committed some notorious sins to merit being reborn as a *mleccha*. The original speaker rose to explain that if it had been the will of the caste's tutelary deity, Lord Bhavanishankar, that a history of the caste was to be written, it would have been known to Him that somebody born in America would have access to the fellowships and resources necessary to the task. "Therefore," he shrugged, "it could all be arranged."

### *The Problem of Caste in Indian History*

Caste—the distinctive moral system of India which defines the population in birth-ascribed, hierarchically ranked corporate units—has stimulated the interest and analytical energies of foreigners for centuries. The Indian tradition itself provides evidence of social stratification and occupational differentiation from early times, and has identified these with the concepts of *varna* and *jāti*. The former derives from a brahmanical theory dividing society into four unequal, stratified parts; the latter originates in the sense of "birth" or "kind," applied socially to the much more numerous segments of society which foreigners called "caste." "Caste" itself is foreign—derived from the Portuguese "casta" and applied by them to describe the social system they encountered upon arriving in India. "Casta" had a meaning of breed or kind which directly paralleled the meaning of *jāti*.[5]

Discussion of caste is complicated by important distinctions of definition arising either from vagaries of observation or levels of enquiry and analysis. Some scholars have defined caste in a strictly

5. A useful discussion of definitions is contained in David G. Mandelbaum, *Society in India*, Vol. 1: *Continuity and Change* (Berkeley and Los Angeles: University of California Press, 1970), pp. 13–22. A stimulating recent interpretation of the institution may be found under "Caste Systems" [by McKim Marriot and Ronald B. Inden] in the *Encyclopedia Britannica*, 15th ed., "Macropaedia," Vol. 3, pp. 982–991.

comparative sociological framework as a type of social stratification which may operate in any culture.[6] Others have emphasized the specific place of caste within the dominant cultural system of India, that associated with Hinduism.[7] The question of cultural specificity is complicated by the cross-cutting issue of composition. Put simply, ought the term "caste" refer only to the whole hierarchical system of endogamous, birth-ascribed units, or may it refer to the component parts of that system? This matter has not been a lexographic quibble, for much of the modern literature on caste in India has assumed an existing caste system and has postulated changes therein which were subsequently found not to be occurring in the component parts, the "castes" themselves.[8] Thus caste could be described as decaying or flourishing, depending upon the perspective of the reporter and the presuppositions of what caste meant. The existence of the brahmanical concept of *varna* added a further element of potential confusion, since if all persons identified within a single *varna* were called members of "a caste," what then about the myriad smaller groups, or *jāti*? These units, recruited by birth, collectively observing endogamy and ritual commensality, are little networks of kin and potential kin that existed throughout Indian society within localities and regions. Some scholars termed these *jāti* "subcastes"; others said that they were the "real castes."[9]

Yet if *jāti*s were "castes," then the groups of which they appeared to be subdivisions must be something else. These larger aggregations of persons of seemingly related *jāti*s, "usually in the same linguistic region, usually with the same traditional occupation, and sometimes with the same name" have been referred to as "caste-categories" and "caste-clusters."[10] It seems clear that the terms "caste" and

6. Cf. Gerald D. Berreman, "Structure and Function of Caste Systems," Ch. 14 in George De Vos and Hiroshi Wagatsuma, *Japan's Invisible Race: Caste in Culture and Personality* (Berkeley and Los Angeles: University of California Press, 1972), pp. 277–307; Edward B. Harper, "A Comparative Analysis of Caste: The United States and India," in Milton Singer and Bernard S. Cohn (eds.), *Structure and Change in Indian Society* (Chicago: Aldine, 1968), pp. 51–77.

7. Cf. Louis Dumont, *Homo Hierarchicus: The Caste System and Its Implications* (London: Weidenfeld and Nicolson, 1970).

8. For a recent survey of the extensive literature on caste, see M. N. Srinivas et al. "Caste: A Trend Report and Bibliography," *Current Sociology* 8 (1959): 135–183.

9. Adrian C. Mayer, *Caste and Kinship in Central India* (Berkeley and Los Angeles: University of California Press, 1960), pp. 3–10; Ghurye, *Caste and Race*, p. 182.

10. F. G. Bailey, "Closed Social Stratification in India," *Archives Europeenes de*

"*jāti*" have been and are employed with varying degrees of specificity, depending upon context or purpose. For matrimonial negotiations, a particular "subcaste" identity would be most potent for the individual; yet in general village affairs, a "caste" identity would be commonly employed, perhaps generalized as a "caste-cluster" name. And it is known that when asked at a pilgrimage site the name of their *jāti*, some persons responded "Hindu."[11]

This matter of definitions is of concern in this book, because in my discussion of the Saraswat origins it has been necessary to examine a "caste-cluster," the Gaud Saraswat Brahmans of Goa, and sections of that cluster in various historical epochs. The available data provide precious little precision of definition. Thus the medieval ancestors of most of the Saraswats seem to have belonged in Goa to two sections of the Gaud Saraswat Brahman cluster. Yet there is insufficient evidence to establish that these sections were endogamous or otherwise corresponding to the idea of *jāti* as "caste." Rather, there is a suggestion that endogamous bounds were not tightly drawn. And when some families of these sections later moved out of Goa, they seem to have incorporated families of other Gaud Saraswat sections in a new connubium. The separateness of the Saraswats cannot be spoken of as a rigid, unchanging concept, but rather as a tendency of an identity to inhere in certain families who subsequently joined to form what is known as the Chitrapur Saraswat Brahman *jāti*. The tangled shrubbery of the narrative in the first chapters of this book reflects this inconsistency. I hope that readers will patiently pursue the overgrown path, for it traces a necessary foundation for comprehending later developments.

The study of caste, whether of caste system, caste-cluster, or *jāti*, has not included much historical research. To the extent that history has an invisible bias that stresses elements of change occurring through time, it might be proposed that early scholarly perceptions of caste as an unchanging and static system would discourage specific historical research.[12] Critics of Indian civilization pointed

*Sociologie* 4 (1963): 107; I. Karve and V. M. Dandekar, *Anthropometric Measurements of Maharashtra* (Poona: Deccan College, 1951), pp. 10–12.

11. Surinder M. Bhardwaj, *Hindu Places of Pilgrimage in India: A Study in Cultural Geography* (Berkeley and Los Angeles: University of California Press, 1973), pp. 231–232.

12. Cf. Burton Stein, "Social Mobility and Medieval South Indian Hindu Sects," in James Silverberg (ed.), *Social Mobility in the Caste System in India: An Interdisciplinary Symposium* (The Hague: Mouton, 1968), pp. 78–94.

to caste as a symptom of India's flaws, and official ethnographers sought to explore the origins of the institution, but relatively little was published specifically on the history of caste.[13] This may reflect other interests and priorities of earlier generations of historians as well.

Historical theorizing on caste was based mainly on secondary materials or translations of texts.[14] At least one of these studies attempted to come to terms with the presumed changes in Indian caste that were even then transpiring in British India. Karl Marx expected that in the modern state arising from British colonial rule, the traditional social order that had been characterized by caste would be shattered and replaced by a modern class society.[15] Later studies surveying the broad features of Indian society implicitly or explicitly accepted this perception that the break-up of the old social order was an inevitable concomitant of modern developments, including urbanization.[16] However, examinations of India since the attainment of independence in 1947 have indicated that, contrary to previous expectations, caste is alive and apparently flourishing in even the most innovative and changeful circumstances.[17] But this finding in part has reflected a scholarly shift in emphasis from caste, the system, to caste, the component. Indeed, "caste" has acquired an additional definition as a quasi-voluntary association recruited on the basis of birth within a single *jāti* or from among related *jāti*s, directed toward protection of corporate self-interests and social amelioration, often in competition with other similar groups in fields of political action.[18]

Because this development entailed competition rather than interdependence among "castes," some anthropologists have been

13. An exception was Shridhar V. Ketkar, *The History of Caste in India*, 2 vols. [Vol. 2 entitled *An Essay on Hinduism: Its Formation and Future*] (Ithaca, N. Y.: Taylor & Carpenter, 1909; London: Luzac, 1911).

14. Cf. J. D. M. Derrett, "The Administration of Hindu Law by the British," *Comparative Studies in Society and History* 4 (November 1961): 10–51.

15. Karl Marx and Friedrich Engels, *The First Indian War of Independence* (Moscow: Foreign Languages Press, 1959), p. 36.

16. Max Weber, *The Religion of India* (Glencoe, Ill.: Free Press, 1958), p. 112; Kingsley Davis, *The Population of India and Pakistan* (Princeton: Princeton University Press, 1951), pp. 170–171.

17. Harold A. Gould, "The Adaptive Functions of Caste in Contemporary Indian Society," *Asian Survey* 3 (1963): 427–438.

18. Lloyd I. Rudolph and Susanne H. Rudolph, "The Political Role of India's Caste Associations," *Pacific Affairs* 28 (1955): 235–253; M. N. Srinivas, *Caste in Modern India and Other Essays* (Bombay: Asia Publishing House, 1962), pp. 15–41.

inclined to see the situation as an antithesis of caste, stressing that caste may be properly understood only as "a system of interrelationship" within a specific, interdependent local arena.[19] This persuasive doctrine has not prevailed, however. The "survival" of castes has continued to be commented upon. This "survival" has itself been reexamined in light of the fact that many of the systemic features which characterized caste organization during the past century seem now to have decayed, even while their caste indentities persevere. One scholar has specifically asserted:

> In many ways that intriguing quality of caste—its ability to bend to the new kinds of social change in India, but not to completely snap—is more an artifact of anthropological vagueness about what "caste" is, than any inordinate elasticity in the social institution itself.[20]

Professor Fox's point is well taken. But it seems to me that some of the vagueness may be laid at the door of the castes and their members themselves. This becomes evident when a *jāti* is made the focus of historical study. The classical definitions of caste do not easily accommodate the full range of possible fission and fusion processes which lie in the background of what at a given moment may be seen as a unified and clearly bounded group. Retrospective consideration of a caste thus pragmatically becomes the study of the identifiable ancestors of that caste. If caste were historically the static, traditionally immutable institution that many have assumed it to be, this qualification would be unnecessary.

Surprisingly little has been published by way of analysis of specific *jātis* in Indian culture and society. Anthropological researches predominate, including Louis Dumont's extensive monograph on the Pramai Kallar of Tamilnad, Stephen Fuchs' study of a central Indian untouchable community, and David Pocock's works on the Patidars of Gujarat.[21] Robert Hardgrave's analysis of

19. E. R. Leach (ed.), *Aspects of Caste in South India, Ceylon and Northwest Pakistan* (Cambridge: Cambridge University Press, 1962), p. 10.

20. Richard G. Fox, "Resiliency and Change in the Indian Caste System: The Umar of U. P.," *Journal of Asian Studies* 26 (1967): 575.

21. Louis Dumont, *Une Sous-Caste de L'Inde du Sud: Organisation Sociale et Religion des Pramalai Kallar* (Paris: Mouton, 1957); Stephen Fuchs, *The Children of Hari: Study of the Nimar Balahis in the Central Provinces of India* (Vienna: Herold, 1950); David F. Pocock, *Kanbi and Patidar: A Study of the Patidar Community of Gujarat* (Oxford: Clarendon Press, 1972). Other recent caste-centered studies include Klass W. Van den Veen, *I Give Thee My Daughter: A Study of Marriage and Hierarchy*

the political mobilization of the Nadars of South India has added another dimension to the study of caste and change.[22] At least two historians, Karen Leonard and Ronald Inden, have completed doctoral dissertations on aspects of caste history.[23] The writing of caste history in India has been proceeding during the past century, particularly in Indian languages. These have generally not focused upon the corporate features and identity of respective castes, but have emphasized Puranic myths of origins and/or the achievements of notable elites within their membership in modern times.[24]

## *The Pattern of Saraswat History*

What then does the history of the Saraswats tell us? It suggests a pattern through which the core of a *jāti* was formed by members of a few families in roughly similar circumstances with a presumption of common background. The endogamy was not absolute, for more families joined in the connubium. Yet the separation implicit in endogamy was underwritten through obtaining recognition from the ruler of the territories wherein the *jāti* members resided. This recognition was held by tradition to be dependent itself upon the agreement of the Saraswats' ancestors to place themselves under a spiritual preceptor. Allegiance to *swami* was a mark of brahmanical status in the region of Saraswat residence. Because earlier preceptorial ties of the Saraswats were to *gurus* who lay beyond the frontiers of the existing regional kingdom, creation

---

*Among Anavil Brahmans of South Gujarat* (Assen: Van Gorcum, 1972); R. S. Khare, *The Changing Brahmans: Associations and Elites among the Kanya-Kubjas of North India* (Chicago: University of Chicago Press, 1970).

22. Robert L. Hardgrave, Jr., *The Nadars of Tamilnad: The Political Culture of a Community in Change* (Berkeley and Los Angeles: University of California Press, 1969).

23. Ronald Inden, *Marriage and Rank in Bengali Culture* (Berkeley and Los Angeles: University of California Press, 1976); Karen Leonard's work has not yet been published. Cf. Karen Leonard, "The Kayasths of Hyderabad City: Their Internal History, and Their Role in Politics and Society from 1850 to 1900" (University of Wisconsin, Ph.D dissertation, 1969).

24. Examples of this literature from the Maharashtra region include Viṣṇu Vāsudev Āṭhalye, *Karhāḍe Brāhmaṇāñcā Itihāsa* [History of the Karhada Brahmans] (Poona: Sitabai Karandikar, Shake 1869 (A. D. 1947]; Vishwanath Ganpatrao Mankar (pub.), *History of a Section of the Pathare Prabhu Community commonly known as Kanchole Prabhus* (Bombay, 1931) Cf. also P. B. Joshi, *History of the Pathare Prabhus and their Gurus and Spiritual Guides* (Bombay, 1914).

of a new alliance within its boundaries was necessary. The effect of this creation of a new, separate allegiance to a distinctive spiritual lineage of *gurus* (*guruparampara*) provided a source of religious guidance, status protection, and preservation of caste purity through the *swamis*' actions as social controllers.

During the eighteenth century A. D. the Saraswats' *gurus* toured among their devotees, calling upon them to fully accept the *gurus*' spiritual guidance and to bring their lives into conformity with the behaviors appropriate to *dharmas* of caste and sect. This was symbolically confirmed in the establishment of Shri Chitrapur *Maṭha* (monastery), which became the spiritual headquarters of the caste *guru*. The creation of a monastic center also provided a focus for material support of corporate religious life. Changes in the relative economic and social position of Saraswats during the nineteenth century influenced the form and degree of caste support for its religious institutions. Indeed, as Saraswats gradually won positions of power and prestige in the British Indian district of Kanara, they invested their new wealth in expressions of corporate religious status and sentiment.

Although the growth of the Saraswats' corporate institutions was uneven, the overall development from about 1830 to 1900 was one of steadily increasing prosperity and status for members of the caste and for their *swamis*. The *swamis*, in fact, worked diligently to further stimulate allegiance and to elaborate the institutions for promotion of *dharma*. The caste, which had established the *guruparampara* in about 1700 to help define and assure their independent social status, had by about 1900 become defined by allegiance to that *guruparampara* and its *maṭha*. Allegiance to the *guru* was expressed in accepting his guidance with respect to purity of behavior and in offering him material support. The seventh *guru*, Shrimat Pandurangashram Swami (r. 1864–1915), gave particular emphasis to Saraswat conformity to his own ideal of what was appropriate behavior, and was prepared to excommunicate those who would not accept this.

The prosperity which had lent support to the *maṭha* was itself the product of Saraswat flexibility and adaptability in responding to changing conditions associated with British rule. Such adaptability in choice of residence, occupation, and education introduced elements of cultural diversity into the Saraswats' world. Diversity could threaten the unity of the caste, particularly with reference to the *guru*'s behavioral standards. Travel across the sea to England, which seemed to offer secular advantages, guaranteed spiritual disadvantage. This issue and certain others associated with the general phenomenon of social reform, coupled with a steadily increasing rate of urbanization within the caste, created a tension which ultimately produced conflict and alienation. The caste, although small, was rent between those who were able to accept the *swami*'s dictum and those who were not. The social costs were unevenly distributed, but it is clear that few escaped inconvenience or anxiety. Apparent violations of the *swami*'s "code" brought the spectacle of virtually all caste members of a single town being excommunicated and then later readmitted by means of mass penance ceremonies. By 1900 it appeared that the unity of the Saraswats might be at an end.

The early years of the twentieth century found the caste members dispersed more widely than ever before in their history, but their actual points of concentration were diminishing to a few cities outside their home Kanara districts, most especially Bombay. The urban migrant members of the caste had relied upon their caste ties for finding employment, housing and fellowship in the cities. Even as these urbanites appeared to be cut off from the spiritual guidance of the *swami* and *maṭha*, they asserted the caste identity as a basis for new institutions to cope with modern problems. The Saraswats took a lead in promoting education for both boys and girls, establishing or supporting schools and scholarship funds. When indebtedness and lack of capital threatened the economic security of urban and rural Saraswats, caste members pioneered the creation of a caste cooperative credit society for their own benefit. A decade later they launched India's first cooperative housing society, to provide members with a better living environment and to give their community a focus of activities.

In this and in the establishment of a caste association, the urban Saraswats avoided the membership criteria, developing since the eighteenth century, that centered upon conformity to the discipline of *maṭha* and *swami*. Instead they articulated a membership criterion of the "natural identity" of a Saraswat—a person whose ancestors were Saraswats. Their action in this may be defined as a form of "substantialization" as posited by Louis Dumont. This process refers to the replacement of the hierarchical and pollution concerns which underlay caste as a system with an ethnic notion of substance in which each caste operates in competition with the rest.[25] To be sure, the Saraswats did not define their acts in these terms; yet it is clear in the aftermath of the changes that they did take pains to develop a distinctive culture reflective of the substance of the caste. And in this they endeavored to reintegrate the religious heritage of Shri Chitrapur *Maṭha* and its *swami* within their group culture. Redefinition of caste and its boundaries was thus a continuous process that has gone on throughout the history of "the caste" and in all likelihood will continue in the future life of the community.

The history of the Saraswat *jāti* has the advantage of having a beginning. Although the exact date cannot be established, the creation of a separate *jāti* may be taken as a starting point in the process of caste identity-building. Because it is necessary to develop a sense of the people who formed this new group, Chapter 1 provides a general picture of the Gaud Saraswat Brahman caste-cluster of Goa from which the Saraswats emerged. Chapter 2 explores what is known of the early stages of separation and caste formation. The imposition of British rule, and the generally improving material situation of many Saraswats, had important implications for patterns of occupation and residence among the caste members generally. These in turn influenced the growth and elaboration of corporate institutions of Saraswat social and religious affiliation. These developments are explored in Chapters 3 and 4.

During the nineteenth century, increased participation in new education, occupations, and public activities by individual Saraswats conditioned them to take new roles in caste affairs and gave them leverage within their caste. The Saraswats came to be a component of the district elite of Kanara, even though many members did not enjoy elite status themselves. The bifurcation of Kanara in 1859, and subsequent transfer of its northern half to the Bombay Presidency jurisdiction three years later, divided the Saraswats' world and set in motion a new stream of migration which ultimately created a major concentration of the caste in Bombay city. These changes, and the implications of urbanism or urbanization, are studied in Chapters 5 and 6, the former focusing upon the Kanara districts, the latter upon Bombay city.

Urbanization and its concommitant redistribution of the caste could not alone explain the changes in the corporate life of the Saraswats. As noted above, Pandurangashram Swami of Shri

25. Dumont, *Homo Hierarchicus*, p. 222.

Chitrapur *Maṭha* was endeavoring to enforce a strict code of behavior as an outward sign of allegiance to caste and *maṭha*. This in itself contained several innovations which severely tested that allegiance. The majority of the caste members had to come to terms simultaneously with his religious orthodoxy, as he developed and elaborated its requirements and standards, and with dynamic forces of social reform associated with new educational and occupational patterns. Most Saraswats were caught between the two forces of change; neither force, reform nor orthodoxy, won a clear victory. Castes cannot exist and prosper in such circumstances. Instead, a compromise emerged through the process of rearticulation of caste identity and renewed endeavors in Saraswat corporate enterprise. These patterns, chronicled in Chapters 7 and 8, were confirmed through the events dealt with in Chapter 9, in which, under Shrimat Anandashram Swami, the Saraswats and their new widely dispersed institutions and population were reintegrated with a revitalized Shri Chitrapur *Maṭha*.

The story does not end there, nor has it been possible to delineate clear periodization for this study. How does one periodize the life of a caste? In the present instance, I feel that the revitalization of the caste link with *swami* and *maṭha* in the early 1930s represented a convenient, if not ideal, cut-off point. My research has included materials of more recent times. I had the privilege of interviewing many persons on events and trends in the Saraswat life down to the most recent past. Yet as this is a history, I have been constrained to identify persons by their actual names. To move beyond 1935 would necessitate commenting too much upon persons who, happily, are still among us. Western readers may stumble and grumble over the number of persons of little renown that populate this text. My Saraswat readers may be able, by the same token, to judge whether my narratives and interpretations conform to their own appreciation of the facts. Here too, time yields a perspective. Events of recent days past do not admit readily to interpretation. It is my hope that, at some time in the future, I may be permitted to develop a companion volume to examine the corporate experiences of the Saraswats in the post-1920 period.

# 1

# AN ANCESTRAL HERITAGE:

## *The Gaud Saraswat Brahmans of Goa to 1700* A.D.

THE ANCESTORS of the Saraswat *jāti* were descendents of brahman families from Goa. Those families were part of the cluster known collectively in later times as Gaud Saraswat Brahmans. Documentation of their past has been eroded by the ravages of monsoon, white ant, and human indifference. Nonetheless, much information has survived, revealing a wide variety of institutions and traditions which made up the heritage of the new caste. This chapter attempts to give a sense of developing order to this diffuse and often confusing collection of historical and ethnographic data.

The land of Goa is much like that of the adjoining territories that form India's western coast. This narrow strip of land between the Arabian Sea and the bold escarpments of the Deccan, the Western Ghats, is segmented by occasional mountainous spines and frequent deep tidal creeks. This littoral has been at once a frontier zone of the dominant political and cultural systems of India and a region of contact with the maritime world beyond India. Its agriculture is dominated by rice and coconut, but only in the lush, adequately watered lowlands. The annual visitation of the monsoon rains clothes the Ghats in green, but the uplands support only grass and scrub jungle and provide a marked contrast to the adjoining paddy fields.[1]

Brahmanical tradition holds that the entire littoral of western India was created at the behest of Shri Parashurama, the axe-

1. O. H. K. Spate and A. T. A. Learmonth, *India and Pakistan: A General and Regional Geography*, 3rd ed., rev. (New York: Barnes & Noble, 1967), pp. 642–643, 665–672.

wielding brahman boy whose revenge of his father's murder cost the life of every kshatriya warrior and king of India. After the bloody deed, this vengeful avatar of Vishnu sought a land where he could obtain purificatory penance. The story is recorded in the *Sahyadrikhanda* of the *Skanda Purana* that he obtained a promise from the sea that it would recede whatever distance he might throw his axe from the crest of the Western Ghats.[2] He then populated the emergent land. Virtually every dominant brahman caste along the coast from the Gulf of Cambay to Cape Comorin has a myth associating their origin with the legendary agency of Parashurama.[3] The Gaud Saraswat Brahmans of Goa spoke of these events as marking their arrival in their new home.[4] The *Sahyadrikhanda* offers another explanation for the settlement of brahmans from the north in Goa. It credits Mayurvarma, king of the Kadamba dynasty, with creation of *agraharam* villages as early as the late fourth century A. D.[5] To be sure, the Gaud Saraswat Brahmans (hereafter GSB) were not the only sacerdotal body in the south Konkan. Pre-brahmanic priests called *gavdos* continued to serve local cults, and other brahmans, notably the Karhadas, were present from early times.[6]

Whatever the circumstances of their settlement in Goa, the

2. Geological data support an emergence pattern only south of Goa; to the north, subsidence is evident. Spate and Learmonth, *India and Pakistan*, pp. 19–21. The *Skanda Purana* houses many local legends and appears in no uniform collective whole. John Dowson, *Classical Dictionary of Hindu Mythology and Religion*, 10th ed. (London: Kegan Paul, Trench, Trubner & Co., 1961), p. 301; J. Gerson da Cunha, *The Sahyadri-Khanda of the Skanda Purana* (Bombay, 1877).

3. Cf. Jarl Charpentier, "Parashu-rama: The Main Outlines of His Legend," in *Mahamahopadhyaya* [*S.*] *Kuppuswami Sastri Commemoration Volume* (Madras, n.d.), pp. 9–16; R. E. Enthoven, *Tribes and Castes of Bombay*, 3 vols. (Bombay, 1920–1922), 1: 242–243, 246, 249–250; B. A. Saletore, *Ancient Karnataka*, Vol. 1: *History of Tulava* (Poona: Oriental Book Agency, 1936), pp. 9–38; K. P. Padmanabha Menon, *History of Kerala*, 2 vols. (Ernakulum: Cochin Government Press, 1924–1929), 1: *passim*.

4. Jose N. da Fonseca, *An Historical and Archgeological Sketch of the City of Goa* (Bombay: Education Society's Press, 1878), p. 10; Gaṇeśa Rāmacañdra Sarmā, *Sārasvata Bhūṣaṇa* [Ornament to the Saraswats] (Bombay: Popular Book Depot, 1950), pp. 54–58.

5. Gerson da Cunha, *Sahyadri-Khanda*, pp. 305, 333. Cf. D. D. Kosambi, *Myth and Reality*: *Studies in the Formation of Indian Culture* (Bombay: Popular Prakashan, 1962), pp. 152–171; George M. Moraes, *The Kadamba Kula*: *A History of Ancient and Medieval Karnataka* (Bombay: B. X. Furtado, 1931), pp. 7–11.

6. Anañt Ka. Priyolkar, "Sārasvata Brāhmaṇa āṇi tyañce Sārasvata," in Pānduranga Sadāśiva Pisurlekar (ed.), *Śri Śāntādurgā catuśatābdī mahotsava grantha*

ancestors of the GSB maintained that they were originally from Kashmir and the Punjab, on the banks of the river Saraswati.[7] Brahmanical lore holds that the brahmans of India are divided into five northern (*pañca gauḍa*) and five southern (*pañca dravida*) divisions. The GSB ancestors identified themselves as of the Saraswat section of the northern Gaud division, in contrast to their Maharashtra and Karnataka Brahman neighbors of the southern division.[8] Those neighbors questioned the GSB's competence to perform all six duties (*shatkarma*) reserved to brahmans. It was said that the GSB could study the *vedas*, but not teach them; give alms to brahmans, but not accept them; and have sacrifices performed, but not perform them. There is no substantial evidence to bear out these assertions. They seem mainly to have rested upon a general suspicion of outsiders, and perhaps the inclusion of fish in the GSB diet.[9]

The GSB's legends of northern origins include the story of their ancestor, the sage Saraswata. During a period of extended famine he had kept alive the recitation of the *veda* by miraculous meals of fish permitted and provided to him by the godess Saraswati. Since fish appears to have been accepted in brahmanical diets well into post-Gupta times generally, this story seems a later, historically superfluous attempt to rationalize medieval status disputes.[10] The appearance of fish in the diet of Bengali brahmans

---

[Shri Shantadurga, Fourth Centenary Celebration Volume] (Bombay: Shri Shantadurga Seva Samiti, 1966), pp. 1–52.

7. Śarmā, *Bhūṣaṇa*, pp. 55–58; Rāmacañdra Narahara Sohanī, *Gauḍasārasvata Brāhmaṇāñca Itihāsa* [History of the Gaud Saraswat Brahmans] (Khanapur: author, 1937), pp. 1–17. For appearance of the term *Saraswata* in Gujarat, see see H. D. Sankalia, *Studies in the Historical and Cultural Geography and Ethnography of Gujarat* (Poona: Deccan College, 1949), pp. 31, 34.

8. These divisions are not uniformly expounded, but most commonly the Gauda includes Gauda, Sarasvata, Kanyakubja, Utkala, and Mithila; the Dravida includes Dravida, Andhra or Teilanga, Maharashtra, Karnataka, and Gurjara. Enthoven, *Tribes and Castes* 1: 216.

9. John Wilson, *Indian Caste*, 2 vols. (Bombay: Times of India, 1877), 2: 29–30; Bhavānī Viśvanātha Kānavinde, *Sārasvata Brāhmaṇa ūrf Śenvī kīvā Koṇkane Brāhmaṇa* [Saraswat Brahmans Alias Shenvis or Konkani Brahmans] (Bombay: Kamaloji Gauroji, Shake 1792 [A. D. 1870]), pp. 3–14, 88–93, 116–124.

10. Om Prakash, *Food and Drinks in Ancient India* (Delhi: Munshi Ram Manohar Lal, 1961), pp. 209–210; Wilson, *Caste* 2: 30. Many modern GSB are strict vegetarians, but the habit of including fish in their diet is widely attributed. Cf. Goviñda Mañgeśa Kālelkar, *Mumbaī Ilākhyāñtīla jāti* [Castes in the Bombay Province] (Bombay: A. A. Moramkar, 1928), p. 170; Irawati Karve, *Hindu Society: An*

and of parallels in Bengali and Konkani languages also led later GSB scholars to trace their migration from Kashmir to Goa by way of Bengal.[11]

In any event, at some time before the tenth century A. D. there were brahmans in Goa who came from "the north." Although the history of their southward migration cannot be expounded, it is possible to identify some distinctive characteristics of the GSB culture on the eve of modern times.

Some of these traits were brought along in the cultural baggage of the migrants: their *veda* and *sutra* and clans, or *gotra*. It is belived by the GSB that some of their ancestors were brahmans of the *Yajurveda* and *Samaveda*, but the dominant pattern which evolved into an exclusive one was the study and following of the *Ṛgveda* in the *shakala* branch and the *Ashwalayana sutra*.[12] Among the migrants were members of ten clans (*gotra*). The full significance of *gotra* in early Indian society remains unsettled. It is clear that the proscription of marriages within *gotra* reflected the value assigned by north Indians to extended networks of kinship.[13] Since all brahmans

---

*Interpretation* (Poona: Deccan College, 1961), p. 3; L. K. Anantha Krishna Iyer, *The Cochin Tribes and Castes*, 2 vols. (Madras: Govt. of Cochin, 1909–1912), 2: 362.

11. Rāmacañdra Bhikāji Guñjīkar, *Sārasvatīmaṇḍala: athavā Mahārāṣṭra Deśātīla Brāhmaṇājātīce varnan* [A Description of the Brahman Castes of Maharashtra] (Bombay, 1884), pp. 9–11. B. S. Guha, "Racial Affinities of the Peoples of India," *Census of India, 1931*, Vol. 1: *India: Part 3, Ethnographical* (Calcutta, 1933), pp. xxix-xxx, cites a study by Voicunta Camotin, *Os Saraswatas de Goa* (Nova Goa, 1929), which employed physical anthropological techniques and concluded that the GSB were "racially akin to the Brahmans of Bengal" but not related to those of the Punjab. Guha states that the GSB did not appear through physical indices to be closely related to other castes of Maharashtra save the Chandraseniya Kayastha Prabhus, who themselves claimed an origin in Oudh. Enthoven, *Tribes and Castes* 3: 237–240. Cf. also A. C. Germano da Silva Correia, *Les Mahrattes de l'Inde Portuguese* (Bastora: Imprimerie Rangel, 1934), ch. 2 and 3.

12. S. S. Talmaki, *Saraswat Families*, 3 vols. (Bombay: author, Kanara Saraswat Association, 1935–1950), 1: 11–12.

13. By most accounts the original ten *gotras* were Atri, Bharadvaja, Gautoma, Jamadagnya, Kashyapa, Kaundinya, Kaushika, Vasistha, and Vatsa. Viṣṇu Rañgājī Śeḷdekar and Mukuñda Sadāśiva Śeḷdekar, *Gomañtakāñtīla Kaivalyapura yethīl Srī Śāntādurgā Sañsthānacā Sañkṣipta Itihāsa* [Brief History of Shri Shantadurga Temple at Kavle, Goa], 2d ed. (Bombay: authors, 1935), pp. 21–22. Variations are noted in Rāmacañdra Nāmdev Punāḷekar, *Bārdeśkara Gauḍa Sārasvata Brāhmaṇca Itihāsa va Jantrī* [Bardeshkar GSB History and Census] (Bombay: author, 1939), p. 21. On the *gotra* institution, see D. D. Kosambi, "Origin of Brahmin Gotras," *Journal of the Bombay Branch, Royal Asiatic Society*, n.s. 26 (1950): 21–80; *idem.*, "Development of the Gotra System," in *P. K. Gode Commemoration Volume*, 2 parts (Poona, 1960), 2: 215–224.

possessed some combination of *veda*, *sutra*, and *gotra*, these elements served as markers by which families could be identified ritually with others, delineating the boundaries of *jāti*. There were other secular markers as well.

Within Goa, the immigrant brahmans settled on lands in villages under distinctive forms of community organization which were preserved into modern times in a somewhat fossilized form under Portuguese law.[14] The original settlers of the ten *gotra*s settled in Sasashti (Salcette), Tisvadi (Tissuary, or Ilhas da Goa) and Bardesh (Bardez) regions of Goa.[15] Recognized as the founders of the villages (*gaonkar*), these brahman families collectively organized and enjoyed the produce of the best rice fields. It is unlikely that they themselves would have cultivated. Cultivation was done by the indigenous laboring castes, who by custom held a share in the produce of the common fields. Not all *gaonkar*s in Goa were GSBs, but most GSB families held *gaonkar* rights and appear to have kept the best and most productive tracts under their control.[16] GSB tradition maintains that at a later time other batches of northern brahmans arrived and settled in Goa. The later migrants were of the Kaundinya, Vatsa, and Kaushika *gotra*s. They ultimately settled in two Sasasthi villages, Kuthal or Kushasthal (Cortollim) and Keloshi (Quelessam).[17] When this occurred cannot be accurately dated, but the Kushasthalikars and Keloshikars became an influential segment of the GSB of Goa by the sixteenth century. Other new migrants or alliances among the GSB seem to have occurred, for by the eighteenth century the number of *gotra*s recognized among the GSB had increased to 19 or 21.[18]

14. Cf. Filipe Nery Xavier, *Bosquejo Historico das Communidades das Aldeas das Concelhas Ilhas, Sclcete e Bardez*, 2nd ed., 3 vols. (Bastora, 1903–1907); B. H. Baden-Powell, "The Villages of Goa in the Early Sixteenth Century," *Journal of the Royal Asiatic Society* (1900): 261–291.

15. The number of families is given variously as 66 and 96. Tisvadi, Bardesh, and Sasashti would suggest 30, 12, and 66 respectively, but Tisvadi actually had 31, and some traditions hold that the 12 of Bardesh were subtracted from the 66 of Sasashti. Guñjīkar, *Sārasvatīmanḍala*, pp. 31–33; Śarmā, *Bhūṣaṇa*, pp. 66–67.

16. Interview with Professor D. D. Kosambi, Poona, Feb. 18, 1966.

17. Talmaki, *Families* 1: 38. Alexander Cunningham, *Ancient Geography of India*, rev. ed. (Calcutta, 1924), p. 707, notes that Kushasthal was an alternate name for the Kanauj or Kanyakubja region.

18. Śrīpāda Vyāñkaṭeśa Vāgḷe (pub.), *Koñkaṇākhyāna* (Bombay: S. V. Vagle, Shake 1831 [A. D. 1909]), 1.7, v. 2–35 (pp. 30–32); Śarmā, *Bhūṣaṇa*, pp. 177–178. Legends of rivalries over prestige, of sons-in-law remaining as members of the bride's household, and of receipt from the family deities of permission to perform marriages

In addition to their landed interests, the GSB ancestors were marked as devotees of distinctive tutelary deities. These family gods (*kuladevata*) were not worshiped exclusively by the GSB, but their origins and the founding of their temples were associated with the immigrants. The most prominent of the deities were Shantadurga, Mangesha, Mahalakshmi, Nagesha, Ramnatha, Ravalnatha, Narasimha, Damodara, and Saptakoteshvara.[19] These deities were not only household gods and goddesses, but objects of devotion shared by extended lineages (*vaṅgaḍ*) of each *gotra*. These lineages shared in the management of their temples, and even after GSB spread out from Goa, pilgrimage to these shrines continued among the devotees.[20] Although in later times some devotees became specifically identified with Vaishnava sympathies, the iconography of the GSB family deities remained uncompromisingly Shaivite in form.

Not all brahmans pursued sacerdotal professions. The distinction of *vaidika* (sacred) and *laukika* (secular) occupations has been long recognized. While GSB families did serve as priests in the temples of the family gods, many, perhaps most, followed secular employments. The GSB constituted the dominant landed elite of Goa, but supplemented enjoyment of the fruits of the soil with employment as scribes and accountants or as masters of trade and commerce. No single occupation defined the boundaries of the GSB.

Another distinctive element in the medieval culture of the GSB emerged during their early centuries in Goa: the establishment of a line (*guruparampara*) of spiritual preceptors (*swami*, *guru*) centring upon a monastic headquarters (*maṭha*). The *maṭha* was a widespread phenomenon of medieval Hinduism, particularly in peninsular

within *gotra* suggest that the *ganokars* continually attempted to expand their landed holdings and to consolidate resources, even at the expense of brahmanical norms. *Koṅkaṇākhyāna*, 11.5, v. 30–113 (pp. 59–64).

19. Viṣṇu Raṅgājī, Śeḷḍekar, *Gomāñtakātīla Gauḍa Sārasvata Brāhmaṇa āṇi tyāñce Kuladeva* [The GSB in Goa and Their Family Deities] (Bombay: Gopal Narayan Patkar, 1938), *passim*.

20. A. Rā. Dhume, "Srīmaṅgeśa-devasthānacī Saṅksipta Māhitī" [Brief Information on Shri Mangesh Temple], *Śrī Sāntādurga catuśatābdī*, pp. 126–128. The *vaṅgaḍs* were the source for the elders or *mahajans* (lit., "great men") who held rights of management and of first worship at festivals. Cf. Punāḷekar, *Bārdeśkara*, p. 26. Portuguese destruction of temples in the sixteenth century probably eliminated some inscriptional evidence relevant to identification of *vaṅgaḍs*. On surviving evidence relating to the founding of Shri Saptakoteshwar temple, see H. Heras, "Pre-Portuguese Remains in Portuguese India," *Journal of Bombay Historical Society* 4 (1931): 24–43.

India. It may have been modeled on the Buddhist *vihara*, a center of ascetic residence which developed into a place of religious instruction. It found its expression in Hinduism in the creation of four *maṭhas* by Shankaracharya (c. 788–820 A.D.), the great *advaita* scholar.[21] During succeeding centuries, *guruparamparas* and *maṭhas* proliferated. They provided their disciples with both spiritual guidance and social control. In Southern India special relationships developed between specific castes of brahmans and particular *swamis* and *maṭhas*.[22]

The earliest recorded alliance of this sort among the GSB was to a line of *swamis* who traced their spiritual descent from Shri Gauda-padacharya, traditionally held to be the *guru* of Shankaracharya and original formulator of the nondualist (*advaita*) teachings which his illustrious student spread throughout India.[23] This *guruparampara* cannot be fully traced, but it is believed that each *swami* selected a pupil-disciple (*shishya*) who would succeed him from among the youths of the GSB community. The *shishya* would be trained in philosophy and religion in preparation for upholding correct belief and behavior among the disciples. A *swami* would visit his disciples and bestow blessings and spiritual guidance. On such visits his feet would be worshipped, and material manifestations of devotion would be given him for the benefit of the *maṭha*. Such visits appear to have had the additional force of social control, for if caste elders of a locality felt that an individual had sinned against his *dharma*, they could punish by prescribing penances or even excommunication. These sanctions would be confirmed by the *swami*. An unrepentant sinner could be refused the right to worship him. Since technically a *swami* was but an occupant of the final stage of life, a *sannyasin*, without possessions, family, or caste, his position was akin to that of a trustee who put aside his own self-

21. K. R. Venkataraman, *The Throne of Transcendental Wisdom: Sri Sankaracharya's Sarada Pitha in Sṛngeri*, 2nd ed., rev. (Madras: Akhila Bharata Samkara Seva Samiti, 1967), pp. 1–2, 4–38; K. A. Nilakanta Sastri, *Development of Religion in South India* (Bombay: Orient Longmans, 1963), p. 117; V. Raghavan, "Methods of Popular Religious Instruction in South India," in Ramakrishna Mission Institute of Culture, *The Cultural Heritage of India*, 4 vols. (Calcutta, 1953–1962), 4:507–509.

22. Nilakanta Sastri, *Religion*, p. 118. Cf. Abbe J. A. Dubois, *Hindu Manners, Custom and Ceremonies*, 3rd ed. (Oxford, 1906), pp. 123–131.

23. *Śrī Śāntādurgā catuśatābdī*, p. 140; J. N. Farquhar, *An Outline of the Religious Literature of India* (Oxford, 1920), pp. 167, 170–76; Śarmā, *Bhūṣaṇa*, pp. 184–185; Guñjīkar, *Sārasvatīmaṇḍala*, Appendix 4, p. 46.

realization to help his devotees. It would not be surprising that *swamis* would be seen as manifestations of the gods themselves on earth. Hence the denial of the right of offering devotion and worship remained a severe and effective sanction in the world of medieval Hinduism.[24]

The *swami* to whom the GSB ancestors first paid allegiance was of the *smarta* persuasion. Although in southern India "*smarta*" often has been taken to mean being inclined toward worship of Shiva as supreme deity, in fact those who follow this persuasion are supposed to reverence equally five deities, Shiva, Vishnu, Devi, Surya, and Ganesha. It is only in the south that the term implied a sectarian affiliation.[25] This became pronounced when in either the thirteenth or fifteenth century a substantial number of GSB families specifically gave up this affiliation in favor of the Vaishnava teachings of Madhvacharya (c. 1199–c. 1278 A. D.), identifying Vishnu as supreme god and adopting the appropriate formal devotional practices associated with his worship.[26] One tradition holds that Madhva himself initiated a GSB disciple after a visit to Goa and converted many GSB families of Sasashti and Bardesh. This disciple subsequently established a Vaishnava *maṭha* in Goa at Mathagaon. Until then all GSB were thought to have been *smarta* devotees of the *swamis* of the Gaudapadacharya *maṭha*. However, a second tradition places the conversion two centuries later, through the actions of a *swami* of the Phalimaru *maṭha*, one of the eight Madhva *maṭhas* associated with the important Krishna temple at Udipi. This *swami* is said to have taken a young GSB disciple known as Narayanatirtha Swami. He in turn founded a *maṭha* at the

24. A comparable role developed among the *jagadgurus* of Virashaivism. William McCormack, "Lingayats as a Sect," *Journal of the Royal Anthropological Institute* 93 (1963): 62–63.

25. Farquhar, *Outline*, p. 180; Nilakanta Sastri, *Religion*, p. 61; Louis Renou, *Religions of Ancient India* (New York: Schocken, 1968), p. 92.

26. This survey is based upon reprinted documents and other data from Śarmā, *Bhūṣaṇa*; M. Govinda Pai, "Nama Hiryaranu Kuritu" (Kannada) [Regarding our Ancestors], reprinted in Gowd Saraswath Brahman Seva Sangh, Mangalore, *Silver Jubilee Souvenir* (1964), pp. 63–85; H. Laximinarayan Kamath, "Brief History of Sri Kasi Mutt Samstan," in *ibid.*, pp. 87–103; Narsimha Bhima Acharya of Udiavar, "Shri Samsthana Gokarna-Partegali Jivottama Maṭha Sañskshipta Itihasa" [Brief History of Gokarn-Partegali *Maṭh*], in *ibid.*, pp. 205–231; G. H. Khare, "The Archives of the Vaishnava Maṭha of Sarasvata Brahmans at Partagali," *Indian Historical Records Commission: Proceedings* 28:ii (1951):50–55; V. P. Chavan, *Vaishnavism of the Gowd Saraswat Brahmans* (Bombay: Ramachandra Govind & Son, 1928), pp. 1–32.

port town of Bhatkal in Kanara in 1475. By that time emigré GSB families were spreading southward from Goa along the coast.[27] The majority of the GSB families accepting the Vaishnava persuasion came from villages of Sasashti and Bardesh. Since it was among those families that mercantile activity had become common and migration to trading opportunities along the coast not unusual, the second tradition probably holds more historical substance.

Many families remained *smarta* devotees of the Gaudapadacharya *maṭha*. The descendents of the later northern migrants, the Kushasthalikars and Keloshikars were included among the *smarta*s. Their principal villages contained the chief temples of Mangesha and Shantadurga, two of the most popular GSB family gods. As *gaonkar*s of the villages, the Kushasthalikars and Keloshikars were counted among the elders of the temples, enjoying prestigious rights of first worship at festivals and lucrative rights in the management of the temples and their extensive landed properties.[28] These rights were apportioned to the lineages (*vaṇgaḍ*) of original founders of the temples.[29] At Kuthal the *gaonkar*s numbered 24, and the same number of *vaṇgaḍ*s were recognized at the temple of Shri Mangesha, divided among 10 Vatsa *gotra* and 14 Kaundinya *gotra* families. Shri Shantadurga's *vaṇgaḍ*s included 12 Kaushika *gotra* families and one each from the Vatsa and Bharadvaj *gotra*s.[30] Inclusion of the latter reveals an assimilation within the Keloshikars of other GSB families of Sasashti who did not accept the Vaishnava persuasion.

The confusing array of corporate identifying names was further amended among the Kushasthalikars and Keloshikars. These *smarta* GSB of Goa came to be known also as Shenai or Shenvi ("learned"), a reference to a growing tendency among them to

27. Khare, "Archives of the Vaishanava Matha," p. 50; Narsimha Pauranika [of Bhatkal] and Kumtha Narayanacharya, *Shriguruparamparamritam* [Nectar of the Line of Gurus] (Khanapur, 1904), p. 22.

28. Dhume, "Śrīmañgeśa," pp. 123–129; Śeḷḍekar and Śeḷḍekar, *Śāntādurgā Sañkṣipta Itihāsa*, pp. 21–23; Xavier, *Bosquejo Historico*, Vols. 1 and 2.

29. Kosambi, *Myth and Reality*, pp. 164. In some contexts the term means simply "the original families." Punāḷekar, *Bārdeśkara*, p. 26n, compares it to "sobati" [companions, associates], presumably the descendants of the founders. It has been asserted that the *vaṇgaḍ* classification was a later device to organize and regulate support for the temples. M. N. Prabhu (pub.), *Sārasvata Samāja* (Mangalore, 1938), pp. 12–13 (translated with assistance of Shri G. Gopinath Bhat).

30. Śeḷḍekar and Śeḷḍekar *Śāntādurgā Sañkṣipta Itihāsa*, p. 23; Dhume, "Srīmañgeśa," pp. 126–127.

supplement their landed incomes with employment in secular literate professions as teachers, writers, and accountants, either in government or private service. The term was later used in the Maharashtra region to identify virtually any GSB, while to the south of Goa it was applied almost exclusively to *smarta* GSBs.[31]

Available evidence suggests that the GSB identity in Goa was neither perfectly nor universally applied. Brahmanical status, *veda* and *sutra*, diet and intermarriage appear to have been shared among the GSB ancestors. But cutting across these elements of identity were others: village, family deity, occupational status and sectarian persuasion. So long as most GSB families remained within the limited area of Goa, this imperfect internal order could be preserved. But the sixteenth century brought major changes to Goa and the world of coastal India.

Intrusion of military and political forces from beyond the limits of the Konkan set in motion the wheel of change for the GSB. The port of Goa had attracted raiding parties of the Bahmani sultan's army from the Deccan in the fourteenth century. It was only in the late fifteenth century, however, that the Adil Shahi rulers of Bijapur made a bid for consolidated control over the below-ghat Konkan territories and their ports. The objective was to assure access for the Deccan powers to the maritime commerce of the Arabian sea, the most important single item of which was the supply of horses from Arabia, much prized in Deccan warfare.[32] Before this Goa had been under the nominal sovereignty of the Vijayanagar empire. Even then not all had been peaceful for occasional intervillage disputes had degenerated into open conflicts as village communities attempted to encroach upon each other's lands.[33] Although these land disputes have been explained as the result of enhanced revenue demands, it seems reasonable that conflicts over productive fields were symptomatic of a growing demographic imbalance in Goa.

31. P. K. Gode, "Antiquity of the Caste Name 'Shenvi,'" *Journal of the University of Bombay* 6, no. 6 (May 1937) : 152–155; [Vāmana Raghunatha Varde Vālāvalīkār] Śaṇai Gōyabāba, *Kāhī Marāṭhī Lekh* [Some Marathi Writings] (Bombay: Gomantak Press, 1945) 1 : 140–166; Prabhu, *Sārasvata Samāja*, pp. 14–15.

32. Kosambi, *Myth and Reality*, p. 159; C. F. Saldanha, *Short History of Goa* (Goa: Imprensa Nacional, 1957), pp. 47–50.

33. Kosambi, *Myth and Reality*, pp. 159–160; *idem.*, *An Introduction to the Study of Indian History* (Bombay: Popular Book Depot, 1956), pp. 308–309. For GSB representatives under Vijayanagar, see P. S. S. Pissurlencar, *Goa Pre-Portuguesà atraves dos Escritores Lusitanos dos Seculos XVI e XVII* (Bastora: Tipografia Rangel, 1962), pp. 22–23.

In spite of its lush appearance, the garden of Goa could not produce sufficient food for all its inhabitants. Village conflicts could not solve the problem; war, famine, and migration were more effective. This demographic problem in the history of Goa has been overwhelmed by the documentary weight of the conquest and later "Christianization" of the territory by the Portuguese in the sixteenth century, but it remained to haunt Goa's rulers into the twentieth century.[34]

The Muslim conquest of Goa did not last long. If the Hindus of Goa did not actually invite Albuquerque to rid them of Bijapur domination, at least they seemed unalarmed when he conquered the island of Tisvadi (Ilhas da Goa) in 1510. Thirty-five years later the adjacent peninsulas of Bardesh and Sasashti were ceded by Bijapur, and the Portuguese consolidated their rule of Goa.[35]

The early years of Portuguese rule produced sustained endeavors by the new conquerors to induce their subjects to accept the Christian religion. Extensive conversions resulted, yet for half a century the Hindu community of Goa did not give up the defense of their faith, even at the cost of violence.[36] In 1545 Miguel Vaz, Vicar General of the Indies, urged the King of Portugal to take stricter measures against the Hindus. He offered a tribute of sorts to the active resistence of the GSB to conversion:

> There exists in this island a caste of people who call themselves Synaes Brahmans, who are much opposed to Christianity and not only do not convert themselves, but also hinder the conversion of others whenever possible and support the error of heathenism. . . . In times of trouble we cannot count upon their loyalty. These Synaes who hinder conversions to Christianity or at least their traders should be banished.[37]

Fortunately for many GSB, the King of Portugal and his officers worshipped at the shrine of the goddess "Expediency." They offered not banishment, but preferment, to members of Goa's Hindu elite. One Krishna served as renter of the customs office,

34. It is not likely that pre-Portuguese Goa escaped famines or epidemics, as they were known from the earliest times of Portuguese rule. Fonseca, *Historical Sketch of Goa*, pp. 5, 29, 84.

35. Frederick C. Danvers, *The Portuguese in India*, 2 vols. (London: W. H. Allen, 1894), 1: 186–219, 465.

36. Anthony D'Costa, *The Christianisation of the Goa Islands: 1510–1567* (Bombay: author, 1965), pp. 4–6. This work views "Christianisation" as a relatively benign process. A more pessimistic interpretation obtains in A. K. Priolkar, *The Goa Inquisition* (Bombay: author, 1961).

37. Priolkar, *Inquisition*, p. 74, quoting J. Wicki (ed.), *Documenta Indica* (Rome, 1948) 1: 66–72.

captain of Indian troops, and broker for the horse trade which the Portuguese were redirecting back to Vijayanagar. Krishna visited Portugal and received honors from King Dom Manuel, but returned home adamantly clinging to the faith of his fathers.[38]

Whether by persuasion or coercion, some GSB families did convert. When they did the Portuguese made it a grand show. In 1548 Loqu Sinoy (Lokanatha Shenvi) was baptized in great pomp as Lucas deSa. He was said to rank just behind Krishna and to be very rich. He had made charitable donations to Hindus to enable them to resist conversion, and it was asserted without a saving remnant of charity that he had converted merely to gain an advantage over his old rival Krishna. At any rate he was thought a prize catch; the Archbishop of Goa himself officiated at his baptism.[39]

It is neither well remembered nor understood in India that the introduction of the Inquisition in 1560 was an act taken primarily against converts to Christianity rather than Hindus. The Iberian experience had created an atmosphere of fear and distrust toward "new Christians." Some had converted no doubt for gain or to save family lands, but the Portuguese suspected all. Until 1561 most new Christians had retained their pre-conversion names, indigenous costume, and use of their Konkani language. When the Inquisitors called this into question, many Christians were as ready as the Hindus to leave the Portuguese territories for the adjacent lands under Hindu rule.[40] "Christianization" represented a disjunction, but Hindus were never eliminated from Portuguese territories altogether. The Portuguese could not run Goa without the Hindus. GSBs were employed in public service and were particularly valued as diplomatic envoys to neighboring Indian powers. Restrictions on worship and later destruction of temples led to a peculiar situation where a Keloshikar, Ramaji Shenai Kotthari, who served as envoy for the viceroy to the Sultan of Bijapur, chose to

38. Danvers, *Portuguese* 1: 366; Priolkar, *Inquisition*, p. 71. Krishna served as envoy to Bijapur and was instrumental in the cession of Bardesh and Sasashti in 1545. P. S. S. Pissurlencar, *Agentes da Diplomacia Portuguesa na India* (Bastora: Tipografia Rangel, 1952), pp. 14, 19–21.

39. Priolkar, *Inquisition*, pp. 71–73.

40. J. H. Cunha Rivara, (ed.), *Archivo Portuguez Oriental*, 6 vols. (Nova Goa: Imprensa Nacional, 1863–1875), 6: Doc. 600.; D'Costa, *Christianisation*, pp. 82–83; C. R. Boxer, *Race Relations in the Portuguese Colonial Empire: 1415–1815* (Oxford, 1963), pp. 81–82.

reside in Bicholem which lay in the territory of the Maratha king of Savantvadi.[41] It appears that some portion of the GSB elite of Goa prospered despite the changed conditions. Professor Pearson's investigations have revealed that a substantial number of positions of wealth and influence were held by GSB in Goa throughout the seventeenth century.[42] Even among those who left Goa, there was an expectation of returning at some time in the future. *Gaonkari* rights were assiduously preserved, so much so that in 1634 the Portuguese prohibited honoring the shares of *gaonkars*—either Hindu or Christian—who had moved from Goa into the adjacent "Terras da Canara."[43]

While GSB families could remain in Goa and prosper, there were costs to be paid. Some migrated across the river with their family deities into a nearby Hindu ruler's territories. Those who remained behind continued to patronize and support the new temples. When the Portuguese extended control over those areas in the "new conquests" of the eighteenth century, the power of the Maratha arms which had been demonstrated in the capture of Vasai in 1739 served to ensure that a policy of toleration would be observed for the Hindu temples.[44]

The rise of the Marathas in the seventeenth century had other implications for the GSB. Shivaji and his successors sought writers and diplomats, and many Shenvi families found fresh opportunities in the service of the Marathas in the Deccan. Some had already accepted hereditary revenue offices in the so-called Southern Maratha Countries.[45] When the Maratha adventurer Khem Savant overthrew a Kudaldeshkar Gaud Brahman subordinate of Bijapur and founded the Savantvadi state, public affairs were largely given over to migrant Shenvis who had left Goa.[46] In the

41. Pissurlencar, *Agentes da Diplomacia*, pp. 22–23.

42. M. N. Pearson, "Wealth and Power: Indian Groups in the Portuguese Indian Economy," *South Asia* 3 (August 1973): 36–44.

43. Cunha Rivara, *Archivo* 6: Doc. 600.

44. *Śrī Śāntādurgā catuśatābdī*, pp. 92–93, 102–110; Śeḍdekar and Śeḍdekar, *Śāntādurgā Saṅkṣipta Itihāsa*, pp. 55–67; Vithal T. Gune, *Ancient Shrines of Goa* (Panjim, 1965), pp. 7–8. On the general impact of Maratha power on the Portuguese, see P. S. S. Pissurlencar, *Portugueses e Marathas*, 6 vols. (Nova Goa, Bastora, 1926–1940), 6: *passim*.

45. Thomas Marshall, *Statistical Reports of Pergunnahs in the Southern Maratha Countries* (Bombay, 1822), pp. 93, 98–100.

46. Selections from the Records of Bombay Government [hereafter SRBG], n.s. 10: *Memoir on the Sawunt Waree State* by W. Courtney and J. W. Auld (1855),

Maratha domain proper, the GSB status as brahmans was challenged by Maharashtra Brahmans, particularly the Chitpavans. Even a successful proof of full standing as *shatkarmi* brahmans before the learned *pandits* of Poona did not eliminate discrimination.[47] Hence as the Chitpavan domination of the Peshwa's territories expanded, the GSB found greater opportunities in the kingdoms of Maratha princes in northern and central India, notably Holkar and Sindhia.[48]

GSB migration from Goa took other paths as well. The Bahmani raids in 1351 appear to have stimulated some Shenvi families to withdraw southward into what would become the Kanara district. At about the same time, some families of Sasasthi and Bardesh were entering commercial endeavors along the coast to the south of Goa. The coastal trade at that time was dominated by Muslims of Gujarat and the Persian Gulf.[49] Nevertheless, the brahman traders of Goa appear to have been gradually increasing their activity and influence even before the assault upon the old commercial system by the Portuguese in the sixteenth century. In the southern ports and trading towns, the newcomers were identified by their language as "Konkanis," a term which has remained in colloquial usage to the present day. Even before the Portuguese annexation of Sasashti and Bardesh in 1545, the "Konkani" merchants began establishing themselves permanently beyond the Goa frontiers. During the sixteenth century they built new temples for their caste members in

---

p. 154; J. A. Saldanha, "Savantvadi Castes and Village Communities," *Journal of the Anthropological Society of Bombay* 8 (1909): 498–502; James C. Grant Duff, *History of the Mahrattas*, rev. ed., 2 vols. (London, 1921), 1:71–72; Viṭhṭhala Purūṣottama Pingulkar, *Sāvantvāḍi Saṁsthanacā Itihāsa* [History of Sawantwadi State] (Bombay: author, 1911), pp. 20–49.

47. Shridhar V. Ketkar, *History of Caste in India*, 2 vols. (Ithaca, N. Y., and London, 1909–1911), 1: 22. For prevailing views at Poona in the 1820s, see Arthur Steele, *Law and Custom of Hindoo Castes Within the Dekhun*, new ed. (London: W. H. Allen, 1868), pp. 79–81.

48. S. N. Sen, *Administrative System of the Marathas*, 2nd ed. (Calcutta: University of Calcutta, 1925), p. 131n; Narahara Vya. Rājādhyakṣa, *Śindeśā kharā Itihāsa* . . . [True History of the Sindhias] (Bombay: Nirnaya Sagar Press, 1907), pp. 311–331; Gaṇeśa Ra. Śarmā, *Sārasvata Ratnamālā* [A Necklace of Saraswat Gems] (Khanapur, 1910), pp. 176–222.

49. V. N. Kudva, *History of the Daksinatya Saraswats* (Madras: Samyukta Gowda Saraswata Sabha, 1972), p. 35; John Huyghen van Linschoten, *Discourse of Voyages into ye Easte and West Indies*, 2 vols. [Hakluyt Society Publications, old series, nos. 70–71] (London, 1885), 1:67–68; Ashin Das Gupta, *Malabar in Asian Trade* (Cambridge: Cambridge University Press, 1967), pp. 5–10.

the port towns along the coast. At Bhatkal, then an important shipping center, inscriptional evidence reveals GSB temples were begun in 1538, 1546, 1555, 1567, and 1590, and a recorded tradition holds that their Vaishnava *swami* established a *maṭha* there in 1475.[50]

The "Konkanis" remember their spread along the coast as a response to Portuguese religious persecution; but it appears that some of them received Portuguese patronage.[51] The Portuguese had created a partial vacuum in their attacks upon the declining "Muslim aristocracy of commerce."[52] Quite apart from any interest in trade goods for Europe, the Portuguese were dependent upon the west coast tracts of Kanara for the rice necessary to cover Goa's chronic deficiencies of food. During most of the sixteenth and seventeenth centuries, Sasashtikar ("Konkani") traders dominated this lucrative opportunity.[53]

At Calicut, the Zamorin's efforts to preserve the freedom of his port had preserved somewhat the position of the Muslims, and the "Konkanis" did not prosper initially. They did settle at Cochin. There in the seventeenth century their commercial interests coincided with the rising fortunes of the Dutch East India Company.[54] The trading ports of the period were numerous and small. Along the coast, petty rulers of little kingdoms sought to recruit the "Konkanis" to build their share of the trade. For example, the ruler of Karnad, a glorified revenue collector whose capital was a hamlet near Mulki in modern day South Kanara, brought

50. Archaeological Survey of India, *Revised Lists of Antiquarian Remains in the Bombay Presidency* (Bombay, 1897), pp. 194–195; Vāmana Ra. Varde Vāḻāvalīkār, *Gõyakārāñcī Gõyābhāyalī Vasṇūka* [The Habitation of Goans Outside Goa] (Bombay: Gomantak Press, 1928), pp. 145–147.

51. Pearson, "Wealth and Power," pp. 38–39. P. C. Alexander, *The Dutch in Malabar* (Annamalainagar, 1946), p. 95, states that the Portuguese brought the "Konkanis" to Cochin and placed them under formal protection which was subsequently transferred by treaty in 1663 to the Dutch.

52. Das Gupta, *Malabar*, pp. 103, 174n. "The dispersal of the Konkanis ... was, beyond doubt, one of the most significant events on the West Coast during the sixteenth century."

53. Pearson, "Wealth and Power," p. 38; Kosambi, *Myth and Reality*, pp. 152–159; "Kyfeat of Concany Casts" ["kaiphiyata" : narrative statements, India Office Library, London [hereafter IOL]: European Manuscripts, MacKenzie Collection, unbound translations, Class VI, Tulava, etc., ff. 48–53.

54. Francis Day, *Land of the Permauls or Cochin, Its Past and Its Present* (Madras, 1863), pp. 308–309; C. Achyuta Menon, *Cochin State Manual* (Ernakulam, 1911), p. 207; N. Purushothama Mallaya, "Saraswaths in History, with special reference to Kerala," unpublished paper read at Kerala History convention, Ernakulam, May 18, 1965, p. 5.

five GSB families from Bhatkal. He settled them and built for their use a temple of Shri Venkataramana, a deity that had become an object of special veneration among the Vaishnava GSB after their departure from Goa.[55]

Associated with this migration for trade was a further intensification of the Vaishnava tradition among the GSB. The spiritual successors to Shrimat Narayantirtha Swami toured the west coast visiting disciples, dispensing blessings and guidance, and receiving worship and tithes. *Maṭhas* were built at Gokarn and Partagal.[56] In about 1540, sixty-five years after the founding of the *maṭha* at Bhatkal, a second Vaishnava *guruparampara* was begun to minister to the GSBs residing farther south along the coast. Some *smarta* families also migrated to the south, sometimes serving as writers for their commercial cousins. There are recorded instances of further conversions to the Vaishnava persuasion at places such as Bhatkal and Udipi. These conversions were not individual, but family actions led by elders who agreed to abide by correct behavior under the guidance of the *swami*, accepting his authority in all matters of custom and sacred law.[57]

The sixteenth century was also a period of political change in the lands south of Goa. The most dramatic change was the decline of the Vijayanagar Empire following its military defeat by the confederacy of Deccani sultanates in 1565. Several small successor states emerged from the debris, ruled by former Vijayanagar feudatories styled *nayakas*. The new kingdoms asserted regional political and military domination at the expense of both the central imperial power and local petty chieftains.[58]

One such *nayaka* kingdom arose in the wild but protected reaches of the *malnad*, the western Mysore plateau. It was founded by a line of Virashaiva (or Lingayat) rulers who had accepted the Vijayanagar overlordship as late as 1509 at the accession of the emperor Krishnadevaraya. But even before the battle of Talikota sounded

55. Kudva, *Dakshinatya Saraswats*, pp. 198–214; V. R. Kilikar, "Marathaka-Pachacha: The Glory of the Emerald Idol" unpublished manuscript, Cochin, 1965), pp. 16–22.

56. Khare, "Archives," p. 52.

57. Śarmā, *Bhūṣaṇa*, pp. 218–222. Examples of pledges to *gurus* are quoted in Khare, "Archives," p. 54.

58. K. D. Swaminathan, *The Nayakas of Ikkeri* (Madras: P. Varadachary, 1957), pp. 12–19; Burton Stein, "Integration of the Agrarian System of South India," in Robert E. Frykenberg (ed.), *Land Control and Social Structure in Indian History* (Madison: University of Wisconsin Press, 1969), pp. 188–196.

the end of imperial power, the *nayakas* had asserted direct control over large tracts of land above and below the Western Ghats. And while they continued to express loyalty to Vijayanagar until 1613, these rulers were consolidating their control of the *malnad* and attempting to undermine the authority of the petty rulers along the west coast.[59] One element in this expansion of control was the creation of a reliable and loyal administrative hierarchy, and here some Shenvis were recruited to fill lower-revenue positions along the coast. Some also were present as diplomats and supervisors in the *nayakas*' successive capitals at Keladi, Ikkeri, and finally Bednur.[60]

Thus by the seventeenth century the GSB of Goa had evolved cultural and social affiliations of village, deity and sect which cut across the tentative unity which had been symbolized by language and marriage. Distinctive subsections had been possible in Goa itself. By the early eighteenth century conflict over rites and precedence between Vaishnava Sasashtikars and *smarta* Kushastalikars and Keloshikars led to the remarkable situation in which the two parties petitioned the King of Portugal praying for official intervention to produce mutual segregation of the two subsections.[61] The dispute faded away without such drastic measures, but its occurrence reveals that internal differentiations among the GSB could become extremely divisive. The petitions also reveal, however, that intermarriage among subsections of different sectarian persuasion had continued.

Beyond internal differentiation, the GSB of Goa had also begun to enter into migration out of their medieval homeland both to the north and south. We shall examine more carefully the implications of migration for the GSB in the following chapter.

Who were the ancestors of the Saraswats? Beyond identification of some family names, gods, and villages, the picture is incomplete. But examination of the history and culture of the GSB reveals a complex mixture of social and cultural elements from which a series of caste identities could be constructed. When descendant generations later endeavored to reintegrate in a new *jāti* in new surroundings, this was a heritage upon which they drew.

59. Pietro Della Valle, *Travels of Pietro Della Valle in India* (ed. Edward Grey), [Hakluyt Society Publications, 2nd series, nos. 84–85], 2 vols. (London, 1894), 1:191.

60. Talmaki, *Families* 1:67–70.

61. Cunha Rivara, *Archivo* 6, suppl. II, docs. 108 and 142:299–300, 371–382.

# 2

# THE BIRTH OF A *JĀTI*:

## *Migration and Fission in the Eighteenth Century*

THE COMPACT world of the Gaud Saraswat Brahmans of Goa had crumbled during the sixteenth and seventeenth centuries. Some GSB families had migrated considerable distances from their ancestral lands as a result. Maintaining social ties with those who remained in Goa was difficult. Unity had been weakened already in Goa by social disputes which had raised barriers to full social intercourse among GSB subsections. By the close of the seventeenth century, as the migrants entered new cultural regions and political domains, their dependence upon the old Goa order weakened. In such circumstances, one segment of GSB families—drawn mostly, but not exclusively, from among the *smarta* Kushasthalikar and Keloshikar Shenvis—who had migrated southward into Kanara broke away and formed their own caste. During the eighteenth century this distinction was reinforced by their allegiance to a discrete *guruparampara* and establishment of a separate *maṭha* for the *swamis* of that lineage. The Saraswat Brahman *jāti* was gradually taking shape.

The migration of *smarta* GSB families to the south actually commenced two centuries prior to the commercial expansion of the "Konkanis." *Gotra* and family deities provide the means of identifying these migrants. The earliest known settlers in Kanara were Kushasthalikars of Kaundinya *gotra* whose family god was Mangesh, with secondary allegiance to Mahalakshmi. They settled in the vicinity of the temple town of Gokarn, centering on a village, Bankikodla. As members of this group found employment as revenue accountants they assumed a new surname reflecting their official capacities: Nadkarni.[1]

The first settlements are thought to date from some time after the 1351 A. D. Bahmani raids on Goa. Thereafter Nadkarni families settled in villages adjacent to Gokarn in Ankola to the north of the Gangavali river. About a century later, further migrations occurred into the same area. Two families, Kulkarni and Balwalli, acquired lands and employment in petty revenue positions.[2] Nothing substantial is known about the migratory process. It seems likely that as more Kushasthalikar and Keloshikar families came to Kanara, they were attracted by economic opportunities, either employment in the service of the expanding "Konkani" traders or appointments in the administration of the rulers succeeding the Vijayanagar empire, the Nayakas of Ikkeri. The old Goa pattern of Shenvis, *smarta* GSB, appropriating opportunities requiring skills of writing and accounting, was repeated. It is likely that the Nayakas of Ikkeri, who were building their own power on the remains of the Vijayanagar system, found it expedient to employ outsiders in revenue capacities to assure their control over and against local power structures.[3] Saraswat traditions assert that their ancestors became local revenue accountants, *shanbhogs*. But as *shanbhog* has a more general meaning of "writer," it is not certain that most Saraswats were actually employed in revenue work.[4]

By the seventeenth century, then, there were Kushasthalikar and Keloshikar Shenvi families in Kanara. While their Vaishnava GSB

1. Talmaki, *Saraswat Families* 2 : 1–4; 1 : 40. 67–68; Ānand Nāḍkarṇī, *Kadrekar-Nāḍkarṇī Kulavrattānt* [Kadre Nadkarni Family History] (Bombay: P. S. Nadkarni, 1965), p. 10. The Nadkarni name was exclusively a GSB usage until the present century. In this chapter "Kanara" is used to designate the area which today constitutes the Karnataka state districts of North and South Kanara, plus the Kasargode taluka of Kerala. The term was not current in the eighteenth century, but is employed for convenience. The traditional names for the regions to the south of Goa are Konkan, Haiga, and Tulava, the borders between these generally being recognized as the Gangavali and Gangolli rivers.

2. Talmaki, *Families*, 2: 33, 38.

3. Cf. Robert E. Frykenberg, "Traditional Processes of Power in South India," *Indian Economic and Social History Review* 1 (1963): 126–127; Burton Stein, "Agrarian Integration," pp. 188–196.

4. *Shanbhog* has a general meaning of "writer" as well as a specific use identifying revenue accountants. This was pointed out to me by Shri Shankar Shetty; Cf. H. H. Wilson, *A Glossary of Judicial and Revenue Terms* . . ., rev. ed. (Calcutta: Eastern Law Book House, 1940), p. 731.

cousins, the so-called "Konkanis," pursued trade, the Shenvis concentrated upon acquisition of land and "service" in revenue administration. The lands sought were fields for cultivation of rice and coconut palms. Ecological parallels with the Goan agrarian pattern facilitated management of the new land. One principal difference was that in Kanara the GSB migrants were not pioneers of cultivation, but rather took over from earlier landed classes. No economic village community of the Goan style developed. In Kanara the productive rice fields were held by families and not by villages. Since, as brahmans, the new landholders would not cultivate, a major portion of a family's lands would be given in tenancy to others. In instances where the tenants were the previous owners of the land rights, the tenancy rights were generally permanent and inalienable (*mulgeni*). Without the community-derived labor force of the Goan village system, the new landlords utilized agricultural slaves for work on fields they retained in direct management.[5]

Modern genealogical research has established that the oldest settlements of Saraswat families were in villages and towns along the coast. As fresh opportunities of *shanbhog* vacancies and other appointments appeared, or as families matured and divided, branch families, known as *dayadis*, moved on to other villages, usually in the hinterland of the original settlement. Thus families at Ankola and Gokarn generated further settlements at Chandavar, Mallapur, and Dhareshvar; those at Bhatkal spread to Shirali, Heble, Sirur, and Baindur. Later entrants who came to the Kundapur–Gangolli harbor settled at Basrur, Hattiangadi, Kandlur, Hemmadi and Amladi. Map 2 illustrates the distribution of villages in Kanara where Saraswat families settled and from which they derived surnames.[6] Some places are omitted for considerations of space.

The social and religious institutions of the migrants could not be sustained in the same manner as in Goa. A notable feature of isolation was the distance from the shrines of the family deities, *kuladevata*. It seems that most devotees of these deities agreed that the principal

5. Francis Buchanan, *A Journey from Madras Through the Countries of Mysore, Canara and Malabar . . .*, 3 vols. (London, 1807), 3 : 100–106, 139–152, 166; D. D. Kosambi, *Myth and Reality*, pp. 152–157; *Gazetteer of the Bombay Presidency*, 27 vols. [hereafter *Bom. Gaz.*] (1877–1904), 15, *Kanara*, part 2 : 1–20, 154–193.

6. Talmaki, *Families* 1 : 70.

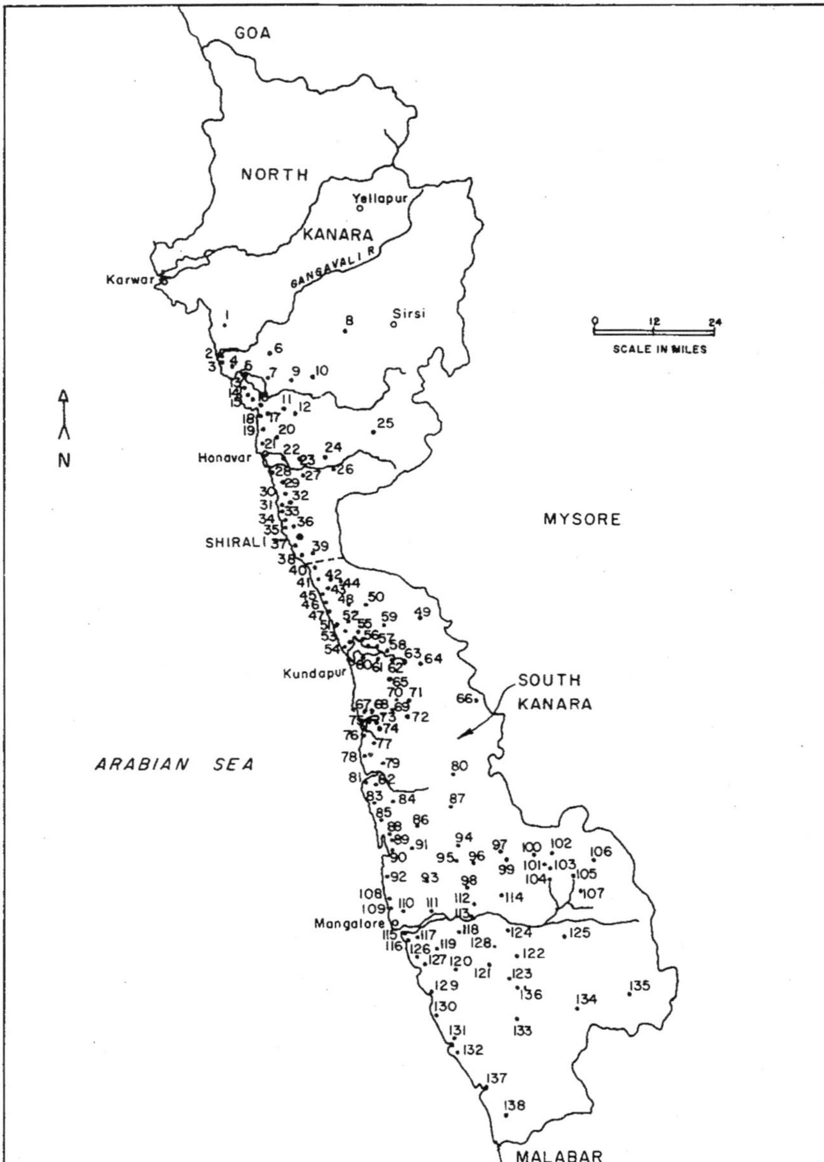


Map 2. Kanara District, Showing Villages Associated with Saraswat Families.

## KEY TO MAP 2: VILLAGES ASSOCIATED WITH SARASWAT FAMILIES IN KANARA.

(Not all villages are shown, owing to space considerations.)

*North Kanara*

1. Ankola
2. Bankikodla
3. Bijur
4. Gokarn
5. Aghanashini
6. Yennemadi
7. Mirjan
8. Nilekani
9. Divgi
10. Harite
11. Mallāpur
12. Chandavar
13. Kagal
14. Kodkani
15. Masur
16. Kumta
17. Kalbag
18. Dhareshvar
19. Haldipur
20. Mugve
21. Karki
22. Mavinkurve
23. Jalvalli
24. Upponi
25. Bilgi
26. Gersoppa
27. Idgunji
28. Kasarkod
29. Samsi
30. Gunvante
31. Manki
32. Chittoor
33. Talmaki
34. Bailur
35. Murdeshwar
36. Kaikini
37. Heble
38. Bhatkal
39. Mudbhatkal

*South Kanara*

40. Sirur
41. Baindur
42. Taggarse
43. Bijur
44. Hoskote
45. Naikinkatte
46. Khambadkone
47. Keregal
48. Kaltode
49. Hosangadi
50. Padukone
51. Trasi
52. Amladi
53. Madiman
54. Gangolli
55. Hemmadi
56. Tallur
57. Hattiangadi
58. Gulvadi
59. Wandse
60. Basrur
61. Kalavar
62. Molehalli
63. Kandlur
64. Haladi
65. Sheriyar
66. Someshvar
67. Kachur
68. Barkur
69. Handade
70. Nilavar
71. Nalkur
72. Arur
73. Betrabet
74. Benegal
75. Brahmavar
76. Kallianpur
77. Nayampalli
78. Udipi
79. Hirebet
80. Andar
81. Udiavar
82. Balsavar (Katpadi)
83. Padbidri
84. Yellur
85. Hejmadi
86. Mundkur
87. Karkala
88. Karnad
89. Mulki
90. Sashittal
91. Kilpadi
92. Posodi
93. Shedde (Mudashedde/Padushedde)
94. Mudubidri
95. Thodar
96. Karanje
97. Aldangadi
98. Karpe
99. Kokrade
100. Shiral
101. Jamalabad
102. Savnal
103. Kapanadak
104. Beltangadi
105. Ujre
106. Charmodi
107. Dharmastal
108. Panembur
109. Pejavar
110. Sujir
111. Amembal
112. Bantwal
113. Panemangalur
114. Kaval
115. Ullal
116. Vombatkere
117. Savur
118. Sajip
119. Invalli
120. Saletore
121. Vithal
122. Puttur
123. Irde
124. Bondal
125. Ichalampadi
126. Udiavar
127. Manjeshvar and Bangramanjeshvar
128. Kodange
129. Kumble
130. Mogral
131. Kasargode
132. Chandragiri
133. Adur
134. Bellare
135. Guttigar
136. Panje
137. Tirkannad
138. Nileshvar

temples of the gods should remain in the Goa vicinity. The only exception was the Vatsa *gotra* devotees of Shri Lakshminarayana, whose principal shrine was relocated at Ankola.[7]

Where several families resided in a single place, as at Gokarn or Bankikodla, a body of elders was formed to oversee the corporate concerns of the community. This body was known as a "ten" [*hattu samastaru* or *dahajana*], and may be compared with the better known term of "five," *panchayat*. Such bodies had guided the village communities in Goa, but in the new setting they appear to have functioned only as a means of settling disputes and maintaining caste behavior in their locality, with no economic powers beyond levying fines for misconduct against *dharma*.[8]

The elders of these "tens" identified themselves in their documents as Kushasthalikars. The sanction of their authority lay with their *guru*, the *swami* of the Gaudapadacharya *maṭha*. Portuguese presecutions in Goa had led to the relocation of this *maṭha* at Kavle in the territory of Sonda.[9] The *swamis* of the *maṭha*, however, had departed for a period in north India at Kashi (Benares). During the sixteenth century it does not appear that they toured among their disciples south of Goa. Sometime around 1600 Shrimat Sachchidananda Saraswati Swami did return to the south, but some of his disciples resisted recognizing him.[10] They may have been turning to other *swamis* for guidance, for there are references in early eighteenth-century documents to special honors paid to the *smarta swami* of Sṛngeri and a Vaishnava *swami* of Udipi. It is clear that *smarta* GSB families in seventeenth-century Kanara were influenced by the Vaishnava persuasion. Certainly their descendents retained a most eclectic tradition, incorporating the observances of the Vaishnava Bhagavata cult; the introduction and widespread adoption of the *Krishna Jayanti* celebration, the wearing of Vaishnava devotional marks and observance of the *ekadashi* holy days, demonstrate their accommodation.[11] The *smarta* GSB families had intermarried with Vaishnavas in Goa, and such exchanges continued in the south.

7. *Ibid.*, p. 151.

8. H. Shankar Rau (ed.), *Shrimat Anandashram Ordination Jubilee Souvenir* (Bombay: editor, 1941), pp. 97–100.

9. Śarmā, *Sārasvata Bhūṣaṇa*, pp. 186–189; Rāmacañdra Va. Na. Karāṇḍe Śāstrī, *Kaivalyapura Maṭhācā Sañkṣipta Itihāsa* [Brief History of Kaivalyapur *Maṭha*] (Mhapsa, Goa, Shake 1832 [A. D. 1910], pp. 15–28.

10. Śarmā, *Bhūṣana*, p. 187; *Bom. Gaz.* 15, *Kanara*, part 1 : 167–168.

11. H. Shankar Rau, *Shrimat Anandashram Ordination*, p. 100.

Several families from among Atri and Kutsa *gotras* of the Saraswats were from among the Sasashtikars prior to the eighteenth century.[12] Given such eclecticism, how did the ancestors of the Saraswats come to break away to form their own caste in isolation?

Three stories from caste tradition purport to explain the division of the ancestors from the rest of the GSB in Kanara. It is more precise to say that these accounts narrate a division among and within the *smarta* Kushasthalikars and Keloshikars who had always been at least nominally distinct from their Vaishnava cousins. Because each tradition addresses different aspects of the division, it is possible that the three in combination reveal various facets of a single problem. The first focuses upon a dispute within the Nadkarni family of Ankola over property and privileges. The second emphasizes an internecine falling-out among former devotees of the Kavle (old Gaudapadacharya) *maṭha swami* regarding recognition of him or of one or the other of his disciples (*shishyas*). The third emphasizes political change and frontiers forcing migrant brahmans to choose their own *swami* in order to preserve their standing and official patronage, even at the cost of separating from those Kushasthalikars and Keloshikars who remained devotees of the old *maṭha* and *swami*.

The Nadkarni family had been the earliest *smarta* GSB or Shenvi settlers in Kanara, centering on Gokarn and Ankola in the fourteenth century A. D. Besides extensive land holdings, members of the family held *shanbhog* appointments in villages from the Kalinadi to the Gangavali river. During the seventeenth century, a dispute arose over some of the properties at Ankola. The intensity of factional conflict was resolved only when the two sides settled on segregation as a solution, and the dissident families removed to the south bank of the Gangavali river.[13] This choice of boundary may have reflected the fact that the Gangavali had become the northern political frontier of the Nayakas of Ikkeri-Bednur. It remained a stable frontier between Bednur and Sonda for more than a century.[14]

12. Talmaki, *Families* 1:31–32, 53–54.

13. Madras District Gazetteers, *Statistical Appendix and Supplement to the Manuals: South Canara* (1937), p. 197; *Bom. Gaz.* 15, *Kanara*, part 1:167–168. Sectarian disputes among the GSB in Goa also resulted in demands for separation. Cunha Rivara, *Archivo Portuguez Oriental* 6, suppl. ii, doc. 142:371–381.

14. Jerome A. Saldanna, *The Indian Caste*, Vol. I: *Konkani or Goan Castes* (n.p. [Sirsi, N. Kanara], n.d. [1904]), p. 62. The capital of the kingdom was transferred from Ikkeri to Bednur in 1639. K. D. Swaminathan, *Nayakas of Ikkeri*, p. 82.

Since some of the Kaundinya *gotra* Nadkarnis remained in Ankola within the Shenvi section of the GSB community, the seceding group were called "Shenvi-paiki," from among the Shenvis. Had a property dispute created a new caste? Since the seceding Nadkarnis must have had established ties of intermarriage with other Shenvi families, under the prevailing preference for cross-cousin matches, support which would have separated the other families also from the Shenvi fold might have been forthcoming. But it is the nature of such ties that they are limited in scope. Relatively few of the families which ultimately formed the new Saraswat caste appear to have had close marital ties with the Nadkarnis. In fact, the earliest surviving documents of agreements between the Saraswats and their *swami*, dated to 1720, include no Nadkarni names, suggesting that the family had not merged into the *jāti* until later in the century.[15]

The second tradition of separation emphasizes a misunderstanding between the *smarta* Shenvis (i.e., Kushasthalikars and Keloshikars) in Kanara and their traditional line of *gurus*, the *swamis* of the Gaudapadacharya *maṭha*, then relocated in Kavle. In the early seventeenth century Shrimat Sachchidananda Saraswati Swami, the sixty-third in the lineage, returned to south India after an absence of the *swamis* in the north for nearly half a century. According to a later successor at Kavle, this *swami* in 1630 issued an order which the *smarta* Shenvis of Kanara refused to honour, with the predictable result that they were excommunicated.[16] Sachchidananda Saraswati Swami had two *shishyas* who were sent to tour in Kanara, which further stimulated the controversy. What was at stake cannot be discovered today, but the disputes were sufficiently intense to be still recalled in the late nineteenth century.[17]

The story is incomplete and the explanation unsatisfactory, if only because the Kavle *maṭha swamis* did not excommunicate all of their devotees in Kanara. Shenvis of North Kanara district still owe allegiance to the old *maṭha*. Also, the Kavle *maṭha gurus* subsequently welcomed members of the Saraswat *jāti* on an equal footing during visits to their family deities in Goa. The fragments of the story do suggest the growing isolation of the *smarta* GSB in

15. Cf. documents reproduced in Ṣhankar Rau, *Shrimat Anandashram Ordination*, pp. 97–98.

16. V. N. Kudva, *History of the Dakshinatya Saraswats*, p. 175.

17. *Bom. Gaz.* 15, *Kanara*, part 1 : 168.

Kanara. If those fragments were current in the Nayaka's capital at Bednur toward the end of the seventeenth century, they might have played a role in the circumstances of the third tradition of Saraswat separation.

The third story is related to the recruitment of GSB to the service of the Nayakas of Ikkeri and Bednur. Several modern Saraswat surnames are derived from this service at the Nayakas' court.[18] The Nayakas' diplomacy seems to have been in GSB hands; Vitula Sinay (c. 1582–1629) was envoy for Venkata Nayaka I in 1623.[19] Dewan Narayanappa Nadkarni was a dominant figure in administration following the shift of the capital to Bednur later in the century. No single caste held a monopoly on appointments. Ikkeri was reported to have several quarters allocated to different groups of brahmans in the rulers' service, including one occupied by "Konkanis," the mercantile GSB who played a critical role in the rice trade.[20]

The antipathy of the various Dravida Brahmans toward the GSB, which was noted in the preceding chapter, manifested itself at Ikkeri and Bednur. The Karnataka Brahmans maintained that the Shenvis were not vegetarian and therefore of uncertain status. A perceptive Italian traveller reported that commensal restrictions were observed:

> Yea, in one and the same Race (in that of the Brachmans, which is the noblest), some Brachmans (as the Panditi and Boti [*pandit*, *bhat*], who are held in great esteem amongst them) will not eat in the company or so much as the House of a Brachman *Sinay* or *Naicke* and other nobles who eat fish and are called by the general name *Mazeri* [*matsyāhārī*, "fish-eaters"], and much less esteemed than those who eat none; yet the Brachman Sinay and Naicke . . . eat in the house of a *pandito* or *Boto* without being contaminated, but rather account it an honor.[21]

During the reign of Basavappa Nayaka I (1696–1714) some persons, not identified, raised a charge that the GSB Shenvis at Bednur were not really brahmans at all. The proof was that they had no *guru*.[22]

18. Talmaki, *Families* 1 : 71–74.

19. Varde Vālāvalīkār, *Gōyakārāñcī*, p. 166; Della Valle, *Travels*, 2 : 195, 210–212, 217.

20. Varde Vālāvalīkar, *Gōyakārāñcī*, pp. 157–158; Pissurlencar, *Agentes da Diplomacia Portuguesa na India*, pp. 23, 33, 57–59.

21. Della Valle, *Travels*, 2 : 232. Gode, "Antiquity of Caste Name 'Shenvi,'" pp. 153–154, notes that in Maharashtra, also, the *matsyahari* term was used.

22. H. Shankar Rau (ed.), *A Chitrapur Saraswat Miscellany* (Bombay: editor 1938), p. 41.

It was unlikely that without a specific caste allegiance to a spiritual preceptor, the brahmanical standing of any group would be recognized by the ruler. Under these circumstances the previous story of loss of contact with the Kavle *maṭha swamis* would be significant. In any event, the elders at Bednur convened their "ten" and then referred the matter to their relations on the coast at Gokarn. Prayers were addressed to Shri Bhavanishankar—the tutelary deity of the Kavle *maṭha*—and to Shri Mahabaleshvara, the great god of Gokarn. Soon after this, a wandering ascetic, who had been a north Indian Saraswat brahman before becoming a *sannyasin*, arrived at Gokarn. He agreed to undertake the duties of serving as a spiritual preceptor to those families among the GSB who would accept him. This event is believed to have occurred in 1708. Thus was set in motion a new *smarta guruparampara*, the disciples of which were evolving as a separate *jāti*.[23]

Following the meeting at Gokarn, and Shrimat Parijñanashram Swami's acceptance of the role as spiritual guide, the effect of the agreement had to be confirmed. Messages were sent by the "ten" of Gokarn to all other "tens" in towns and villages as far south as Mangalore and Vithal, informing them that there would be a *guru* touring among them offering sermons on religion and social behavior and giving all householders blessings.[24] Not all of the Kushasthalikar and Keloshikar families appear to have accepted the new *swami* immediately. For example, the Nadkarnis, Kulkarnis, and Balwallis seem to have remained outside the fold for at least a generation. Families north of the Gangavali river remained disciples of the Kavle *maṭha*. So did a few farther south, including the Kinis of Udipi, the Shanbhogs of Haldipura, the Gaithonde-Shenais of Karkala, and the Nayakas of Calicut.[25] Those who did embrace the new discipleship agreed to support the expenses of the *swami* and his retinue by paying an annual tithe, *vantiga*, which was supposed to be equivalent to one month's income every two years. They also agreed to offer worship and hospitality whenever he toured among them.[26]

But other recognition was necessary. Parijñanashram Swami

23. *Ibid.*, pp. 41–42.

24. H. Shankar Rau, *Shrimat Anandashram Ordination*, p. 97.

25. Kudva, *Dakshinatya Saraswats*, p. 171, gives these examples. Some families cited as disciples of Kavle *maṭha* are clearly not from Kushasthalikar or Keloshikar *vangaḍs*, e.g., Kaushika *gotra* devotees of the family god Nagesha.

26. H. Shankar Rau, *Shrimat Anandashram Ordination*, pp. 97, 99–100.

visited Basavappa Nayaka at Bednur, then obtained recognition from the Sṛngeri *maṭha*. This confirmed the status of the *swami*'s disciples and continued their royal patronage for the remaining years of Bednur's independence. In 1739 Basappa Nayaka II granted land in support of the construction of a *maṭha* at Gokarn for the Saraswats' *guruparampara* and the consecration of the image of its tutelary deity, Shri Bhavanishankar.[27] Thus the Lingayat rulers of Bednur had played the role of Hindu monarch, granting recognition and patronage to castes and religious activities.

The spiritual lineage was maintained through the adoption of a *shishya* who would be close disciple, student, and then successor of the *swami*. Parijñanashram Swami attained final extinction, *mahasamadhi*, in 1720. Prior to that the householders of the caste had arranged for the adoption of a son of one of their number to be the *shishya swami*. An agreement was made by the "ten of the Kushasthalis" of Bednur and other caste elders with one Krishnaya Shanbhog. In return for his sacrifice of giving his son to be *shishya*, he and his family would thereafter be given a share of the management of the *maṭha*. The family, known as the Shukla Bhats, would be given first consideration in the affairs of the community and in subsequent adoptions of *shishya*s (*śiṣya svikār*).[28] The new *guru*, Shankarashram Swami, remained the guide of the community until 1757. His career was one of extensive touring, accepting *vantiga* and giving spiritual services to the householders of the caste. A *maṭha* was erected at Gokarn at the *samadhi* memorial of the first *guru*.[29]

Apart from a few legends, very little is known of the detailed activity of the first and second *swamis*. A fire in the early nineteenth century destroyed most of the records of the *maṭha*. It appears that the management of *maṭha* affairs was in the hands of members of the Shukla Bhat family. Because the *swami*s were men in the fourth and final stage of life, *sannyas*, they were themselves obliged to possess nothing beyond the necessities of life and their office. Nonetheless, the personal qualities of the *guru*s were reflected in the activity of the institution. Traits of retiring piety, rigorous scholar-

27. *Ibid.*, p. 101; S. N. Koppikar, "The Shri Chitrapur Math," *K. S.* 11, no. 1 (July 1927):47.

28. H. Shankar Rau, *Shrimat Anandashram Ordination*, pp. 98–99.

29. The original *maṭha* structure, which was completely rebuilt in this century, is located a short distance southeast of the Kotitirtha tank at Gokarn.

ship, or active interest in affairs of caste were differently mixed in each succeeding *guru*. In 1757 Shankarashram Swami passed away to *mahasamadhi* while on tour at the village of Shirali near Bhatkal. The Nagarkatte family, that held extensive lands there, donated a site for Shankarashram Swami's *samadhi* memorial around which was built a new *maṭha*. Because of its centrality to the dispersed settlements of its disciples, this new *maṭha*, named Shri Chitrapur, became the premier religious institution of the Saraswats and was thereafter the principal seat of the *gurus*.[30]

There was another problem maintaining continuity of the *guru-parampara*. Shankarashram Swami had not selected a *shishya*. In order to preserve the spiritual succession, the caste elders persuaded one who had been initiated by the old *swami*, and who had been a member of the caste, to serve as the new *guru*. He agreed and took the title Parijñanashram Swami II. His saintly piety led him to avoid secular duties connected with the *maṭha*, and he soon adopted a *shishya*, Shankarashram Swami II, to act in his stead. This new guru served the community until 1785, when he was succeeded by Keshavashram Swami. During his reign of 38 years, Keshavashram Swami actively toured through Kanara, successfully urging Saraswats to give up Vaishnava practices and building up endowments of lands in support of Shri Chitapur *maṭha*.[31]

Apart from the altered circumstances of social and religious identification which had defined a new *jāti*, the ancestors of the Saraswats found the world around them changing as well. Political and economic forces reshaped the political system that dominated Kanara, inhibiting the opportunities of the Saraswats at some points, opening fresh chances at others. A brief survey of these changes and of the social life of the caste during the late eighteenth century will complete the background of the Saraswats' emergence into the nineteenth century.

Kanara from 1763 to 1800 witnessed a rather dreary political drama of conquest and misrule. The curtain was raised in the conquest of Bednur in 1763 and annexation of its territories by Haidar Ali of Mysore.[32] It was rung down in the Fourth Anglo-Mysore War in 1799 with the conquest of Mysore under the general

30. S. N. Koppikar, "Shri Chitrapur Math," 46–48.
31. *Ibid.*, pp. 50–51.
32. Mark Wilks, *Historical Sketches of the South of India*, 2 vols. (reprint ed., Mysore, 1930), 1:505–509.

direction of the future Duke of Wellington. The intervening scenes are a combination of despotic ineptitude on the part of the Mysore rulers punctuated by equally inept military interventions by the English East India Company forces. In 1768 Bombay troops captured Mangalore and promptly lost it to Haidar Ali's son Tipu, who then won the respect if not love of the town's inhabitants by plundering them as a punishment for failure to assist the Mysore cause.[33] Another English intervention in 1783 collapsed in another victory of Tipu Sultan, confirmed the next year by the Treaty of Mangalore. Tipu concluded that the substantial Christian population of the Kanara coast might constitute a threat to his sovereignty, and he embarked on a program of forced migrations and seizures of property to suitably chastize "the Nazarenes." Quite apart from the horrors visited corporately and individually upon this segment of the region's people, the action represented only one more disruption of life's pattern in what should have been a smiling land. The disruptions kept much of the countryside in a state of continued disorder, with consequently reduced security for life and property.[34]

Haidar Ali's conquest had immediate effects for the Saraswats. His armies had overrun much of the territory of the ruler of Sonda, who fled to Goa, where he ceded the rest of his territory to the Portuguese in return for personal security.[35] Once again the temples and shrines of the GSB family deities lay under Portuguese rule, but Maratha military strength and Hindu influence in Goa itself were sufficient to prevent any recurrence of persecution. For the Saraswats at Bednur, Haidar's victory in 1763 ended their tenure in administration. For the most part they removed back to the coastal regions, where their families held land and where they might obtain local revenue positions.[36]

Mysore rule in Kanara further weakened the petty chieftains already eroded by the efforts of the Bednur rulers. Removal of such local sources of rebellion ought to have encouraged the growth of rural stability and prosperity, but both Haidar and Tipu introduced fresh taxation which, Sir Thomas Munro later observed, had

33. George M. Moraes, *Mangalore : A Historical Sketch* (Bombay: Indian Historical Research Institute, 1927), p. 44; *Bom. Gaz.* 15, *Kanara*, part 2:313–315; Wilks, *Historical Sketches* 1:608.

34. Wilks, *Historical Sketches* 2:217–218; 262–279.

35. *Bom. Gaz.* 15, *Kanara*, part 2:140.

36. Talmaki, *Families*, 1:44–45.

brought the agricultural economy of the district to the brink of ruin.[37] Some Saraswat families suffered loss of lands—one Kaundinya *gotra* family of Kodikal, near Mangalore, gave up their holdings, as tax burdens mounted in Tipu's final decade, and fled. Their only connection with the village after the 1790s was their surname.[38]

In fairness to those rulers, particularly the much-maligned Tipu, it seems likely that the Mysore revenue policy demanded a good deal more than it received. Both Haidar and Tipu attempted to control land alienations and to introduce their own men for efficient administration. It appears that these officers were fully frustrated in this by the prodigious energies of the local revenue officials. Since Saraswats were counted among the *shanbhog*s and landlords of the district, it is likely that they shared in the task of frustrating the Mysore *amildar*s' attempts to obtain accurate knowledge and control of the cultivated land and its produce.[39] Some Saraswat families were able to expand their lands and influence during the time of troubles. The Kolegar family acquired lands at Koppa and Bailur, two villages between Shirali and Honavar on the coast. About 1760 a representative of the family, one Bhanappa, acquired the headmanship (*patelki*) of Bailur. A generation later, in 1776, his son Devanna obtained appointment as *patel* and *shanbhog* of Koppa.[40] Further acquisitions of lands ensured that the family, which now adopted the surname of its new village, Koppikar, entered the nineteenth century with a sound financial base. The prevalence of the personal name Bhanappa among this family and another at Honavar seems to have led in time to a general use of the nickname "Bhanap" when referring to themselves. It had the connotation of cleverness and quickness.[41] In subsequent chapters

37. Thomas Munro's report of Nov. 9, 1800, quoted in Wilks, *Historical Sketches* 1 :171.

38. Talmaki, *Families* 2 :93.

39. *Bom. Gaz.* 15, *Kanara*, part 2 :142–158; MRO, selections from the records of the Collector of South Canara [hereafter SRSC]: *Letters of Sir Thomas Munro Relating to the Early Administration of Canara* (Mangalore, 1879), p. 81.

40. Shankāra Nārāyaṇa Koppīkar and Rāmamohan Ve. Koppīkar, *Bailuru Śri Lakṣmināṛāyaṇa Devara hāgū ā devara bhajakarāda Koppīkara Kuṭumbada Itihāsa* [History of Bailur Shri Lakshminarayan Temple and Its Devotees, the Koppikar Family] [Kannada] (Udipi: authors, 1932), pp. 78–81 (translated with assistance of Shri. H. V. Nagaraja Rao); Talmaki, *Families* 3 :22–23.

41. Talmaki, *Families* 3 :24. Interview with V. M. Chickramane, Gokarn, Feb. 11, 1971; interview with Gourish V. Kaikini, Gokarn, Feb. 12, 1971.

"Saraswat" and "Bhanap" will be used interchangeably, in the manner of their usage among members of the caste.

Warfare in the district left destruction in port towns, and whenever Mysore rule slackened, local chieftains sallied forth to extract what they could from the countryside. In 1799 land was unsalable, many fields lay in waste, and formerly flourishing ports and market towns like Honavar, Ankola, and Kundapur were decayed, containing "only a few beggarly inhabitants."[42] But those inhabitants had watched kings and conquerors come and go, and when Munro began his settlement operations in Kanara after the war in 1799, they granted him the same expedient welcome with which, no doubt, others had been greeted before. They praised his compassion and justice, bewailed their poverty and the sins of previous despots now deposed, and looked over their new masters to discover their strengths and weaknesses.

During the late eighteenth century, many Saraswat families were experiencing internal readjustments. Pressure on extant family lands increased with each generation, and branches of families moved, usually to nearby villages, to take up fresh fields. The very instability of property which ruined the Kodikal family might offer another new opportunity for acquiring choice paddy lands.[43]

The spread of families may be illustrated by the example of a Keloshikar Kaushika *gotra* family of the Vaidya *vangaḍ*. It had been settled at Manki, near Honavar, where it held valuable lands in the early eighteenth century. With succeeding generations, branches of the family hived off first to nearby hamlets: Talmaki, Chittoor, and Samrodi. Other descendants moved to more distant points, Yennemadi and Gokarn to the north, Shirali and Sirur to the south.[44] These developments were memorialized in the adoption of new surnames based upon village of present or previous residence. The process of branch (*dayad*) formation obscures the relatively small circle of relations which had formed the new *jāti* during the eighteenth century. In one reported case, five generations used five surnames:

> One Devappaya of Padbidri settled at Hejmadi and was called by the latter surname. His son Santappa called himself Karanje when he went to live with his sister, Karanje Tungamma. Santappa's two sons,

42. MRO, SRSC-*Letters of Sir Thomas Munro*, p. 85.
43. Talmaki, *Families*, 1:41–42, 70.
44. *Ibid.*, p. 135; Kudva, *Dakshinatya Saraswats*, p. 168.

Shamaya and Venkatraman, went to Yellur and assumed it as their new surname. Shamaya's son Shantamurti left Yellur and lived in Kumta and called himself by the latter surname.[45]

Genealogical materials are by no means complete for the pre-1850 period, but on the basis of common deities, *gotras*, and customs, the full range of 507 Saraswat families with 315 surnames may be linked tentatively with some 80 ancestral families drawn from among 10 distinct stocks of migrants from Goa.[46] The uneven numerical and geographical distribution of these 10 stocks offers indirect evidence of a core of constituent families from among Kaundinya, Kaushika, Vatsa, and Bharadvaj *gotra* devotees of Mangesh and Shantadurga, i.e. Kushasthalikars and Keloshikars, who subsequently incorporated through marriage some GSB families of other *gotras*, *vangads*, and deities (see Table 1). These incorporations of other GSB families of other *gotra* or deity are more apparent than later additions of other families of the predominant Kushasthalikar and Keloshikar identifications. One GSB family of Atri *gotra*, devotees of Shri Mhalasa, had settled at Khambadkone and subsequently intermarried with Saraswats, effectively becoming part of the *jāti*. All eleven Atri *gotra* surnames today may be traced to this one family.[47] In a similar fashion, GSB families of Kutsa *gotra* who were devotees of Shri Narasimha entered the fold in the eighteenth century. Sometime before that, one Vatsa *gotra* family of Hattiangadi whose *kuladevata* was Shri Lakshminarayan of Ankola had joined the Saraswats in intermarriage and in devotion to the new *guruparampara*. Most devotees of Shri Lakshminarayan were and are Vaishnavas, yet as early as 1720 the names of Saraswat elders included the Hattiangadi name.[48]

The incomplete and often confusing record of stray documents, oral traditions, and property partition deeds cannot yield a comprehensive picture of the Saraswat caste in the eighteenth century. But a view emerges that reveals dimly the workings of migration, fission, and fusion in corporate identity and activity.

45. Talmaki, *Families* 1 : 66. The period of time represented by these five generations is approximately 1750 to 1859.

46. Analysis based on Koppīkar and Koppīkar, *Bailuru Śrī Lakṣminārāyaṇa*, Ch. 17; Talmaki, *Families* 1 : 62–66. "Family" is used here in the sense of a group of persons of the same surname, *gotra*, and deity, but not necessarily of one household.

47. Talmaki, *Families* 1 : 65, 118, 128.

48. *Ibid.*, pp. 151–152; Shankar Rau, *Shrimat Anandashram Ordination*, p. 98.

DISTRIBUTION OF SARASWAT *Gotras*, DEITIES, AND FAMILY NAMES

| *Gotra* | *Principal Family Deities* | *Original District Settled* | *Number of Surnames* | *Percentage of Surnames* | *Percentage of Gotra in caste census in:* 1932 | 1956 |
|---|---|---|---|---|---|---|
| Atri | Mhalasa | S. Kanara | 11 | 2.1 | 1.95 | 1.82 |
| Bharadvaj | Shantadurga | S. Kanara | 42 | 8.3 | 8.26 | 8.72 |
| Kaundinya | Mangesh | N. & S. Kanara | 164 | 32.3 | 35.20 | 34.83 |
| Kaushika | Shantadurga | N. & S. Kanara | 142 | 28.0 | 28.33 | 28.93* |
| Kutsa | Narasimha | S. Kanara | 12 | 2.4 | 0.60 | n.a.* |
| Vatsa (1) | Mangesh | N. & S. Kanara | 104 | 20.5 | | |
| Vatsa (2) | Mangesh and Shantadurga | S. Kanara | 14 | 2.8 | | |
| Vatsa (3) | Mangesh, Shantadurga, Mahalakshmi, Nava Durga, and Simha Purusha | N. Kanara | 4 | 0.8 | | |
| Vatsa (4) | Nagesh | N. Kanara | 3 | 0.6 | | |
| Vatsa (5) | Lakshminarayan of Ankola | S. Kanara | 11 | 2.1 | | |
| Vatsa : total | | | (136) | (26.8) | 25.64 | 25.40 |

SOURCES: S. S. Talmaki, *Saraswat Families*, 3 vols. (Bombay, 1935–1950), 2 : 38 and 1 : 65; H. Shankar Rau, *Chitrapur Saraswat Directory* (Bombay, 1933), p. 29; Kanara Saraswat Association, *Chitrapur Saraswat 1956 Census Report and Directory* (Bombay, 1956), pp. 70–71.

NOTE: *Because of similarities in pronunciation, Kaushika and Kutsa gotras were entered together in 1956.

Was the new caste fully functional and complete, its members fully dependent upon each other in matters of kinship? In all probability it was not. And just as some families of other *gotras* and deities merged among the Saraswats, presumably others slipped away from among the major *gotra* and *deity* groups. The caste's independent identity—whether known as Kushasthalis, Keloshikars, Shenvipaiki, Saraswat, or Bhanap—had been the product of multiple causes: disputes, misunderstandings, and political changes. It seems evident that it was in the creation of the new *guruparampara* and *maṭha* that the amalgam of families acquired coherence and cohesion. By sharing in their allegiance to *maṭha* and *swami*, all families' members would join in common patterns of worship and could dine together in ritual purity (*pankti bhojana*). Since cross-cousin patterns of marriage were preferred, the growth of a web of kinship would be necessarily slow. With succeeding generations, the divisions of landed property led to spatial relocations. The Saraswat families were thus established in a territorial pattern of relative dispersal, settled in over 300 towns, villages, and hamlets along approximately 200 miles of the Kanara coast. In the tours of their *gurus* and in visits to the *maṭha*, the Saraswats found a significant bond by which their social fabric could be patched together and preserved. The basic identity and institutions of the *jāti* had taken shape.

# 3

# CONSEQUENCES OF CONQUEST:

## *Early British Rule in Kanara, 1799–1834*

TIPU SULTAN and his kingdom were both casualties of the British victory at Seringapatam in 1799. While the Mysore plateau was to remain under nominally independent Indian rule, several frontier areas including the lands along the west coast were annexed to the East India Company's Madras Presidency. A new district called Kanara stretched from Malabar to the southern frontiers of Portuguese Goa. A not yet well known young officer, Thomas Munro, was given the charge of its pacification. What did the change of rulers mean for the district and its inhabitants? Analogy to other parts of British India suggests that beyond establishment of relative stability and security, there were few dramatic changes for the next half-century.[1] In the absence of detailed scholarly research on Kanara's history in the nineteenth century, it is possible only to outline aspects of British rule and their impact on the district. The "impact" of British administration upon all members of the Saraswat *jātī* was not uniform. But with their landed interests, social standing, and heritage of literacy and "government service," members of the caste would necessarily have to come to terms with the new order.

### *Establishment of British Rule*

One of the first accomplishments of British rule in India generally was the disarmament of rural warrior aristocracies. In Kanara

1. Cf. Eric Stokes, "The First Century of British Colonial Rule in India: Social Revolution or Social Stagnation?," *Past and Present* no. 58 (Feb. 1973): 136–160.

various petty chieftains had reasserted themselves during the confusion of the Fourth Anglo-Mysore war. Some were military adventurers, others were scions of old warrior families that had been objects of the previous rulers' repression.

The case of the Hegade of Vithal illustrates the problem. Though little more than an itinerant bandit during Tipu's reign, this chief raised a small force in 1798 and announced his presence to his would-be subjects by plundering extensively in the land south and east of Mangalore. Isolated farmsteads and temples were looted with ease, to the despair of their owners and patrons. Those with property were fair game. The Saraswat community at Vithal endured the plunder and destruction of the oldest temple of their caste in the area, Shrimat Ananteshwar.[2]

Thomas Munro took a hard line against the petty pretenders, captured most, hanged a few, and thereby overawed the rest. "Where there has been seven years of anarchy," he said, "order can be established only by being inflexible; indulgence may be thought of afterwards."[3] By the spring of 1800, the district was judged to be pacified. Munro and his assistants could turn then to the next most pressing concern—the assessment and collection of the land revenue.

In this, Munro found fresh obstacles. The landholders of the district withheld their active cooperation from the official attempts to ascertain the extent of cultivated lands and their productivity. Because the agriculturists of Kanara were scattered in farmsteads and hamlets rather than in nuclear villages, it was difficult to bring them together to settle with the officials. When they did assemble, they uniformly reported the ruinously high taxation of Tipu Sultan and proclaimed their present abject poverty.[4] But Munro perceived that their reluctance "originated entirely in the inhabitants having once been in possession of a fixed land rent and in their still universally possessing their lands as private property."[5] Here, in a remote

2. MBRP, July 2, 1821 [IOR: P/293/85/ff.5570–5572]; Madras District Manuals: *South Kanara*, 2 vols. (Madras, 1894–95), 1:77–80; MRO, SRSC: *Letters of Sir Thomas Munro*, pp. 6–18; H. Shankar Rau, *Chitrapur Saraswat Miscellany*, p. 68.

3. Alexander Arbuthnot (ed.), *Major General Sir Thomas Munro: Selections from His Minutes*, 2 vols. (London, 1881), 1: lxxv.

4. MRO, SRSC: *Letters of Sir Thomas Munro*, p. 1.

5. *Ibid.*, p. 77.

corner of the peninsula, were the vigorous proprietary interests which British experiments in both *zamindari* and *ryotvari* land revenue systems had sought for a generation.[6]

The rights may have been ancient as Munro believed, but their enjoyment was not. During the preceding two centuries there had been a transfer of landed rights to new proprietors, including Saraswats. Although no survey had ever been made, the lands were divided into estates, or *varg*s, that varied in size from one-fifth acre to 1600 acres within a "revenue village." Owners, known as *varg-dar*s, might cultivate their own lands, but in most instances these proprietors relied upon others to carry out the work. To this end they would have some lands of the *varg* cultivated on their own account. But most had formal agriculturalist tenants. Tenants and landlords alike depended upon the labor of agrestic serfs and slaves.[7] Two forms of tenancy prevailed: *mulgeni*, which was permanent and at a fixed rental; and *chalgeni*, which was short term and with renegotiated rents.

The land revenue demand in Kanara was said to be based upon a standard assessment to which various rulers had added increments. The Bednur rulers had made heavy demands, but Haidar and Tipu were credited with greatest imagination in developing ways of extracting the district's wealth. Munro said the agrarian economy of the district was near to ruin, but assumed that the revenue demands of 1762 reflected a realistic tax. The new British land revenue settlement returned to the assessments of late Bednur rule plus a percentage of Haidar Ali's additions. The rate was between one-third and one-half of the gross produce. Because the estates had not been surveyed, the Madras *ryotvari* system was out of the question. Munro adopted the view that although much of the countryside had fallen out of cultivation during the chaos of Tipu's last years, the number and intensity of disputes over land demonstrated the probable profitability of the estates. He did not see the

6. G. R. Gleig, *The Life of Major General Sir Thomas Munro*, 3 vols. (London, 1830), 3:160–163. This account of the settlement in Kanara is based on MRO, SRSC: *Land Assessment and Land Tenures of Kanara* (Mangalore, 1853); MRO, SRSC: *Reports on Revision of Assessment and Disturbances Known as Koots in Kanara, by John Stokes, 1832–1833* (Mangalore, 1895).

7. Francis Buchanan, *A Journey from Madras Through the Countries of Mysore, Canara, and Malabar* 3:35–36, 140; "*Slavery in India*," in Great Britain, *Parliamentary Papers* (Commons) 125 (1828):548–553.

settlement as a permanent one, although subsequently the *vargdars* and not a few collectors made that assumption. The immediate goal was to promote expansion of cultivation in lands that had gone to waste during the period of depopulation.[8]

While a detailed agrarian history of Kanara is beyond the present scope, it must be recognized that the new settlement had important implications for landholders, including Saraswats. Munro had been confident about the landlords' ability to meet the revenue demand, since he had been shown the accounts kept by the *shanbhogs*. These were represented to be imperfect, but reliable, records of revenue affairs for upwards of four centuries.[9] It seemed too good to be true. Munro and his successors soon decided that it was. The government had to face increasing difficulty in realizing its revenues in Kanara. Succeeding collectors determined that although the country gave every appearance of an increasing prosperity, the assessments were too high. In 1819 modifications were made, reducing the demand on each estate to the average of the previous sixteen years' collections; the basic system remained, however, into the 1860s.

The inequalities of the operations were enormous. Because *vargs* were not surveyed for quality or extent, it was possible for an enterprising *vargdar* to encroach upon public "waste" lands. If local officials could be compromised, estates would be divided, separating the most profitable portions from the inferior sections. These latter would then be "sold" to an indigent cultivator or an entirely fictitious person, and a new *varg* registry created in his name. After two years the new *vargdar* would be reported to have absconded, leaving his estate fallow. The lands would be reclassified as "waste" and the revenue demand remitted, whereupon the original *vargdar* would commence encroaching upon the now untaxed lands. Within a few years he could possess all that he ever had held, but at a greatly reduced assessment.[10] The opportunities for fraud were limited only by the imagination and ambition of the *vargdars*. Poor cultivators were forced to bear a heavier proportion of tax than was paid by the wealthy.

The true value and extent of landed wealth of Kanara was

8. MRO, SRSC: *Letters of Sir Thomas Munro*, pp. 83–84, 103–104.
9. *Ibid.*, p. 77.
10. MRO, SRSC: *Mr. H. M. Blair's Report on Modification of Beriz, 1842* (Mangalore, 1897), p. 11.

like treasure secured in a chest. One man, the *shanbhog*, held the key. Munro had praised the skills of the Kanara *shanbhogs* and the scope of their records. But the skill most widely practiced in Tipu Sultan's time had been concealment of revenue from the Mysore officials.[11] By the time he prepared to leave Kanara, Munro said that to expect the local functionaries to provide accurate accounts and ready co-operation would be "madness."[12] It is clear that Munro did not like Kanara; he sought another assignment even before his arrival. He hated the climate, with what seemed five months of rain and an excessive hot season. And he seems to have not much appreciated the enterprising qualities of the district's population. His remarks call to mind the phrase coined by the humorist S. J. Perelman, "It's not the heat, it's the cupidity."[13] As it has not been possible to locate records from the early nineteenth century of specific estates held by Saraswats, it may be said only that landholders of Kanara appear to have suffered disadvantages under the British revenue system, but that many were nonetheless able to prosper.

### *Access to Government Service*

It has been noted that the Saraswats possessed a nickname, "Bhanap," believed to be derived from the personal name of an especially clever member of the Koppikar family who had held an official post in pre-British Kanara. Whether true or not, it was a fitting tradition for a caste that came increasingly to supply a major proportion of local administrative personnel in Kanara. But this did not transpire rapidly.

The English East India Company's growing domain in India was supervised by Europeans, but managed by Indians in its civil and military hierarchies. The structures of administration differed in each part of India, but the functions of pacification, taxation, and administration were invariably dependent upon recruitment of

11. Gleig, *Life of Munro*, 3 : 161.

12. MRO, SRSC: *Letters of Sir Thomas Munro*, pp. 6–7. MRO, SRSC: *Collector's Report on Appointments Held by Potails and Shambogues in Kanara, 1815* (Mangalore, 1919), p. 1, notes that Tipu's officers were so dependent upon *shanbhogs* they actually subsidized them, hoping to gain their cooperation.

13. Gleig, *Life of Munro* 3 : 113–114; 1 : 229. S. J. Perelman, *Westward Ha!* (New York: Simon and Schuster, 1948), p. 96.

suitable Indian employees in the subordinate levels. These recruits usually were drawn from among the same social strata that had supplied such functionaries in pre-British regimes. Because the British were still learning the lessons of South Asian rule, they were as dependent upon old administrative elites as their predecessors.[14]

In the growth of the Madras Presidency, the major base of recruitment to administrative service had been among members of several brahman castes. Some were Tamil- or Telugu-speakers, others were descendents of Maharashtra Deshastha Brahmans who had been recruited to southern India for such service in earlier centuries.[15] These groups could not fully monopolize positions in British service. Yet by virtue of their skill and support, British officers came to depend upon these "revenue brahmans." Young Thomas Munro did so during the creation of the *ryotvari* system in the Baramahal. When the chore of pacifying and settling Kanara was fixed upon him, he recruited some of them to accompany him into the new district to help establish and govern the new administration.[16]

The introduction of outsiders into Kanara administration had been a common practice under Tipu Sultan, for potential local recruits were judged neither trustworthy nor competent. Munro filled gaps in his staff with the brahmans who had come to Kanara under Tipu.[17] Munro's successor, Alexander Read, complained, "None are found on this coast for revenue business. . . . I have never yet been able to procure more than two writers, and only one of these [is] capable of conducting the monthly accounts or any other business without assistance." When Read had to replace his chief writer, he stated he could find a replacement only from

14. Robert E. Frykenberg, *Guntur District: 1788–1848: A History of Local Influence and Central Authority in South India* (Oxford: Clarendon Press, 1965), pp. 24–37; Kenneth Ballhatchet, *Social Policy and Social Change in Western India, 1817–1830* (London: Oxford University Press, 1957), pp. 77–103.

15. Frykenberg, *Guntur District*, pp. 8, 15–22; Mahratta Education Fund, Madras (pub.), *South Indian Maharashtrians* (1937), pp. 129–144.

16. MRO, SRSC: *Letters of Sir Thomas Munro*, p. 6; MRO, MBRMR, no. 19: *Report of Mr. Stokes, Commissioner, on the Discontent in S. Kanara* [18034], para. 294; *Bom. Gaz.* 15, *Kanara*, part 1 : 129; MBRP, Jan. 5, 1829 [IOR: P/296/79/ff. 406–407]; MBRP, July 3, 1820 [IOR: P/293/56/ff. 4649–4653].

17. An example was Hannumantharao (b. 1748), who served Tipu and was subsequently appointed by Munro in 1800 as *tahsildar*. MBRP, July 17, 1820 [IOR: P/293/56/ff. 5548–5550].

Madras or Seringapatam.[18] But recruiting from that distance was costly.

The Indian officers brought to Kanara had to be given greater pay than in the Baramahal, to offset a higher cost of living. Although Kanara was the legendary rice bowl of the west coast, little of the grain found its way into the bazaars; that which did was 10 to 15 percent more costly than in the Tamil districts. Most local people obtained their staples from their own lands or tenancies. Only outsiders depended on the market, which was dominated by the export trade. The climate seemed uncongenial; contagious diseases threatened; Kanara was, for the "revenue brahmans," a hardship post.[19] Nevertheless, for over a quarter century Deshastha and Karnataka Brahmans dominated the administrative offices of the district.[20] So long as Munro's system of "double daftar" was maintained—that is, two parallel chains of command and accounts in Kannada and "Hindvi" (Marathi or Hindustani)—the outsiders held the advantage.[21] British collectors, when making new appointments, looked with special favor upon the sons of the men already in their service. It served as "a solid proof to the respectability of the native departments that their children, following the correct path of their fathers, are certain to find encouragement under the British."[22]

So long as the British officers were themselves stationed in the district for lengthy periods, there appears to have been little concern that corruption might threaten the administration. Except for a few of the men who had come with Tipu, none of the favored group had lands in the district, so they were presumed to be free of participation in any local combinations to avoid revenue payments.[23] Hence the British officers continued to patronize their old servants, diligently defending their inflated salaries.[24]

18. MBRP, July 1, 1802 [IOR: P/287/12/ff. 6441–6442].

19. Munro's Report, May 4, 1800, quoted in MBRP, July 3, 1820 [IOR: P/293/56/ff. 4649–4653; MBRP, Sept. 26, 1816 [IOR: P/291/93/ff. 10867–10892]; MBRP, Jan. 5, 1829 [IOR: P/296/79/ff. 406–407].

20. MBRP, Jan. 25, 1830 [IOR: P/297/39/ff. 1476–1479]; Oct. 28, 1830 [IOR: P/297/62/ff. 12202–12203].

21. MBRP, June 10, 1816 [IOR: P/291/82/ff. 6282–6285].

22. MBRP, July 22, 1822 [IOR: P/294/25/f. 6831]; MBRP, March 14, 1803 [IOR: P/287/27/ff. 2608–2621].

23. MBRP, March 14, 1803 [IOR: P/287/27/ff. 2608–2621].

24. MBRP, July 3, 1820 [IOR: P/293/56/ff. 4649–4651].

The costs associated with the system were high. It became evident by 1817 that the "double daftar" was not working. The majority of all records in the district were in Kannada, and the proportion continued to grow. Kannada was not the mother-tongue of all the district inhabitants—Konkani and Tulu were strongly represented—but Kannada was the language generally understood as the vehicle of law and administration. Adoption of a single official language would simplify procedures and widen the scope of recruitment for government service. With the elimination of the double language requirement, local residents, whose families already possessed lands from which they could obtain their rice and other necessaries, could be recruited, and at lower rates of pay.[25]

In 1817, Collector Thomas Harris moved to fill an important post in his revenue establishment with a local man, Dhareshwar Narnapah, a Saraswat who had been unemployed since an earlier retrenchment from a minor clerical post.[26] Harris determined to increase the numbers of local men, both Saraswat Brahmans and Christians, to balance what he believed to be an overrepresentation of a single caste in his office; "I consider it a matter of primary importance to introduce those of another persuasion gradually, in order to incite a competition which has little or no existence at present".[27] From this time forward, local men were appointed to higher posts in the district administration, but the local offices, *patels* and *shanbhogs* (village heads and clerks), still offered the best opportunities for Saraswats and other district residents.[28]

The accountancy of a revenue village was pivotal in the assessment process and in the collection of taxes. This post *(shanbhog)* offered some voice in the management of temples within the village and carried the responsibility for disbursing government funds and

25. MRO, SRSC: *Letters of Sir Thomas Munro*, p. 164; MBRP, Dec. 4, 1828 [IOR: P/296/72/ff. 12513–12516]. The Sea Customs department, which was one utilizing only Kannada language records, offered early advancement to local men. Cf. "Record of Services" of Tonse Mangeshaya and Boniface Fernandez, MBRP, May 28, 1848 [IOR: P/308/34/ff. 8126–8129], MBRP, May 16, 1842 [IOR: P/303/46/ff. 5985–5987].

26. MBRP Dec. 15, 1817 [IOR: P/292/48/f. 15230].

27. *Ibid.*

28. Because identification of persons in district establishment lists (*moyen zabitah*) is lacking, it is not possible to quantitatively measure local recruitment. District local records that would throw further light on the matter were destroyed during the Coorg invasion of 1837. Cf. MBRP, May 15, 1800 [IOR: P/286/35/ff. 4169–4193]; MBRP, July 21, 1803 [IOR: P/287/37/ff. 8134–8153].

serving as a link from the village to officials at the *tahsildar*'s taluka (district subdivision) headquarters.[29] Such power offered myriad opportunities for posing local or personal interests against the regular priorities of the administration. It was discovered in 1817, for example, that the *shanbhog* of Vithal, one Mangeshayya, had been regularly holding back a percentage of his revenue collections. With this he had created a sort of floating fund which his son then employed for investment in trade. Mangeshayya had also given his son priority in the right to stand security for debts and revenue arrears of cultivators. Thus his son was in a position to expand the family's landed holdings. Furthermore, his son had been enabled to obtain favourable prices in government sales of goods that had been put in distraint for arrears of rent or revenue.[30] The *shanbhog* was dismissed and a successor selected from among "those who are expert at accounts and otherwise qualified as landholders and in knowledge appertaining to their duty." Except under circumstances such as detailed here, British policy was to appoint "the next descendant or near relation, if fit, in preference to . . . strangers."[31]

Thomas Harris, the collector of Kanara from 1816 to 1823, thought that the *shanbhog*s were growing in power and prestige. This was partly due to the fact that they had begun to serve not only as channels for the government, but also for moneylenders in dealings with the cultivators.[32] Sixty years later it was observed that the pattern of land-holding often entailed:

> The descendants either of village accountants or of the relations of village accountants, officers who had every facility for enlarging their own holdings and allowing those in whom they were interested to enlarge theirs by encroaching on Government waste. Moreover, those people formed the educated class of the community and rapidly became the moneyed class and acted as village bankers. In the course of time the lands of their debtors passed into their hands, and the debtors fell from the rank of occupants to that of tenants.[33]

Thus while continued occupation of local revenue offices in Kanara enhanced the position of Saraswats and other local caste members,

29. MBRP Nov. 22, 1827 [IOR: P/296/40/ff. 14375–14376].

30. MBRP, Nov. 3, 1817 [IOR: P/292/43/ff. 13079–13081]. In some villages the posts were hereditary, notably in the northern talukas. Some of these rights, however, had been granted only during Tipu's time, in return for payment of a fee (*nazar*) MRO, SRSC: *Collector's Report . . . Potails and Shambogues*, p. 1.

31. MRO, SRSC: *Collector's Report . . . Potails and Shambogues*, pp. 2–3.

32. MBRP, Feb. 20, 1823 [IOR: P/294/46/ff. 2514–2518].

33. *Bom. Gaz.* 15, *Kanara*, part 2 : 185.

a British decision during the 1820s to adopt a new policy of recruitment in district administration opened new opportunities. Lower costs, simplification of language use, and a balance of castes and communities in district offices as a check on corruption were the influential points governing the decision. So long as the British collectors maintained substantial tenure in their appointments, the control over combinations and corruption was relatively effective in Kanara. Peculators were charged and dismissed occasionally, but continuity was the watchword. After 1823, however, the collectorate charge changed hands frequently; continuity and control suffered.[34]

The process of accommodation of local talent in administration was accelerated unexpectedly in 1831. The annual revenue settlement commenced as usual when the *tahsildar*s of each taluka called the local landlords together to accept the assessment papers for the coming year. But this year in several of the meetings near Mangalore the assembled *ryot*s became unruly, loudly protesting that the demand was beyond their means and refusing to accept the papers.[35] These "tumultuous assemblages," or *kut*s, were attributed in part to the steady decline in demand for and price of rice over the previous decade.[36] A similar outburst in the adjacent Nagar division of Mysore provided the occasion for British intervention in that state's administration.[37] In Kanara, the pettions were peculiar in that several Christian employees of the revenue department were singled out for complaints of alleged misconduct. When the Madras Board of Revenue sent a special commissioner to Kanara to investigate the "*kut*s," he determined that the whole affair had more to do with jobs in government service than with the price of rice.

The commissioner concluded that the decline in prices had worked only marginal hardships which could have been adjusted with little difficulty. Rather, the petitions and complaints had been

34. Alexander Read was collector from 1800 to 1816 (jointly with J. G. Ravenshaw from 1800 to 1805); Thomas Harris served from 1816 to 1823. During the next 10 years the charge changed hands 11 times, involving 6 different men. Madras District Manuals: *South Canara* 2:275.

35. *Ibid.* 1:104–105; MRO, SRSC: *Reports of Mr. Stokes on Revision, passim.*

36. MBRP, July 1, 1830 [IOR: P/297/50/f. 6947]; MBRP Sept. 16, 1830 [IOR: P/297/57/f. 9076].

37. M. Shama Rao, *Modern Mysore*, 2 vols. (Bangalore, 1936), 1:420–432, 446.

started by a clique of Deshastha Brahmans in the district offices, led by Krishna Rao, the *huzur sheristedar*, and others. The object had been to discredit the employment of local men.[38] Several of the preceding district collectors had shown favor to Christians and/or Saraswats. One of the conspirators testified that the original draft of the complaint had stated "among other things, that Christians and Sarushwut [*sic*] Brahmins ought not to be employed in the public service." He further testified that he had urged that reference to the Saraswats be stricken, for otherwise some *ryots*, including a number of Saraswats, would refuse to sign.[39]

The conspirators felt threatened; the previous collector had given patronage to Christians, and the new collector was believed to be partial to Saraswats. The only real evidence of such partiality was the fact that the new collector, N. S. Cameron, had been a subcollector in the district and at that time had employed a Saraswat, one Yellur Devapaya. When Cameron was transferred out of the district, he had invited Devapaya to come with him to serve as his assistant in Trichinopoly. The offer had been declined, but Cameron's high regard remained.[40] The "*kuts*" led to the departure of one collector and the appointment of Cameron in his place in 1831. The machinations of the clique bore fruit; the maligned Christian *naib sheristedar* was suspended. But the fruit was bitter, for Cameron filled the vacancy with his old, trusted subordinate, Devapaya. Within a year the plot had been laid bare. The Deshastha *huzur sheristedar* was suspended and Devapaya was promoted to the post which he held until his death in 1841.[41] Although his success was singularly great, it symbolized the gradual opening of district administrative bureaucratic posts to members of his caste.

The rise of Saraswats in the district bureaucracy spawned, among later generations of "Bhanaps," a stereotypical view of the quantitative and qualitative extent of their ancestors' employment in government service. Analysis of available records shows that relatively few Saraswat individuals rose in government service until the 1830s and that there was nothing resembling a caste

38. MRO, SRSC: *Reports of Mr. Stokes on Revision*, pp. 109–118.

39. Testimony of Derebyle Ramiah in MRO, MBRMR no. 19: *Report of Mr. Stokes on Discontent* [18034], para. 62.

40. U. Ananda Rao, *A Life Sketch of Karnick Devapah: Head Sheristedar, Canara District* (Cocanada, 1915), Appendix, p. 1.

41. *Ibid.*, pp. 1–4; MBRP, June 24, 1833 [IOR: P/299/6/ff. 7910–7911].

monopoly of appointments at the higher level. The "ethnic variable," a perception by British officers that it was best to balance castes and communities in district administrations, was clearly at work.

Ethnic balance notwithstanding, the path of advancement for the outside men had been smoother than for the Kanara residents. Krishna Rao, the suspended *huzur sheristedar*, had cóme with his father accompanying Munro in 1799 and had been appointed cash-keeper in 1800 in the headquarters of the northern division at Kundapur. A year later he was *huzur gomastha* (chief accountant). In 1807 he became the *sheristedar* (secretary to the District Collector; highest-ranking post open to an Indian) of Mangalore taluka, and when his father, the *huzur sheristedar*, died in 1810, Krishna Rao was appointed *naib sheristedar*, which post he enjoyed for fifteen years, rising to his father's old rank in 1825.[42]

By contrast, his successor, Yellur Devapaya, had long remained in the lower ranks. He began as a village *shanbhog* and then held petty appointments in judicial offices before he won Cameron's patronage.[43] The first Saraswat ever to hold a *tahsildar* appointment, Chandavar Mangeshaya, had also begun in 1799 at age 20 as a *shanbhog*. Ten years later he obtained entry into the salt department—as a *gomastah* from 1809 to 1817, then to 1824 as a *mutsidi* (supervisor). He left the salt department for one year to serve as a police *amin* (taluka officer) before being appointed taluka *sheristedar* for two years. After brief service as a cash-keeper and sea customs supervisor, Mangeshaya was made *sayar kamavisdar* (superintendent of excise collections) from 1828 to 1832, when Cameron appointed him *tahsildar* at Honavar. Of the ten *tahsildar*s in Kanara in May 1834, Mangeshaya had served longer in subordinate positions than all others save the one other local man, a Shenvi, Subbarao of Ankola.[44] Where the sons of outsiders had been granted preference, local men had to prove themselves.

The chance coincidence of patronage and opportunity which Cameron's collectorship offered a few Saraswat individuals such as

42. MRO, MBRMR no. 19: *Report of Mr. Stokes on Discontent* [18034], para. 294.

43. U. Ananda Rao, *Life Sketch*, p. 2.

44. MBRP, June 30, 1834 [IOR: P/299/40/ff. 5639–5649]. The salaries of the lower posts were commensurately reduced. A *shanbhog*'s monthly compensation was about Rs. 5; salt *gomastah*, Rs. 10/8, *mutsidi*, Rs. 21; taluka *sheristedar* and sea customs agent, Rs. 50 to 60. Mangeshaya's salary as *tahsildar* doubled to Rs. 120. An experienced *huzur sheristedar* received Rs. 280 per month; his deputy, Rs. 175. MBRP, Jan. 5, 1829 [IOR: P/296/79/ff. 406–446].

Devapaya and Mangeshaya provided a base for further opportunities. When Cameron left the district in 1833, he wrote to Devapaya, "I regret that my removal from this district will prevent my affording you all that assistance which, had I remained in authority, I should have been most happy to have rendered."[45] Cameron need not have worried. Devapaya won the praise of succeeding collectors—playing a major role in frustrating the success of the Coorgi rebels during the later invasion of the district in 1837. Within a year of his promotion to *huzur sheristedar*, several relatives and caste fellows had been accepted in service and/or promoted.[46] Position brought other opportunities, as evidenced by approval in 1834 by the Board of Revenue of the purchase by Devapaya, in the name of his son Venkatrao, of an estate in the Bantwal taluka, at the cost of Bahaduri Pagodas 995 (about Rs. 3,410). By that time his son was serving in the collector's office at Mangalore as *huzur gomastha*.[47]

Devapaya's success did not usher in a golden age of Saraswat monopolies in Kanara government offices. Rather, the field of recruitment for district offices had expanded to include residents of the district. Christians, Shenvis, and other local brahmans were also found on all establishment rolls with increasing frequency from 1832 to 1852. For example, only a few highly visible Bhanaps held the prestigious and lucrative *tahsildar* appointments during the period. Six individuals—Chandavar Mangeshaya, Kachur Mangeshaya, Mulki Rangappa, Mangalore Annappa, Kalyanpur Anantaya, and Tonse Mangeshaya—served in the post, out of a total of 52 during the two decades.[48] There was not much room at the top.

45. N. S. Cameron to Devapaya, April 30, 1833, quoted in U. Ananda Rao, *Life Sketch*, Appendix, p. 1.

46. Although Devapaya diligently protected government interests during the Coorg invasion in 1837, one relation, a cousin, Murtyappa, had been coerced into service of the Coorg leaders. IOR, Board's Collection 79971, Vol. 1882, pp. 331–357. Murtyappa had been accused once of using Devapaya's influence to obtain the *shanbhog* appointment of Bungadi. *Ibid.*, p. 357. On the "Kanara Insurrection," see *ibid.* and Vols. 1881 to 1886 in the same series; G. Richter, *Manual of Coorg* (Mangalore, 1870), pp. 360–361; F. C. Brown, *Letters . . . Relative to the Disturbances in Canara* (London, 1838), pp. 36ff.

47. MBRP, Oct. 9, 1834 [IOR: P/299/50/f. 10257]. The other *huzur gomasthas* at the time were Padokon [Padukone] Santappa and Amladi Santappa. IOR, Board's Collection 79981, Vol. 1885, p. 282; 79973, Vol. 1883, p. 177. Cf. Talmaki, *Families* 3:29–30; MBRP, Oct. 21, 1850 [IOR: P/309/20/ff. 14392–14425].

48. Based on Tahsildari Returns, MBRP, June 30, 1834 [IOR: P/299/40 ff. 5639–5649]; MBRP, May 16, 1842 [IOR: P/303/46(ff. 5985–5988]; MBRP, May, 28, 1849 [IOR: P/308/34/ff. 8126–8129]; and MBRP, June 10, 1852 [IOR: P/310/24/ff. 6763–6767].

With each new generation, fresh recruits presented themselves for appointments. With the coming of formal education to Kanara in the 1830s, the British enhanced their requirements for employment, beginning a pattern of raising standards of admission to even lowly clerkships which culminated in the elaborate educational qualifications demanded by the close of the nineteenth century. For the moment, young Saraswats aimed at the lower ranks and hoped that their rise would follow, whether from their own capacities or the whims of chance.

Although the Saraswats were among the castes in Kanara who came to be seen as apt recruits to the growing district bureaucracy, they seem to have had no visible impact upon its development. They learned its routines and tried to meet its qualifying demands. The administrative structure of a Madras Presidency district could be diagramed in a way to suggest a small model bureaucracy. Yet the routines and recruitment were neither so established or so rational as the abstract ideal. Service in administrative positions had a long tradition among the Saraswats. The development of British rule contributed new levels of opportunity. The highest ranks offered substantial salaries and chances for promotion of family or caste interest. While most Saraswats who entered the new administration seem to have remained in the low-paying clerical strata, those who did rise won wealth and influence. Their experience offered fresh models of success to following generations. The British practice of not identifying their lower-ranking civil servants save by personal name frustrates any effort to quantify the proportion of Saraswats in the administration before 1870. Nevertheless, what is known of individual careers suggests a slowly expanding structure of opportunity. The developments had some implications for the corporate life of the caste as well. The growing importance of the district town, the availability of education, and the rise of individual government servants altered the balances within the caste that had been functional since the days of Haidar Ali. These alterations will be examined in detail in the following chapter.

# 4

# THE RISE OF THE SARASWATS AND SHRI CHITRAPUR *MAṬHA*: 1785–1865

THE LATE eighteenth and early nineteenth centuries were a time of gradual change in the situation of the Saraswat Brahmans of Kanara. Their *swamis* successfully promoted the distinctive discipleship to Shri Chitrapur *maṭha*, expanding the effectiveness of that institution as a definitive link for the caste. As we have seen, some of those disciples were themselves experiencing changed circumstances of increased wealth and influence arising from landholding and government service. These disciples made substantial contributions to the maintenance and extension of caste religious institutions, and became increasingly interested in the affairs and activities of the *maṭha*. The period was marked among the Saraswats by a reaffirmation of ancestral *dharma*, but it was also a time of confrontation with new knowledge and values. Foreign missionaries offered increasingly valuable English education to those anxious to advance in government service, but at the price of exposure to another religion. The threat of religious conversion put Saraswat families on the defensive, and ultimately pushed them into Kanara's first organized political mobilization—a campaign for the establishment of a government school at Mangalore.

## *Social Change and Religious Elaboration*

Ever since the Saraswats had entered the Kanara region, they had built temples in their villages of residence, usually dedicated to their specific household deity (*ishtadevata*). Such construction of "private" temples by castes or families of single castes was common in Kanara.[1] It was particularly compelling that the Bhanaps, as a brahman *jāti*, establish their own shrines. It appears that even when a temple was built by a single family for its use and the use of the caste, the sponsors could not always preserve and maintain the structure with their own resources.[2] Those who could faced another difficulty in the turmoil of the transfer of power to the British, for the temples were targets of looting and destruction.[3] After the establishment of British rule in Kanara, the growth of public stability and private prosperity stimulated Bhanap families to considerable activity in temple construction and renovation.

One major obstacle was availability of revenue remissions or even direct subsidies (*tastik*) to temples from the government. The British had followed the fashion of Haidar Ali and Tipu Sultan, cancelling most *inam* grants of revenue-free lands in support of temples.[4] Subsequently a cash payment from the treasury was set for those temples that had previously had support, at a rate based on the estimated productivity of lands formerly held. The Saraswats were a relatively small community and relatively recent arrivals, and consequently were not eligible for much government support.[5] In lieu of *tastik* they could only apply for special grants and loans. Thus in 1821 Collector Thomas Harris requested sanction for granting a loan to cover the expenses of rebuilding "the pagoda of Mahdanaut Eswarra"—Shrimat Ananteshwara at Vithal.[6] He explained that the temple had been given assistance in 1804 in recovery from the depredations of the Hegade of Vithal; In April 1821, a fire had consumed the entire structure, and now the Saraswats of the area petitioned for assistance. The collector reminded Madras that the petitioners were "the head inhabitants of Mogany Vittal, . . . Koojistul Brahmins, one of the Concany sect, who are the chief cultivators in this valuable part of Bekul

1. MBRP, Nov. 11, 1863 [IOR: P/315/3/ff. 6617–6618].

2. *Kanara Saraswat* [hereafter *K. S.*] 13, no. 4 (October 1929): 10–11.

3. For example, the Lakshminarayan temple at Bailur was looted of its idols and ornaments and its temple priest murdered. Koppīkar and Koppīkar, *Bailuru Sri Lakṣminārāyaṇa Devara hāgū*, pp. 87–88.

4. MBRP, Sept. 25, 1820 [IOR: P/293/64/ff. 8102–8118].

5. M. Coelho's Petition in MRO, MBRMR, no., 19: *Report of Mr. Stokes on Discontent* [18034], para. 73.

6. MBRP, July 2, 1821 [IOR: P/293/85/ff. 5570–5572].

talook."[7] Because the temple did not receive *tastik*, it was ineligible for the regular decennial government loans for temple renovations. The Board of Revenue approved a loan of Rs. 2000, which was repaid by the collective efforts of the Saraswat community residing at Vithal, Bantwal, and nearby hamlets.[8]

A Saraswat temple at Mangalore, Shri Umamaheshwar, passed through several financial storms. It had been founded in 1744 as a family temple, but the sponsoring family could not maintain it and handed it over to the "ten" of the Saraswats at Mangalore. Public management could do little to expand or improve the shrine. The temple was finally put on a strong footing by a well-to-do Bhanap and by the *swami* of Chitrapur *maṭha*. In 1832 the newly appointed *huzur sheristedar*, Yellur Devapaya, underwrote the costs of badly needed renovations, and subsequently utilized his powers to obtain a place for the temple on the government *tastik* lists.[9] During the 1830s the sixth *guru*, Vamanashram Swami, spent much time at Mangalore and stayed at the temple. When he passed to *mahasamadhi* there in 1839, the *samadhi* monument was erected within the temple precincts and management of the temple was handed over to direct control of the Chitrapur *maṭha*.[10] The stability of the Shri Umamaheshwara shrine was assured.

Devapaya's intervention was not an isolated act of pious investment. He went on to build and endow a pilgrim rest house (*dharmshala*) near the adjacent Ganapathi temple. It served as a stopping-place for pilgrims and as a lodging for Bhanaps visiting Mangalore for religious purposes or on business with the government and courts. It would not be the last time that this influential government servant would employ his growing wealth for the corporate religious benefit of his caste.

The *swamis* of Shri Chitrapur *maṭha* were no less active in building religious linkages among the Saraswats. From 1785 to 1864, three

7. "Koojistul" is a rendering of Kushasthali. The usage "cultivator" is substituted for "*ryot*," which meant not the actual agriculturalist, but the person with whom the revenue assessment was settled. This is evident in Harris' assurances that none of the "humbler class," i.e., the tenants, "would be compelled to help pay off the loan save by their own free will."

8. H. Shankar Rau, *Chitrapur Saraswat Miscellany*, pp. 68–69. MBRP, July 24, 1821 [IOR: P/277/46/f. 2256].

9. U. Ananda Rao, *Life Sketch of Karnick Devapah*, pp. 3–4; "Shri Umamaheshwar Temple," *K. S.* 13, no. 4 (October 1929) : 10–11.

10. "Shri Umamaheshwar Temple," p. 11.

*gurus*, Shrimat Keshavashram, Shrimat Vamanashram, and Shrimat Krishnashram, diligently labored to strengthen the *maṭha* and to define its core of disciples among the Saraswat *jāti*. It will be recalled that when the Saraswats had been threatened with a break in their *guruparampara* in 1757, they had recruited a new *guru*, Shrimat Parijñanashram II, who had soon chosen a successor, Shankarashram Swami II, a young boy of the Shukla Bhat family who was the appropriate choice in light of the earlier agreements. But when Shankarashram Swami's ill health threatened to again cut off the line, the laity urged him to adopt a *shishya* without regard to family. A *guruparampara* is in fact only a tradition of spiritual learning and intellectual discipline passing from one *sannyasin* to another. But by its association with the *maṭha* and its import for the Saraswat community, the survival of this *guruparampara* took on a larger meaning in the social life of the caste. In 1781 Shankarashram Swami II was prevailed upon to designate a boy from a family other than the Shukla Bhats to be his *shishya*. As had been feared, the old *guru* did not live long thereafter, and the new *shishya*, Keshavashram Swami assumed his responsibilities as head of the *maṭha* in 1785.[11]

The new *swami*'s career was an appropriate response to the concerns of the caste elders. He adopted a policy of vigorous promotion of the *maṭha* and emphasized its centrality in defining the boundaries of the caste. Whereas heretofore the activities of the *swami*s had been largely in the vicinity of Gokarn and Shirali, Keshavashram Swami commenced tours to the places of Bhanap settlement farther south, including Kundapur, Mangalore, Bantwal, and Vithal. He took the occasion of these visits to urge his flock to foreswear any accretions of Vaishnava practice in their ritual lives. While, as *smarta*s, the Saraswats would certainly continue to reverence Vishnu, they ought not wear Vaishnava sectarian marks, he decreed. Unfortunately, no text of Keshavashram Swami's sermons is known to exist, and we may only speculate as to the style and tone of their delivery as the young *guru* attempted to reclaim his putative flock. He claimed that they ought to pay tithes (*vantiga*) only to Shri Chitapur *maṭha*, and that they should accept *mantra*s and blessings from no other *swami*.[12] By his efforts, the *maṭha* began to acquire

11. He was from the Talageri *dayad* of the Kandlur family of Kaundinya *gotra*. H. Shankar Rau, *Miscellany*, p. 50.
12. *Ibid.*, p. 51.

some extensive landed properties in Kanara, the income of which was directed toward renovations of the *samadhi*s of earlier *swamis*. Special appeals were also made for other donations.[13]

The obligatory observance of a spiritual retreat during the rainy season (*chaturmas*) was also converted to constructive purpose by Shrimat Keshavashram. By staying in various centers of Bhanap residence each year, he strengthened close ties with the laity. In 1816, for example, Keshavashram Swami went to the site of the *samadhi* of his predecessor in the village of Mallapur, east of Kumta. During the retreat there, he gave sermons and blessings to the householders of the region, who flocked to have a sight (*darshan*) of their *guru*. He also raised funds with which the small *maṭha* and *samadhi* memorial of Mallapur were renovated.[14] On an earlier occasion, when Shrimat Ananteshwara temple at Vithal was reopened in 1804, the *swami* made a special journey to attend the consecration ceremony. Six years later he returned for the installation of a new image. Such visits were occasions for collection of overdue *vantiga* and receipt of special gifts given by the devotees.[15] In the closing years of his reign, Keshavashram Swami turned these resources to the construction of a new building for the Chitrapur *maṭha* at Shirali.[16] Upon his passing in 1823, he was succeeded by his *shishya*, Vamanashram Swami.

Vamanashram Swami had been formally initiated as *shishya* in 1804. Some of his early training was at Mangalore with specially retained brahman teachers, and his short career from 1823 to 1839 centred on the southern part of Kanara. His tours included a visit to the sacred shrine of Taḷa Kaveri at the source of that holy river in Coorg.[17] Saraswat tradition recalls that Vamanashram Swami was inclined toward a retiring, spiritual life, and that he gave less attention to *maṭha* management than his predecessor.[18]

13. Account of Samvatsara Poridhavi, Ashvija, Shuddha 15 [A. D. 1792], re construction of addition to Shri Bhavanishankar temple in the *maṭha* at Bandikeri in Gokarn. Copy in records of Shri Chitrapur *Maṭha* [hereafter R. S. C. M.]. Shri Sujir Sundarrao kindly assisted me in making translations of this and other *maṭha* documents written in old Kannada.

14. R. S. C. M., letter from Keshavashram Swami to Shamayya of Mallapur, dated Dhatu Samvatsara, Jeshta, Shuddha [n.d.; A. D. 1816].

15. "Manuscript notes on the history of Shri Chitrapur *Maṭha* prepared by Shri Sujir Sundarrao," unpaginated (Shirali, 1964).

16. *Ibid.*

17. R. N. Saletore, "A History of the Community, *Maṭh* and *Guruparampara*," G. S. Hattiangadi (ed.), *Fifty Years of Bliss* (Bombay : editor, 1965), p. 334.

18. H. Shankar Rau, *Miscellany*, p. 51.

However this may have been, the surviving records of Vamanashram Swami's time reveal the guru actively seeking to obtain *vantiga* payments from the recalcitrant laity. To the "ten" of Honavar he wrote:

> We are here in the *maṭha* and for many days have not received *vantiga*. We have purchased some lands for the *maṭha* and these must be paid for. For the last two years you have not paid *vantiga*. We have many expenses here. We have to pay the assessment [i.e., the land revenue installments due on lands held by the *maṭha*]. We must borrow the amount from others. So you must send *vantiga* regularly. If you do not, . . . it is very difficult to manage here to continue *vinayogas* [rituals]. We require more money. [We] will be touring on the northern side one year and southern the next for *vantiga* collections. In order to make this this institution [the *maṭha*] permanent, we are purchasing paddy fields and estates. So you will have to collect for each man one *varaha* [equivalent to Rs. 4].[19]

Clearly there was irregularity in the *vantiga* payment; some attributed this to dissatisfaction with the management of the *maṭha* by the *swami*'s former relatives, the Shukla Bhats. Apprehension among the laity concerning secular aspects of the spiritual institution at Shirali were not unique to this period, however.

Shrimat Vamanashram Swami was soon urged to adopt a *shishya* who might relieve the *guru* of worry and the *maṭha* managers of their apparent temptations. Hearing that the *guru* was ill, 48 Bhanap householders at Kundapur urged Vamanashram Swami to move quickly to take a *shishya*. They said that once he had consented to the ordination (*shishya svīkār*), the village's *vantiga* would be collected and sent.[20] The influential Yellur Devapaya was also pursuing the same matter, pressing the claims of one candidate—a young boy, Parameshvara, from the Nagar family, who had been a servant in Devapaya's household. An astrologer stated that the boy was meant for more elevated ends than menial work, and this view was confirmed when the question was put to a spirit-medium oracle at the Shrimat Ananteshwar temple at Vithal.[21] Although by the agreement noted in Chapter 2 the Shukla Bhats were to be given first consideration in choice of a *shishya*, and were also to have

19. R. S. C. M., letter from Vamanashram Swami to Honavar *Haṭtu samastaru* ["ten"], dated Hevalambi Samvatsara, Kartika, Shuddha 9 [A. D. 1837].

20. R. S. C. M., letter from *Hattu samastaru* ["ten"] of Kundapur and other places to Shrimat Vamanashram Swami, dated Manmatha Samvatsara, Phalgun, Shuddha 13 [A. D. 1836].

21. H. Shankar Rau, *Miscellany*, pp. 43–44.

the right to nominate any substitute from other families, the government servants at Mangalore and other southern towns, led by Devapaya, actively supported the candidacy of Parameshvara. One letter to the *guru* noted the "tens" of Gokarn, Bantwal, Manjeshvar, Ullal, and Bekal had urged adoption of Parameshvara, and that the *shishya svikar* had nonetheless been postponed: "You have promised to adopt a *shishya* in Ashadh and now it must be done; Parameshvara must be selected."[22] In 1836 Nagar Parameshvara was ordained as Krishnashram in ceremonies which, significantly, were held in Mangalore. Some fifty years after the event, it would be remembered that Devapaya "in the face of all opposition . . . [had] installed Shri Krishnashram Swamiji as our Guru." "That the *Maṭha* regained its prestige and extended its usefulness justifies the step taken."[23] Once again the influence of the advancing government servants was felt in the caste.

This new balance of power was not appreciated altogether by some members of the Shukla Bhat family, who wrote from Shirali to Vamanashram Swami in Mangalore pointing out that since Krishnashram had come from another family, they might be entitled to some consideration, including a supply of rice. 'When we were going on tour with swamiji, we were getting *dakshinas* [gifts] and clothes from among the 'tens.' We have to pay thirty *varahas* [Rs. 120] assessment. We need a little more for our expenses. You must explain this about our difficulties to the 'tens' and that they should give *vantiga* accordingly, not just for the *maṭha*, but also for the Shukla Bhat family."[24] But it appears that with or without the additional reason, the disciples' contributions were slow to materialize. Even in Mangalore, it was reported, "Some people pay little *vantiga* and some do not pay." Caste elders there and in other towns suggested that Vamanashram Swami should send Krishnashram on tour so that collections could be ensured.[25]

22. R S. C. M., letter from Gauda Saraswat Brahman *Hatthu samastaru* of Mangalore to Shri Vamanashram Swamiji, dated Dharmukhi Samvatsaru, Chaitra, Shuddha 12 [A. D. 1836].

23. U. Ananda Rao, *Life Sketch*, p. 4.

24. R. S. C. M., letter from Dassappa Bhat, Lakshman Bhat, and Shankar Bhat, Shirali, to Shrimat Vamanashram Swamiji at Mangalore, dated Vikari Samvatsara, Ashvija, Bahula 8 [A. D. 1839].

25. R. S. C. M., letter from *Hattu samastaru* of Mangalore to Shrimat Vamanashram Swami, dated Hevilambi Samvatsara, Jeshth [n.d.]; letter from Shrimat Vamanashram Swamiji to Hosangadi Subraya, dated Vikari Samvatsara, Chaitra, Bahula 4 [A. D. 1839].

Shrimat Vamanashram Swami was more successful in stimulating householders to contribute to projects in their own locality. At the then important town of Bantwal, the Bhanaps had no temple where the *swami* could stay while breaking his journey from Mangalore to Vithal. He blessed a plan to provide such a facility, which would also serve as a center for caste dinners and celebrations of festivals. Government servants in the town, led by Nagarkatte Manjappaya, a *munsif* [judge], and Kombrabail Subraya, a *shanbhog*, took steps to construct a new Shri Sitarama temple in 1836. The work was temporarily halted during the Coorgi invasion the following year, but after order was restored, the temple was completed and consecrated in the presence of the *swami* in 1838.[26] Originally the costs of daily rituals were met from random donations; but at the instance of a later *munsif*, Venkappaya, the contributions were invested for capitalization and acquisition of productive lands to support the shrine. Thus the *swami*'s tours, which had created the occasion for requiring quarters for the *guru* in each substantial place of Bhanap residence, also contributed to the establishment of a caste temple. Vamanashram Swami's successor made a similar suggestion at the seaport town of Mulki, which resulted in the construction of a new Shri Umamaheshwar temple consecrated in 1854.[27]

The counterpoint of initiatives from householders possessing secular influence and from the *swamis* of the *maṭha* continued through the mid-nineteenth century. In the previous century, leadership in caste affairs had been vested primarily with the landholders and petty officials in the more northerly sections of Kanara, as well as those at Bednur, but British rule had now altered the focus of the district. The dominant personalities were now found more in the south, clustering in Mangalore or in the taluka towns where government servants and court pleaders resided.

When Vamanashram Swami attained *mahasamadhi* at Mangalore in November 1839, a special *vantiga* collection was made to meet the expenses of the rituals and preparation of the *samadhi*. A lengthy accounting of *vantiga* collections reveals that within a week Rs. 875—a considerable amount in those days—had been collected.

26. R. S. C. M., letter from Bantwal *Hattu samastaru* to Shri Maṭha, dated Vilambi Samvatsara, Jeshta [n.d.]; Ugran Sunder Rao, "Shri Seetarama Temple, Bantval," *Citrāpura Ravikiran* 18 (January 1971): 11–12.

27. "Shri Umamaheshwar Temple, Mulki," *K. S.* 13, nos. 10–12 (April-June 1930): 4–5.

The preponderance of Mangalore influence may be judged by reference to the details of the donations. The Saraswats employed in the collector's office, led by Devapaya, contributed Rs. 73, and employees and pleaders at the District Court, Rs. 75/8.[28] Almost 17 percent of the total collection had come from 54 men, estimated to be 2.2 percent of the adult male population of the caste at that time. Fully half of the total collections were donated from Mangalore town alone.[29] Given the condition of the Chitrapur *maṭha* records for this period, it must be recognized that some more contributions may have come later from northern Kanara, or that landlords may have contributed rice rather than money after the harvest. But on the basis of available documentation, it appears that the southerners, and particularly the government servants and pleaders, were ascending to dominance in caste affairs.

The newly influential men invested much of their wealth in piety and devotion to their *swamis*. But occasionally the exercise of power in secular life had unexpected results in relations with the *maṭha*. It was recalled later that the *maṭha* was "too weak to stand on its legs . . . [and] had very frequently to bow to the haughty and domineering Government servants who bossed the community."[30] When Krishnashram Swami had chosen a *shishya* in 1858, he had selected Nagar Kalappa, his nephew, giving him the title Pandurangashram. The young *shishya* was thought by some householders to be slow in giving up the few worldly pleasures in his otherwise ascetic existence. One district *munsif*, Ullal Mangeshaya, upbraided Pandurangashram: "Is it for this, you *pora* [literally "child," but with an imputation of whelp or brat] that your head has been shaved and you have been set up over us as Guru?"[31] Such criticism from a brash government servant could be accepted in support of a

28. R. S. C. M., *vantiga* account of contributions, dated Vikari Samvatsara, Kartika, Bahula 9–13 [A. D. 1839].

29. Calculations based on *vantiga* accounts and an estimate in Buchanan, *Journey* 3 :5, of 762 Kushasthalis in the southern talukas of Kanara in 1801. *Maṭha* records and extant family histories suggest that this area held about 40 percent of the caste; thus a projection for the entire caste in 1801 would be approximately 1900 persons. Assuming a population growth rate equivalent to that of the Mangalore taluka (17 percent from 1800 to 1830), the caste size in 1830 would be about 2440.

30. Gulvadi Annaji Rao, "Reminiscences of Eminent Kanara Saraswats," *K. S.* 19, no. 6 (July 1935) :5.

31. *Ibid.*; see also G. S. Hattiangdi, *Pandurang, Pandurang* (Bombay: author, 1966), p. 20.

traditional ascetic ideal. Pandurangashram Swami's life thereafter was marked by extreme asceticism. Later, other equally outspoken critics in favour of modern social reform measures would be ignored if not silenced.

The encouragement of regularity in accounts and management of the *matha* and temples was a sustained theme in the modern history of the Bhanaps. An important alteration in procedures of *vantiga* collection was agreed upon in 1869. Six years earlier, the British government had moved to withdraw from its responsibilities for the supervision of Indian religious institutions. Act XX of 1863 established demi-official public committees to oversee the religious endowments and institutions of each district.[32] Upon nomination by each taluka *tahsildar*, district collectors were to appoint supervising committees for each religion. Members would have life tenure—the British desired to avoid "the excitement and party contention" of elections. No member should be a trustee or manager of any temple under supervision of the committee. Government employees were neither forbidden nor encouraged to participate.[33]

By this time Kanara district had been divided, and only South Kanara remained under Madras jurisdiction. The collector found that "members of one caste and religion as a rule keep perfectly aloof from that of all others and never in any way interfere with their religious observances or establishments."[34] Hence it was necessary to submit long lists for each important caste within each taluka. Otherwise the interests of the lower and poorer castes might not be consulted at all. The nominees were very carefully chosen by the *tahsildar*s from among men who paid at least Rs. 50 annual income tax or land revenue. At the time, half the *tahsildar*s in South Kanara were Saraswats; hence once again government servants could exercise their influence with respect to caste institutions.[35]

32. Act XX of 1863, section 3. This was an act of the Government of India which was adopted by the provincial government.

33. MRP, June 24, 1863, no. 1121; MBRP, July 1, 1863 [IOR : P/315/1/f. 3716].

34. MBRP, Nov. 11, 1863 [IOR : P/315/3/ff. 6617–6618].

35. *Ibid.*; MRP, Dec. 1, 1863 (G. L. Morris, Ag. Collector, South Canara, to W. Huddleston, Board of Revenue sec'y, Oct. 27, 1863, para. 8). Taluka committee members for Saraswats were, in Mangalore: Manjeshvar Babannaya Mangeshaya, Ullal Ramanaiya Ramachandraiya, and Bantwal Subrau Timmaiya; in Kasargod: Savkar Manjeshvar Rangappaiya and Sheshappaiya of Hosabettu, and Kumbla Ramaiya (Pensioner) of Palkarekod; in Udipi : Pandit Anantaiya of Brahmawar, Putu Devarahitla Mangeshaiya of Kachoor, and Ramaiya of Kallianpur; and in

A major exercise of that leverage came a few years later when one temple committee member, Manjeshvar Babannaya, approached young Pandurangashram Swami with proposals for revising the rules governing relationships between the *maṭha* and its disciples. A special meeting was called at Mangalore in 1869. Dominated by lawyers and government employees, it petitioned the *guru* for alterations in *vantiga* collection practice. The ideal had been that a fixed portion of a family's income would be given whenever the *swami* or his representative visited. This scheme had worked adequately when most Bhanaps were landlords and petty revenue servants. But as some had begun entering government services or the profession of law, they had been expected to regularly remit an amount equal to 2 to 3 percent of their salaries. The petitioners asserted that while they were paying regularly, the landholders were paying a smaller proportion of income, and that irregularly.[36] The *swami* gave his assent, and it was therefore resolved, "for the well-being of the Gauda Sarasvata community," that all would pay a regular annual *vantiga* according to terms agreed upon in a new charter, known as the *vantiga shasana*.[37]

The tithe would be paid at from 1 to 3 percent of yearly income or land revenue, of which two-thirds would go to the *maṭha* as before, the remainder being used according to local wishes. Provisions were made for installment payments and for fines and punishments for nonpayment, the ultimate sanction being excommunication, or *bahishkar*. To avoid this becoming a tool of factional disputes, false accusations of nonpayment would also be punished by fines. Any unpaid fine would result in social boycott. Local initiatives and investigations were specified, but the ultimate sanction lay with the *guru*. The charter could be changed later, but only with the consent of the *swami*.[38]

When compared with earlier documents of agreements between Saraswats and their *swamis*, the *vantiga shasana* is rather heavily structured and legalistic. It seemed a monument confirming the

---

Kundapur: Khambadkone Krishnappaiya and Gurikara Annappaiya of Puduvali, and Sheshgiriappa of Chilare.

36. Hattiangdi, *Pandurang*, pp. 30–31.

37. H. Shankar Rau, *Shrimat Anandashram Ordination*, reproduces the document on pp. 102–104 [translated with the assistance of Shri Shankar Shetty]. Some 25 of the participants were constituted a managing committee for the Shri Umamaheshwar temple. *K. S.* 13, no. 14 (October 1929): 11.

38. H. Shankar Rau. *Shrimat Anandashram Ordination*, p. 104.

dominance of those Saraswats who had mastered the bureaucratic styles of their occupations and professions. That mastery of those modes of thought and behavior enforced their power within the caste itself. It is not possible to document the actual progress toward this situation, but the circumstances in which it transpired are relevant.

### *Education and Employment in a District Town*

The instrumentalities of British rule in Kanara were of great consequence to Saraswats, whether they were payers of revenue, accountants for traders and other landholders, litigants in property disputes, or candidates for clerical vacancies in district offices. It should be evident that they were not alone in this. And not all of them would have an equal measure of concern with such subjects. Nevertheless, the economic and social circumstances of most Bhanap families meant that they were among those citizens of Kanara most conscious of the new British rule and its apparatus. Their cultural heritage of literacy, education, and scribal employment, which had brought them from Goa in the first place, would encourage immediate attention to the new rulers—even when, as we have seen in Chapter 3, the new rulers did not immediately reciprocate.

It has been observed of British rule in India that "the frontier of administration did not enter the villages, it stopped short of them."[39] In most respects it was the headquarters town of each district that was the significant terminal of the apparatus of central authority. As Professor Frykenberg put it, "The collision between the new world and the old took place at the district level."[40] The district town was the seat of power, and it was a commonplace among the subjects of that power to refer to it in traditional terms as the *huzur*, the "presence." In Kanara between 1800 and 1862 the "presence" lay at Mangalore, the site of the collectorate offices, courts, and a small military cantonment. Honavar, 113 miles up the coast, was intermittently the seat of the district court.[41] While both towns

39. F. G. Bailey, *Caste and the Economic Frontier* (Manchester : Manchester University Press, 1957), p. 3.

40. R. E. Frykenberg, *Guntur District*, p. 236.

41. Madras District Manuals: *South Canara*, 2 :274–275; Judicial Dispatch to Madras, June 2, 1814 [IOR: L/PJ/3/1385/ff. 9–78], para. 25. Location of the court in the north was in anticipation of heavier criminal case load, due to the

had suffered severely in the close of Tipu's reign, Mangalore, which had long been an important port and fortified place, had made the more rapid recovery, because of growing mercantile activity centering on the export trade of rice and other commodities.[42] Trade, not administration, had been its persevering function.[43]

As an urban setting, Mangalore had a distinctly rural appearance. Its bazaar and center resembled the countryside around, houses within walled compounds, shaded by vast groves of coconut palms. Inland lay adjoining hamlets on steep laterite hills divided by small rich valleys carpeted in the bright green of rice fields. British occupation had little impact on this scene. The court and offices were built on the breezy Balmatta hill behind the town, and the military cantonment was established on a vacant tract to the north. The urban environment of Mangalore was distinctive only in the diversity and concentration of its population, which increased from less than 12,000 in 1836 to 19,000 in 1855, and almost 41,000 by 1885.[44] As the hinge of British administration, the town contained a miniscule European community and a larger cluster of other outsiders—the Indian administrators and families who had been recruited from other parts of the East India Company's domain. Both provided elements of heterogeneity in the life of Mangalore, without disturbing the rhythm of life among most district residents.[45] But the landed and the literate of Kanara had to attend more closely to the strangers and their institutions.

Perhaps no district town in the Madras Presidency was more isolated from the capital. Initially, few Europeans came to Manga-

---

unsettled conditions and proximity to the Maratha frontier. The court was shifted back to Mangalore to handle a heavy pressure of civil disputes over landed properties in the southern talukas.

42. Buchanan, *Journey* 3 : 58–60, 137–138

43. Madras District Gazetteers: *Statistical Appendix . . . South Kanara*, p. 173; James Forbes, *Oriental Memoirs: A Narrative of Seventeen Years Residence in India*, 2nd ed., rev., 2 vols. (London, 1834), 1 : 10; G. M. Moraes, *Mangalore*, pp. 1–4, 54–57; B. A. Saletore, *History of Ancient Karnataka* : Vol. I: *History of Tulava, passim*, discusses other places as centers of political power of local chieftains in the region.

44. *Medical Topography of Malabar and Canara* (Madras, 1844), p. 41; Pharaoh & Co. (pub.), *Gazetteer of Southern India* (Madras, 1855), p. 554. An earlier visitor estimated the population at 20,000. K. S. Haridasa Bhat, *Mangalore : A Survey* (Manipal, S. K., 1958), p. 62, citing *Oriental Herald* 22 (1829) : xviii.

45. Buchanan, *Journey* 3 : 5, notes that the outsider Indians in the district did not know it very well; one of Munro's appointees gave Buchanan information of local castes "in the usual confused manner with which they are spoken of by the native officers of revenue." Other Indian outsiders at Mangalore included Vaishya and Parsi merchants from Cutch, Surat, and Bombay. Pharoah, *Gazetteer*, p. 551.

lore; certainly few nonofficial visitors bothered to make a record of their tours. As a "civil station," Mangalore might have been expected to receive the attention of Christian missionaries after restrictions on their activity were lifted in the East India Company's new charter of 1813. But the quest for Kannada-speakers' souls was found to be adquately repaid in the more accessible and salubrious environs of Bangalore and Bellary.[46] Mangalore and its inhabitants stood near the end of the queue to receive the somewhat mixed gifts of change.

When influence of change did come, they were unevenly distributed among the Kanara population. Saraswats were among the major recipients. The slow rise of district residents into higher posts of administration became increasingly predicated upon the act of qualifying for office. European superior officers chose their new appointees from among the men and boys who served as unpaid volunteers (*umedvar*), learning the ropes of the office. But literacy and an ability to cast accounts had to be acquired beforehand through some form of training. The quest for adequate education would remain a constant preoccupation for most Saraswats during the nineteenth century. In Kanara there were few foundations upon which this interest could be built.

Collector Thomas Harris, like his predecessors, had little regard for the general level of achievement among the district inhabitants. In a report on education in Kanara in 1822 he observed, "Probably there is no district in the Peninsula so devoid of artists or scientific men."[47] It was not easy to even speak of an educational system; nor were there many places where one might develop, since it was "a country of cottages, dispersed in valleys and jungles, each man living on his estate."[48] Few could be induced even to show an interest in schooling. Harris had "endeavoured to persuade some of the original farmers, the Bunts, to send their nephews to Mangalore for education, without success." Education in Kanara was little more than the collective quest for some degree of literacy by "Brahmins of the country, the Conkany and Shrinnaivee and to the second class of the former."[49]

46. Julius Richter, *A History of Missions in India* (Edinburgh, 1908), pp. 155, 196–197.

47. MBRP, Sept. 5, 1822 [IOR: P/294/28/ff. 8156–8160].

48. *Ibid.*

49. *Ibid.*

> The education of the few Brahmin children of the higher classes in the towns or villages is conducted in the house of the principal man. He selects a teacher, who receives for each child a small sum; a present of cloth at particular ceremonies, and the same for a few others. . . . It is entirely private . . . and the master is as often changed as the scholars.[50]

The subjects of study were chosen pragmatically: reading, writing, and accounts. Kannada, the official administrative language, was taught rather than Konkani or Tulu. Occasionally an ambitious family might launch a son into the study of Persian or Hindustani, in preparation for seeking a job in the district courts where those languages were in use until 1835.[51]

The Madras Presidency was not forward in development of schools, and an isolated district like Kanara was little touched. A plan instituted in 1833 foresaw public vernacular schools in district and taluka towns. Only three schools opened in Kanara, at Mangalore, Udipi, and Sirsi, with 22, 20, and 28 students enrolled respectively. But few finished. Honavar, which at the time was a taluka headquarters and seat of an auxiliary court, was proposed for a school, but no action was taken. Nor was any firm policy adopted to employ only the successful products of the schools in vacancies arising in the public service.[52]

The most significant expansion of educational opportunity in Kanara was the product of private rather than public initiative. Following the revisions of the East India Company charter in 1833, permitting foreign missions entry into India, the German Evangelical Missionary Society of Basel established a mission station at Mangalore.[53] A new form of Christianity had come to Kanara. The district had a large Christian population already, of course, dating from the sixteenth-century Portuguese activity. But in the early nineteenth century that community concentrated on rebuilding its fortunes after Tipu Sultan's persecutions; it

50. *Ibid.*

51. MBRP, Dec. 4, 1828 [IOR: P/296/72/ff. 12513–12516]; Ananda Rao, *Life Sketch*, p. 2.

52. Madras Board of Education to Governor in Council, Dec. 6, 1834, Appendix, p. 117, in IOR: Board's Collections 79196, Vol. 1864, pp. 97–122.

53. Basel Mission, *A Retrospect of the Work Done by the Basel Mission . . . for the people of South Canara* (Mangalore, 1907), p. 3; R. Scheurmeir, "History of the the Basel Mission Churches in India" (unpub. ms., 1964, in possession of Rev. B. Furtado, Kanara Theological Seminary, Mangalore), *passim*; Richter, *History of Missions*, p. 196; B. H. Badley, *Indian Missionary Directory and Memorial Volume* (Lucknow, 1881), pp. 142–144.

manifested little interest in proselytizing. Indeed, in many ways it appeared to be but another caste in the complex layering of the district's society. The German and Swiss evangelicals represented a different approach.

Upon opening their station in 1834, the missionaries attempted to quickly contact the widest possible audience by adopting the mode of public preaching in Kannada and Tulu. But with an eye to reaching the elite of the district—both Hindu and Catholic—the missionaries turned to education, where a religious message could accompany a valuable public service. A Kannada school opened in 1836, and two years later the district's first formal English-language school was inaugurated in the Mangalore bazaar.[54] Although schooling was open to all, the ranks of scholars were filled largely by young men of the higher castes. They saw knowledge of English as a new means to obtain government appointments. It was also clear that British officers in the district patronized the mission; hence to participate might win favor.[55] Enrollment grew from a few boys in 1838 to 55 in 1840–41 and 80 in 1842.[56]

The missionaries' efforts bore fruit in the conversions of several low-caste agriculturalists and a few members of the ritually still lower Billava caste of toddy-tappers. The dogma of the equality of all believers could not conceal the missionaries' regret that "not one convert had joined us from any of the higher castes."[57] European patronage continued to be given to the enterprise. In 1842 the district collector purchased land on Balmatta hill, where his office had stood before the Coorg rebels had burned it down five years before, and presented this to the mission as a site for a new school. The mission gratefully shifted from the bazaar to the new location, where their students would not be exposed to "the daily exhibitions

54. [Basel Mission], *A Retrospect*, p. 6. A Mr. Walker had opened a "charity school" for children of Indians to learn English, but he left the district and was not replaced. IOR: Board's Collections 94762, Vol. 2065, pp. 5–18. The mission school curriculum consisted of reading, writing, arithmetic, Bible history, geography, grammar, and elements of geometry. Basel Evangelical Mission [hereafter B. E. M.], *First Annual Report* (Mangalore, 1841), p. 1.

55. B. E. M., *Second Report* (1842), p. 20. Other mission societies similarly employed promotion of the English language after 1835 as an opportunity to spread the Gospel. Cf. John C. Lowrie, *Two Years in Upper India* (New York: Robert Carter & Bros., 1850), p. 47.

56. IOR: Board's Collections 79196, Vol. 1864, p. 122.

57. B. E. M., *Second Report*, p. 17; Madras District Manuals: *South Canara* 1:171–173, 187; B. E. M., *Third Report*, (1843), pp. 34–35.

of heathenism"—a reference probably to both the "Konkanis'" Shri Venkateshvara temple which dominated one end of the bazaar and the recently enlarged and rebuilt Shri Umamaheshwara temple of the Saraswats. A year later the evangelicals' prayers were answered: three students of the English school embraced Christianity, two of them "Konkanis" and the third a Saraswat.[58]

These conversions caused immense shock and stir. The converts were from brahman castes; their families were well known and influential. After the Billava conversions, other Billavas had protested to the degree that a mission school for them at Padubidri lost most of its pupils. But other Hindus had given scant attention. Now the stakes were higher.[59] The two "Konkani" converts, aged 25 and 28, had studied English in the hope of obtaining government appointments. Frustrated in that ambition, they had taken jobs in the mission's printing press. Economic motives do not seem to have figured so prominently in the conversion of the third, a Saraswat youth, Ugran Anandarao.

Ugran Anandarao was the son of Ugran Rangappaya, a pleader in the district court until his death in 1833. Thereafter Anandarao had been cared for by his uncle. At the age of 14 he was enrolled in the mission school to learn English, preparatory to finding employment in government service. At the same time he was married to Savitri, the 10-year-old daughter of Santappa, a prominent Saraswat who was then the Mangalore taluka *munsif*.[60] The arrangement was made that Santappa would provide support for his new son-in-law to pursue his studies, and thus enhance future earning prospects. Later in the century this pattern of support by a bride's family for the groom's education became virtually standard practice among the Saraswats—a new adaptation of the traditional practice of dowry.

When it became known that Anandarao was contemplating joining the Christians, his father-in-law attempted to intervene. Anandarao later recalled: "My relatives and many other persons of my caste spoke to me day after day on the subject of religion and

58. B. E. M., *Third Report*, p. 36; Ananda Rao, *Life Sketch*, pp. 3–4; "Shri Umamaheshwar Temple," *K. S.* 13, no. 4 (October 1929): 10–12; B. E. M., *Fourth Report*, (1844), pp. 9–16.

59. B. E. M., *Third Report*, pp. 34–35.

60. Petition of Santapah and others, IOR: Board's Collections 94762, Vol. 2065, pp. 5–18.

tried to turn my mind."[61] The district collector used his personal influence to restrain Santappa and the rest, giving the youth an opportunity to flee to the mission. A near riot ensued, but Anandarao ate with the missionaries and then was baptized as Hermann Anandarao Kaundinya, taking his surname from his old *gotra*. His relations made a lengthy appeal to the Madras government, complaining of interference in their religion by the collector, but the evangelical Lord Tweedale and his council refused to accept responsibility for what they termed the private acts of public officers.[62] Such legal niceties did nothing to repair the tragedy that wrenched Anandarao's family and caste. It was as if he had died—his wife Savitri was reported to have torn off her wedding necklace as if widowed. Her sentiments were interpreted in the petition to the governor:

> I am now only 15 years old; in our caste females are married but once, and should they lose their husbands in any way they cannot marry again as women of other persuasions do. Should I not meet with relief . . . my life shall be of no worth and it will be better for me to give it up.[63]

Anandarao's uncle cried out in a caste meeting assembled by the "ten" of Mangalore, "He is gone, shall all his family be also ruined? Go and perform his funeral as a man lost to his caste and country."[64] Subsequently Hermann Anandarao Kaundinya studied in Switzerland, then returned as a missionary himself to work in his native district.

For a while it appeared that the major casualty of the conversion would be the English school itself. Within a day, the Saraswat, "Konkani," Muslim, and Catholic parents withdrew their sons from the school. Attendance fell from about 60 students to 7.[65] In time some of the Catholic and Muslim boys returned, but at the end of 1845 only two Saraswats were enrolled. The missionaries reported that while Saraswat parents were anxious for their sons to learn English, they chose "to employ as masters natives who

61. Letter of Anandarao to H. M. Blair [n.d.], reprinted in B. E. M., *Fourth Report*, p. 17.

62. IOR: Board's Collections 94762, Vol. 2065, pp. 5–197.

63. *Ibid.*, p. 17; H. Moegling [trans.], *Twelve Letters* (Mangalore, 1859), p. 31 [the work is a translation of a Kannada work of the same title, *Irarupatrike*, by Anandarao, based on his conversion]).

64. Moegling, *Twelve Letters*, pp. 29–31.

65. IOR: Board's Collections 94762, Vol. 2065, p. 9; B. E. M., *Fourth Report*, p. 24.

happen to know a little English than to avail themselves of a Missionary institution of which they are so much afraid."[66] Nor was the furor restricted to Mangalore. A Kannada-language mission school that had operated at Honavar could attract few pupils after news of the conversions reached the town. The missionary there found most people suddenly hostile, "stricken with terror and dismay." When he and one of the ex-"Konkani" converts visited a Hindu festival at nearby Murdeshvar, they received a barrage of earth clods "and other things."[67]

However, the accommodation of English education in the culture of the Saraswats proved to be enduring. Knowledge of English was simply too vital to be foregone. British officials in Kanara continued to promote the link of education and advancement in public service. Findlay Anderson, the district judge and long-time patron of the mission, had found when he returned to Kanara in 1842 that "not two public servants had the slightest acquaintance with geography. Few knew anything of English." Patronage, not competence, had governed recruitment. "Men received appointments . . . because they stood with folded hands in court, had made interest with an influential [person], or had attracted the eye of the presiding officer by activity and zeal."[68] Anderson set a policy that after 1849 he would only employ assistants who passed a competitive examination and possessed a certificate of English competence from the mission school master. Boys would be accepted as volunteers, then made candidates. If successful, they would then be in line for regular appointments and promotions.[69]

Saraswat families had little choice but to again take up the formal training at the mission school. A second school was set up by an Englishman in 1853, but the majority of students remained at the mission's institution. By 1854 it boasted 120 scholars including

66. B. E. M., *Fifth Report*, (1845), p. 8; *Sixth Report*, (1846), p. 13.

67. B. E. M., *Sixth Report*, pp. 20–21.

68. *Friend of India* (Serampore), January 26, 1854, p. 50. [I owe this reference to the courtesy of Mr. John Roberts.]

69. *Ibid.*, pp. 50–51. The volunteers would attend class from 6 to 10 A. M., then attend court for practical experience from 10 A. M. to 4 P. M. After one year they would, if found satisfactory, be promoted to copyist work, still as unpaid volunteers, and on successful completion of a second year would be eligible to enter the ranks. When in 1852 four Billava youths passed the examination and were accepted as volunteers, the Brahmans of the court staff protested bitterly, even petitioning the Governor in Council. It is not clear whether pollution or employment was uppermost in their concerns.

a large proportion of young Saraswats, sons of public officials.[70] They were steering by the Charybdis of missionary English education to avoid the Scylla of unemployment. The lessons were still steeped in Christian teachings, but the students did not respond. Parents appeared to be giving greater attention to making their sons conscious of the ancestral faith. The missionaries were pleased at the size of enrollments, but could regret that "for many years not one of the many hopeful youths who there acquaint themselves with the Gospel should have given his heart to its truth. We sincerely lament the serious fact that so many leave the school for Government employ."[71]

Since Mangalore was the important center of official and educational activity, boys from other places were often sent to live with uncles or cousins in the town to permit them access to opportunity. In one instance, a successful pleader in the taluka *munsif*'s court at Mulki gave up his practice there and moved into the more competitive arena of Mangalore so that his sons might continue their education.[72]

The inauguration in 1854 of a system of educational grants-in-aid to private institutions did not stimulate growth in Kanara of new schools.[73] The government schools also did not flourish, in part because of a lack of competent teachers. It was reported that "the profession of a schoolmaster is in such low esteem on this coast, *and the opportunities in other departments so much more tempting*, that well-educated men could not be got."[74] The one bright spot was the instruction of the European teachers and their Indian assistants at the Basel Mission schools. The Saraswats continued therefore to enroll their sons. What was more remarkable, perhaps, was that they were willing to enroll their daughters in a new mission enterprise—the Brahmin Girls' School, which offered elementary training in reading, writing, and arithmetic.[75] Although limited to some girls of a few families in one town, it marked the commencement

70. B. E. M., *Fifteenth Report*, (1855), p. 19.

71. B. E. M., *Sixteenth Report*, (1856), p. 11. Cf. *Mangalore Almanac for 1854* (Mangalore, 1853), pp. 65–66; *Mangalore Almanac for 1855* (1854), pp. 48–49.

72. Selections from the Records of Madras Government [hereafter SRMG], n.s. (2nd series), 35: *Report on Public Instruction in the Madras Presidency, 1855–56*, pp. 36–39.

73. *Ibid.*,p. 39.

74. SRMG, n.s. (2nd series), 69: *Report on Public Instr. 1859–60*, pp. 44–46; SRMG, n.s. (2nd series), 35: *Report on Public Inst. 1855–56*, p. 39.

75. B. E. M., *Seventeenth Report* (1857), p. 10.

of a progressive support within the Saraswat caste for female education, which remains a distinctive hallmark to the present day.

Conversion, however, once again disrupted the educational routine. Ganeshrao Kaushika, the son of the *tahsildar* of Honavar, was recruited to Christianity in 1862 by none other than Hermann Anandarao Kaundinya. The caste members at Honavar were thrown into an immediate uproar and were dissuaded from violence only by the restraint of Ganeshrao's father. Ganeshrao had already passed the examination for government service, but announced that he intended to follow Hermann Anandarao's example and join the ministry. He left Honavar and went to the mission station at Mangalore. There he was the object of considerable abuse from his mother-in-law and others of his wife's kin.[76] Their remonstrance was in vain; another young Saraswat was lost to his caste. Suddenly the fears of conversion were again renewed. Once more, students were withdrawn from the mission English school. The missionaries expressed concern over "a determined attitude by the heathen at any price to establish an opposition school."[77]

Ullal Mangeshaya and other prominent Saraswats led a deputation of Hindus to the district collector to urge the need for a secular public institution of learning. Although no record of the meeting is preserved, the spokesmen might easily have gone beyond the specific grievances of the moment to invoke the pledge of Queen Victoria's proclamation of four years earlier that her government would not injure the religious sensibilities of her Indian subjects. In any event, they were told by the chief educational officer of the region "that the sincerity and force of their desire should be shown in a substantial manner by coming forward with a sum sufficient partly to endow the Government school."[78] Immediately a public subscription drive was begun. When, two years earlier, the Madras government enquired about the potentials of organizing municipal self-government in towns of Kanara, the collector had replied that

76. *Church Missionary Gleaner*, n.s. 13 (November 1863), 130; B. E. M., *Twenty-third Report*, (1863), pp. 24–25, 27.

77. B. E. M., *Twenty-fourth Report* (1864), p. 18. Unlike 1844, the Mangalore Catholic community in 1863 did not enter the controversy, because their bishop had established a separate school for them.

78. Madras Education Proceedings [hereafter MEP], Sept. 21, 1865, no. 51, enclosure from Director of Public Instruction to Secretary to Government, Sept. 11, 1865, para. 2; SRMG, n.s. (2nd series), 87-B: *Report on Public Instr., 1864–65*, p. 88.

"attempts to induce self-taxation" for improvements would prove fruitless. He was convinced that "to look for purely voluntary subscriptions for such purposes in the mofussil [the provinces] is utterly hopeless in the present state of society."[79] Such pessimism was unjustified. By the autumn of 1865, the public drive had netted actual payments of over Rs. 65,000. This unprecedented manifestation of public concern and fiscal support won immediate sanction for establishment of a new provincial school, which opened the following year.[80] Mangalore had now been linked directly to the provincial educational network that led up the new university at Madras. As we shall see, a new pathway had opened upon which Saraswats would soon enter. In the short run, the Saraswats of of Mangalore and its environs had demonstrated new capacities for innovation and leadership, both for their town and for their caste.

British rule in Kanara had introduced a new order of opportunities during the first half of the nineteenth century, without substantial disruption of the existing social and economic fabric. The limits of change were obscured, perhaps because the greatest transformations were concentrated in highly visible administrative centers and their associated institutions. Similarly, the inhabitants of the district had responded differentially to the new order. Saraswats, by virtue of their heritage of literacy and service as well as their landed interests, were among the first to confront the new opportunities. Not all Saraswats did so; unfortunately, much of the documentation for the period only identifies the most visible individuals, who were pioneering new jobs and new learning. Yet we can be sure that others held back, clinging to the old and familiar ways, perhaps grumbling about the pushing ambitions of new government servants and pleaders who had so much influence in the caste as to even select the new *shishya swami*. In the good old days, the *shanbhog*s and *zamindar*s of rustic villages around Gokarn or Shirali had held initiative; now the southerners were in the ascendant.

Even as such apprehensions were being felt, a British administrative action which split off North Kanara and attached it to the Bombay Presidency set in motion new developments which would again alter the balance within the caste. In the meantime, many

79. MBRP July 7, 1860 no. 3293 [IOR: P/314/58/f. 41].

80. MEP, Sept. 21, 1865, no. 50, from Collector, South Canara, to Secretary to Government, August 29, 1865, para. 2.

of the Saraswats experienced some contact with the emergent bureaucratic order of British district administration. They found not only employment therein, but also new techniques and concepts which they could and did apply to their own caste's internal organization. Education, which was the increasingly necessary key to bureaucratic appointments, had also challenged their religious culture through the agency of Christian missions. But few succumbed. Much of the new wealth and influence was being invested in the promotion and elaboration of the Saraswats' own heritage. Temples and *dharmshala*s were endowed, and Shri Chitrapur *maṭha* prospered as never before, even though the *swami*s still had to regularly appeal to their faithful, reminding them of unpaid tithes. From the troubled times of the late eighteenth century to the stability of the 1860s, the Saraswat *jāti* had prospered, and developed its distinctive institutions. Their strength would be severely tested in the coming decades.

# 5

## A DISTRICT DIVIDED:

### *Modernization in the Mofussil, 1860–1890*

THE BORDERS of the Saraswats' world coincided almost perfectly with the Madras Presidency district of Kanara. Apart from a few families settled on the western fringe of Mysore, virtually the entire *jāti* dwelt in Kanara. Except on occasions of pilgrimage to sacred shrines, the individual and corporate horizons of the Saraswats were localized. So too, for that matter, were most aspects of district life, including education and employment. After 1860 the growth of centralized provincial school systems and administrative structures and services might be expected to widen the world of the Bhanaps, and the growth of new urban institutions in the mofussil district towns might also be expected to alter the opportunities and priorities of members of such a caste. These processes were complicated for the Saraswats, however, by the bifurcation of their home district in 1859 and the transfer in 1862 of the northern half from the Madras Presidency to the Bombay Presidency.

The new frontier line between the two districts and their respective provinces was not an impenetrable barrier, but by 1862 the Madras and Bombay presidencies were each experiencing stronger forces of centralization than in any previous era. Administrative procedures under revised orders, legal and judicial practice under the new codes and High Courts, and educational standardization under the new universities all served to draw each district further into its own province's distinctive patterns. Indians in any district with interests or ambitions involving administration, law, or education began to look beyond their district towns back up the imperial network to its provincial capital at the presidency.

The Saraswats in South Kanara had begun to enlarge their capacities to pursue new opportunities presented by British rule. Logically they looked to Madras and its network. Their compatriots in North Kanara, however, were presented with a new situation. They had been in a most distant corner of Madras in the least developed talukas of a substantially unchanging district. Their caste fellows at or near Mangalore already possessed foundations of experience and institutional life that had hardly filtered into the north. Now in 1862 the citizens of North Kanara were truly rusticated. They were situated on the outermost extremities of the British system that centered on Bombay, and they were in a district bereft of any institutions that could match those of South Kanara. In fact they even lacked an established district town. Historically the Bombay government had ignored its three "Karnataka" districts, Belgaum, Bijapur, and Dharwar. Now there was a fourth to disregard, save for the specific reason of its transfer to Bombay—the development of facilities for transport of cotton from Dharwar to the sea. As we shall see, the new district's *raison d'être* offered some jobs in lower government service and the offices of cotton brokers at port towns. North Kanara's inherent limitations, however, ultimately pushed Bhanaps out into adjacent districts and Bombay city, in a manner quite dissimilar from what was developing for their caste fellows of South Kanara. Two districts that had been one now faced in different directions. In each, Saraswats formed a part of the district's Indian elite. The southerners operated in a growing urban center at Mangalore; the northerners helped establish a new town at Karwar, and then slowly moved toward the urban world of Bombay that lay beyond.

### *Saraswats and Education at Mangalore*

Mangalore's citizens might have appeared advanced, urbane, and cosmopolitan in the eyes of their northern neighbors, but in 1862 the town was still a quiet mofussil backwater with little visible hint of potential growth. Technological and economic change advanced slowly in South Kanara. For Saraswats or anyone else, there were few new opportunities aside from those associated with the growth of government service. These entailed requirements of educational qualifications beyond any previously enforced. The Madras government was elaborating educational requirements for appointments to all but the most menial public service.[1] In Mangalore the principal schooling source had been the Basel Mission until the furor over Ganeshrao's conversion stimulated the public subscription drive that ultimately produced a government provincial school.[2] When that school opened in 1865, the pent-up demand for education was dramatically revealed in an initial enrollment of 315 boys and young men. The Basel Mission school's advanced classes ceased altogether. A Catholic school survived only when the bishop forbade attendance at the new secular institution.[3] The government school was to have been staffed by experienced schoolmasters recruited from Mysore, but few were willing to transfer. Instead the staff was supplied almost entirely by young men of South Kanara who had studied at the mission school.[4] The results were more promising than might have been expected. In the 1867 Madras University Matriculation examination—an entrance examination which was the formal test for successfully completing secondary education—seven Mangalore scholars passed, one at the top of the presidency list. Two years later, a "First Arts" class was added to allow preparation for the second university exam, and 12 out of 19 boys who journeyed to Madras for the test passed.[5]

Teachers as well as students were drawn from among the Saraswats. British education officers still worried about the educational backwardness of the district. Little improvement could be expected, it was thought, "until a better class of men come forward to enter the Educational Department." Most teacher trainees were recruited from the higher castes.[6] To ensure a supply of competent teachers, the government established a Normal School at Mangalore in 1869. This provided an unusual opportunity for young men of South Kanara since the training could also qualify one for the

1. C. Maclean, *Manual of Administration of the Madras Presidency*, 3 vols. (Madras, 1885–1893), 1:560–572.

2. MEP, Sept. 21, 1865, no. 52; MEP, April 5, 1866, nos. 9, 10.

3. SRMG, n.s. (3rd series), 5: *Report on Public Instr. 1866–67*, p. 72; R. Scheuermeir, "History of Basel Mission Churches" ms., p. 21.

4. MEP, June 4, 1866, no. 1; MRO, *List of Officers in Madras Educational Department . . . 1868* [ACL 974], pp. 16–17; SRMG, n.s. (3rd series), 15A: *Report on Public Instr. 1868–69*, pp. cxlviii-cxlix.

5. SRMG, n.s. (3rd series), 5: *Report on Public Instr., 1866–67*, p. cviii, n.; SRMG, n.s. (3rd series), 15A: *Report on Public Instr., 1868–69*, p. cxlix.

6. SRMG, n.s. (3rd series), 15A: *Report on Public Instr., 1868–69*, pp. cxliv, cxlviii; analysis of MRO, *List of Officers, Educational Dept., 1868–1875.*

matriculation examination or an appointment in the revenue or judicial departments.[7] It appears that these alternative job opportunities rather than caste preference attracted young Bhanaps. Schoolteaching was not a materially rewarding profession. Many graduates of the Normal School were found unwilling to accept posts in villages. "Mangalore men when sent to distant rural schools will not stay there." An exasperated educational Inspector examining the school at Mulki bitterly reported that "the headmaster seems to have devoted himself to passing the various 'Revenue Tests' rather than those of the Educational Department."[8] Interest in schoolteaching as a career declined further with the passage of the Local Fund Act in 1871, which provided that local taxes would support primary education. "The idea has got abroad that Government will go no further in middle-class [secondary] education. Hence not only are young men afraid to devote themselves to the profession of teacher lest they should find no employment, but those already employed are anxiously looking for any small appointment in other departments."[9]

Education in South Kanara advanced generally, but by 1884–85 the district had the lowest percentage of male students to school-age population of any district in the Madras Presidency, 38 percent. (The backwardness of neighboring North Kanara may be seen in the fact that its student-to-population ratio was only 8.5 percent.[10]) Although accurate and comprehensive figures are not available on a caste-by-caste basis, a rough calculation of this ratio among Saraswats in Mangalore town in 1896 produces not quite 90 percent.[11] Official efforts to interest other communities in education were only marginally successful.[12] Clearly the Bhanap families saw the usefulness of schooling. It was not long before they turned their organizing skills to education.

Having helped launch the government school, several Mangalore

7. Maclean, *Manual of Administration* 1 :598.

8. SRMG, n.s. (3rd series), 51: *Report on Public Instr., 1874–75*, p. 86; see also SRMG, n.s. (3rd series), 35: *Report on Public Instr., 1871–72*, p. clxx.

9. SRMG, n.s. (3rd series), 41: *Report on Public Instr., 1873–74*, pp. 329–330.

10. *Report of the Director of Public Instruction, Madras, 1884–85*, pp. 157–158; *Bom. Gaz.* 15, *Kanara*, part 2 :210.

11. Chitrapur Sangha (pub.), *Chitrapura Panachanga* [Chitrapur Almanac] (Bombay, 1896), Appendix 1.

12. *Report of the Director of Public Instruction, Madras, 1887–88* p. 158. A Saraswat employed as educational inspector, Nagarkar Raghavendra Rao, had tried to interest Bants in attending school, but found they resisted.

Saraswats experimented with the idea of a school where their young men could prepare adequately for admission and success in the new institution. In 1867 some Bhanap staff members of the government school opened a class in Kannada at the Umamaheshwar temple. Two years later they moved ahead to create an "Anglo-vernacular" school which would offer schooling up to the upper fourth standard.[13] A popular government school teacher, Kallianpur Raghavendrarao, joined with Saraswat lawyers and government servants including Kagal Devappaya, Nayampalli Shivarao, and Ullal Raghunathaya, to solicit funds and organize a managing committee to operate the new school.

Classes were moved to an outer structure of the temple in 1876, and in 1890 to a separate independent building on a nearby road. Although it might be presumed that during the years the school met in the temple only high-caste Hindu boys could attend, in fact several Muslims were enrolled. The staff was almost exclusively drawn from the Saraswat community. Frequently, young matriculates would serve as teachers while awaiting appointments in government service. In the late 1870s Mudabidri Devarao and Katre Mangeshrao, who later entered the judicial and public works departments respectively, were employed as instructors.[14] The student body lists read like a "Who's Who" of the South Kanara Saraswat community; future doctors, judges, social reformers, and title-holders all attended.

The utility of the school's "middle-school" curriculum was enhanced in 1879 when the Madras government decreed that the middle-school test could be substituted for the uncovenanted civil service examination. In order to qualify for grants-in-aid from the Education department, the official curriculum was scrupulously followed.[15] English and Kannada were recognized for instructional purposes in South Kanara schools, even though the mother tongue

13. SRMG, n.s. (3rd series), 28: *Report on Public Instr., 1870–71* (Madras, 1871), p. 197; Ganapathi High School, *Diamond Jubilee Souvenir: Ganapathi High School, Mangalore* (1930), p. 1; *Saraswat Quarterly* 1, no. 1 (April 1919): 12.

14. Maclean, *Manual of Administration* 1 :583; Ganapathi High School, *Diamond Jubilee Souvenir*, p. 2.

15. Ganapathi High School, *Diamond Jubilee Souvenir*, p. 2. Ullal Raghunathaya has been credited with originating the idea of a caste school. *K. S.* 13, no. 4 (October 1929) :11. In 1871 the school received Rs. 94 from government grants, Rs. 100 from subscriptions, and Rs. 378 from fees, against costs of Rs. 755. Though 117 students were enrolled, average daily attendance was only 48. SRMG, n.s. (3rd

of many of the inhabitants was Tulu, Konkani, or Malayalam. Thus even the medium of instruction in "vernacular" classes was unfamiliar to many students. Schoolmasters who did not themselves know Kannada well could not excel it its use as an instrument of instruction.[16] By employing matriculates as teachers, the Saraswat school assured high quality while providing reinforcement among its students for developing linguistic skills beyond their Konkani mother tongue. It appears that no resources were dedicated toward teaching about the caste and its culture. Rather it was expected that rigorous pursuit of academic success would best serve corporate interests.

For lack of attentive management the school very nearly failed financially, but it was resuscitated by a Bhanap matriculate, Trasi Parameshwarayya, who with his brother Subbarao reorganized its management during the late 1880s, enabling the school to again prosper and expand. Although the school faced fiscal crises again, the Saraswat community of Mangalore provided support for what had come to be seen as an important mechanism which would enable each new generation to obtain education and advancement.[17]

The Mangalore public had made sacrifices in the 1860s to obtain the provincial school. Twenty years later they looked again to the government to raise the school's status to a First Grade Government College, to obtain means for studying up to the Bachelor of Arts degree without having to undergo the costs of residing at Madras. When Governor Mountstuart Elphinstone Grant Duff visited Mangalore in 1883, he was told:

> Kanara is an out-of-the-way district, and hence it is that the means of liberal education are not within easy reach of our children. Under the present circumstances they have to proceed to Madras to study for degree examinations, and the heavy expenses incident to a sojourn in the distant presidency town are too restrictive to admit of men in the middle station of life affording to pay for the higher education of their children.[18]

The governor avoided the issue of cost and, recalling that in his

series), 28: *Report on Public Instr., 1870–71*, Appendix B, table 8. SRMG, n.s. (3rd series), 58: *Report on Public Instr., 1875–76*, Appendix B, table 11.

16. SRMG, n.s. (3rd series), 51: *Report on Public Instr., 1874–75*, pp. lx, cxxviii; Indian Education Commission, 1882, *Report by the Madras Provincial Committee, Indian Education Commission: Evidence* (Calcutta, 1884), pp. 261–263, 267.

17. Ganapathi High School, *Diamond Jubilee Souvenir*, pp. 2–3.

18. M. E. Grant Duff, *Tour Minutes (1882–83) by the Right Honorable M. E. Grant Duff, Governor of Madras, and Orders of Government Thereon* (Madras, n.d.) 8 : 16.

home county in Scotland there was also resistance to going to Oxford, advised that "There is nothing, I think, so good for young men as early transplantation."[19] No change in the status of the college was allowed. By 1892, the district had sent to Madras 94 young men to who passed the B.A. examination. Of these 94, 48 were Saraswats.[20]

Saraswat interest in education was not an abstract reflection of a cultural legacy, but a pragamatic endeavor to assure to themselves and their kinsmen access to economic opportunity. During the nineteenth century, Saraswats and the Mangalore Catholic community shared the achievement of a secular elite status, expressed primarily in their domination of professions and public service. The Bhanaps' anxiety to ensure an inexpensive and reliable availability of education led them both to act in the arena of public mobilization and to create special institutions which could serve their corporate interests.

### *Saraswats and Government Service in South Kanara*

Ambitions and energies directed toward the achievement of appointments at prestigious levels of government service usually outstripped the potentials of realization. The preference among Saraswats for a "writer's" employment was a dominant theme throughout the ninteenth century. Later, Saraswats would look back at the last third of the centruy as a golden age of opportunity, when Bhanaps had held choice posts in Kanara administration. Examination of the record suggests that the situation was neither so simple nor so attractive. If some Bhanaps in public service did occupy seats of power and prestige, there were many whose career reached no further than a low-paid clerical appointment.

The expansion of employment opportunities in South Kanara's district administration did not keep pace with Saraswat ambition. The population of the district was growing more rapidly than were jobs, yet the district bureaucracy was expanding proportionately when compared to its numerical strength before the partition. The

19. *Ibid.*, 17. The college did not achieve First-grade status until 1948, but the gap was filled by a new Jesuit college, St. Aloysius', founded in 1882 and raised to first grade in 1887. *History of Higher Education in South India*, 2 vols. (Madras, 1957), 2:48, 70.

20. *The Hindu*, Oct. 5, 1893, p. 3. The rest were 17 Catholics, 15 Konkanis, 9 other brahmans, and 5 others.

talukas which formed the district had held in 1856 about 648,000 persons, rising to 840,000 in 1866 and nearly 920,000 in 1871.[21] Administrative bisection of Kanara had only briefly reduced the proportionate size of the South Kanara establishment. By 1870, excluding village officers and adjusting for officers temporarily on leave, South Kanara's administration employed, from the collector down to the office sweeper, 1,688 persons, only 165 fewer than had operated the entire undivided district thirteen years earlier, and as a cost reduction of only Rs. 4,204 per month.[22] Proportionately, the reduction in the size of district area and population might have been expected to yield at least a 35 percent drop in overall staff strength, but the 1870 figure was only 9 percent less than the figure for undivided Kanara in 1857. How had this affected the chances of ambitious Saraswats?

The 1870 evidence is unmistakable; individuals who were Saraswats, a caste that made up about 0.4 percent of the district population, held 37.5 percent of all appointments below posts reserved for Europeans and above menial ranks that paid under Rs. 10 per month.[23] It might seem that Saraswat ambition had been gratified; that wealth and prestige of service could confer innumerable advantages upon the caste and its members. Analysis of the salary structure of the district bureaucracy dispels this vision quickly. The realities of colonial rule are immediately apparent. Of an adjusted monthly salary total of Rs. 34,097, Rs. 11,890 were tied to 16 appointments held by Europeans. Rs. 5,934 paid the wages of 1,183 peons, messengers, sweepers, lamplighters, and other menials. In between were 504 appointments ranging in pay from Rs. 10 up to Rs. 500 per month. Saraswats held 189 of these positions. The vast majority of these were anything but influential—mostly

21. Madras District Manuals: *South Canara* 2:2; F. Lushington, *Comparative Tables of Provincial Establishments, Madras, for 1857* (Madras, 1858), p. 21. Lushington's figures were probably underestimated, for a ten-year growth rate of 29.5% is high. Kundapur taluka, which was included in North Kanara in 1859, was not not transferred to Bombay in 1862 and so is calculated with South Kanara in the 1856 figure.

22. Based on comparisons of figures of appointments and salaries in Lushington, *Comparative Tables*, pp. 12–33; and "Madras Civil Establishments as of 1870, April 1st" [IOR: L/F/10/130–131/ff. 88–98, 113, 129, 130, 199–202, 204–207, 222–224, 263, 290, 300, 309–310, 318, 337–340, 361, 363, 385, 395–396, 420, 431].

23. Analysis calculated from "Madras Civil Establishments." The estimated at about 4,000 in 1870; no reliable caste figures appear in the decennial census of the Madras Presidency taken in 1871.

clerical or other subordinate positions requiring literacy. The salary distribution calculated for the Saraswat appointees reveals a range from Rs. 10 to Rs. 250 per month. The top pay was received by two district *munsifs*; four others, a *tahsildar*, a police inspector, and two other *munsifs* received Rs. 200 per month or more.[24] At the other extreme of the range, Rs. 10, were the greatest number of Saraswats, 44. There were 42 Bhanaps receiving Rs. 15 per month, the median income for the 189 men; of the total, only 50 had salaries over Rs. 20 per month.[25] To be sure, many of these men may have had shares of income from family lands, but the overall picture conveyed by the figures is that all Saraswats in South Kanara were by no means well-to-do, nor were they of equal economic standing. As the limits of opportunity in Mangalore became more pronounced, Bhanaps would consider emigration to more distant places.

Would further expansion of the bureaucracy in the district have opened still more posts to Bhanaps? The demonstrated capacities of persons of the Saraswat *jāti* could not disqualify them from appointments. However British officers, mindful of governmental fear of family combinations and caste monopolies in its offices, deliberately endeavored to restrict the number of high-ranking appointments made to persons of any one caste. When the *tahsildar* of Kasargode died in 1863, applicants for the vacancy included Tombat Subbarao, a Bhanap submagistrate of Mangalore with 34 years' service.[26] Although he might have been disqualified for lack of sufficient revenue experience, he was instead passed over by the collector on the grounds of his caste—within South Kanara there were already two Saraswat *tahsildars*. The collector proposed seeking an officer from Bellary or Malabar districts. The Board of Revenue suggested that he instead find a suitable candidate among the Christian population of Kanara, for to go outside the district would ignore the difficulties of the subordinate employees of the district "who from peculiarity of local climate and languages can scarcely ever look for employment in any other part of the

24. *Ibid.* Ullal Ramappaya was *munsif* at Bekal, and Ullal Manageshaya *munsif* at Kundapur; Tombat Subbarao was *tahsildar* at Kasargode; Kabad Rama Rao was First-class inspector of police, and Labadaya Ramachandraya and Kallianpur Subbarao were *munsifs* at Barkur and Udipi, respectively.

25. *Ibid.*

26. MBRP, April 1, 1863, no. 1991 [IOR: P/314/77/ff. 2086–2087].

country."[27] When a Christian individual was nominated, however, Madras instead sanctioned appointment of a Deshastha Brahman. In less than two years Tombat Subbarao overcame his superior's doubts and was appointed *tahsildar* of the again vacant office at Kasargode.[28]

The issue of monopolization of offices in South Kanara was often raised, but never settled. Allegations that Saraswat officers gave their caste fellows special patronage were made, but not proved.[29] The usual remedy proposed was increased interdistrict transfer of personnel. But language limited this possibility—Bellary was the only other Kannada-using district administration in Madras—and the expense of transfer could only he justified for persons in the higher ranks of the pay scale. Those South Kanara men who were rising were readily subject to transfer once their monthly emoluments passed Rs. 200. One prominent Bhanap, Dhareshwar Ananthaya, who had started as an unpaid volunteer in the collectorate at Mangalore, rose in ten years to be a *tahsildar*. Thereafter, in order to continue promotions, he had to serve outside the district. Knowledge of English rather than Kannada was now critical. He was posted in Bellary, Coimbatore, Kurnool, Anantapur, and Nellore before he returned permanently to South Kanara as the Treasury Deputy Collector in the very office where he had begun 33 years earlier.[30]

If competition for jobs and schooling had prompted some consciousness of caste in Mangalore, it would be not surprising that local self-government politics could also invoke this force. The Mangalore Municipality was dominated by British officials from its founding in 1866 until the introduction of Lord Ripon's reforms in 1885. Election of nonofficials to the council had begun in 1872, but the councillors had not attempted to shake free of official control.[31] Under the new rules the town was divided into wards "to secure the due representation of minorities," and the franchise

27. MBRP, May 16, 1863, no. 2930 [IOR: P/314/78/f. 2837].

28. The appointment was in April 1865. "Madras Civil Establishments" [IOR: L/F/10/130/f. 199].

29. Cf. *The Hindu*, Oct. 5, 1893, p. 6; Oct. 7, 1893, p. 6; Nov. 13, 1893, p. 6; Nov. 17, 1893, p. 6; *Vijayadhwaja* (Bellary), March 22, 1888 [Madras Native Newspaper Reports (1888), p. 72].

30. Madras. *History of Services of Gazetted and Other Officers in the Civil Department Serving in the Madras Presidency 1 July 1902* pp. 785–787.

31. Madras. *Reports on the Mofussil Municipalities for 1882–83*, para. 3 [IOR: M/4/II]; *Appendices to Report on the Local Self Government in Madras, 1882*, p. 136 [IOR: (71) 2042]. Cf. J. G. Leonard, "Urban Government Under the Raj," *Modern Asian Studies* 7 (April 1973): 227–252.

was defined on a very limited basis of income or property.[32] Saraswats, Christians, and Konkanis were well represented in this elite. Questions of caste domination were invoked very soon.

Although several Bhanaps held office as nominated "official" councillors, their caste's influence in the council came to be symbolized by the standing of Nayampalli Shivarao, a leading lawyer who was described in 1889 as "the recognized leader of the district."[33] In the previous year, when Lord Connemora, the governor, had visited Mangalore, Shivarao presented the address from the municipality, which highlighted the good work of the council. Yet the governor also received a petition requesting that the elective council be ended and autocratic official rule restored. It was believed that this arose from envy toward the influence of Shivarao and other Saraswats in municipal affairs.[34] In 1890 Shivarao and a Konkani, K. P. Ramarao, fought a bitterly contested election which Shivarao won only on a technicality. In 1891 he was elected chairman of the municipality. He held the post for three years and was succeeded by Dhareshwar Ananthaya, who occupied the chair until 1900.[35] This Saraswat presence in local urban politics was continued by Shivarao's son, Nayampalli Subbarao, who was chairman from 1905 to 1913. So long as "politics" existed within a limited franchise, the local elites' rivalries and feuds would color public life in Mangalore.[36]

32. Madras. *Reports on the Mofussil Municipalities for 1886*, para. 5, and Appendix A for details of franchise definitions [IOR: M/4/II].

33. *The Hindu*, Dec. 13, p. 3. Among early council members elected were Ullal Mangeshaya, Ullal Raghavendra Rao, and Labadhaya Ramarao. Madras Financial Proceedings [Municipal], Sept. 19, 1885, no. 537M: *Annual Report of Mangalore Municipality*, p. 162 [IOR: P/2632].

34. [Lord Connemora], *Tour Minutes: Seventh Tour of H. E. The Rt. Hon. Lord Connemora* (Madras, 1888), p. 5; *The Hindu*, Oct. 22, 1888, p. 3; Oct. 7, 1893, p. 6. Similar rivalries were found in the taluka towns of the district. A. S. Panchapakesa Ayyar, *Twenty-Five Years a Civilian* (Madras, 1962), p. 114.

35. *The Hindu*, Oct. 18, 1890, p. 5; Madras Municipal Proceedings, September 1891, no. 1405M: *Report on Mangalore Municipality, 1890–91* [IOR: P/4014]; Mangalore Municipality, *Centenary Celebration Souvenir* (1966), p. 15. Shivarao had 88 votes, his oppoent 89. Shivarao challenged several ballots and votes were thrown out on both sides, resulting in a draw, whereupon the district collector ruled that Shivarao was elected by virtue of having paid higher taxes. *The Hindu*, Oct. 18, 1890, p. 5.

36. *Svadeshabhimani* (Mangalore), Nov. 14, 1913 [Madras N. N. Rept., 1913, p. 1785]. Subbarao's political strength lay not in caste connection but in a self-conscious block of Muslim merchants. Interview with Nayampalli Ramarao, Mangalore, Feb. 20, 1971.

Saraswat-Konkani rivalries were particularly visible in Mangalore. Apart from the political contests of local government, education became a bone of contention. In 1891 a group of Konkani graduates organized the Canara High School at Mangalore. It was expected to assist young Konkanis to "catch up" in the educational race. There was little question at the time about whom the Konkanis had to overtake. Although in later years the Canara High School was a fully cosmopolitan institution, in the 1890s it provided a symbol of challenge to Bhanaps.[37] The details of the petty squabbles of the time need not detain us. Suffice it is to say that leaders on both sides fully lived up to the description by one observer who characterized them as "the Montagues and Capulets of Mangalore."[38] South Kanara's political backwardness was proverbial. One inhabitant wrote that the district's water and air contained no germs of patriotism, for there were no newspapers and no associations to ventilate political grievances.[39] The slow rise of politics had not heralded the far-reaching changes in economic life and public affairs of the district which would come later. Also, it was only in a setting of limited political dimensions that a small *jāti* could be considered as a vital corporate force. Such a view could not be sustained with the emergence of mass politics a few decades later.

## *Coming to Terms with New Forces*

Although in a rustic district town like Mangalore the winds of change were little more than an intermittent breeze, the town was the chief point of encounter between district residents and the institutions and ideas of modern western culture. This encounter was quite uneven in incidence; many were touched hardly at all. Some Saraswats with interests in government service, law, and education experimented in accommodating the new forces, and through ties of caste and kinship involved a substantial number of the other members of the *jāti* in Mangalore in the encounter.

When Lord Connemora visited Mangalore, members of his party attending the collector's reception had found it "startling to

37. *The Hindu*, July 2, 1891, p. 3; July 16, 1891, p. 3; Oct. 11, 1892, p. 3; Canara High School, *Diamond Jubilee Souvenir* (Mangalore, 1951), pp. 1–4.
38. *The Hindu*, Oct. 11, 1892, p. 3.
39. *The Hindu*, Sept. 25, 1896, p. 3.

see Hindus of high position and caste drinking iced whiskeys and sodas with Europeans."[40] Not many Bhanaps appear to have indulged in such marked deviations from customary behavior in their dealings with Europeans, but if they had, they could restore their "purity" through bathing and a change of sacred thread. That might not have satisfied purists, but it had been a customary means of allowing Saraswat students to attend schools with other castes and not injure the ritual purity of the home.[41] Brahmanical restrictions of diet might similarly be accommodated. Bhanaps recognized that this was an investment in their continuing achievement of public service position. While Lord Connemora was visiting Kundapur, his secretary, an Englishman, paused to admire one house elaborately decorated for the occasion of the governor's visit. He and another officer were accosted by the owner, a Saraswat Brahman, who invited them to take tea and some cakes and sweetmeats "made on the spur of the moment by the ladies of his family." The secretary recalled that "remembering an official account of the Nambudri Brahmans who dwell lower down the coast, one might hesitate to shake hands with such a personage," but "our host, whose learning was greater, if his holiness was less, had no scruples. He seized our right hands in both of his and protested that we must come in."[42]

Moments of elite social behavior that departed from customary standards were infrequent, however, and usually were ignored beyond nominal acts of purification. But other challenges come that were more direct and sustained. Religious practice and belief had been confronted by Christian missionaries since 1834. The trauma of conversions had occasionally stunned the Saraswat *jāti*, but the very traumatic quality of the act served to limit its growth or acceptance. On the other hand, various forms of "reformed Hinduism" that had been developed elsewhere in India began to trickle into South Kanara during the late nineteenth

40. Lord Connemora, *Tour Minutes*, p. 6.

41. Gangolli Krishnarao recalled that "It had become customary for a parent to ask his son to wear a different sacred thread at home on return from school," quoted in *The Hindu*, March 12, 1896, p. 8.

42. Lord Connemora, *Tour Minutes*, p. 8. The host was Ullal Babu Rao, newly appointed district *munsif*. *Quarterly Civil List corrected to 1 October 1887* (Madras, 1887), p. 137. Babu Rao was the first Saraswat graduate of the University of Madras, obtaining a B. L. degree in 1869. He had been a successful pleader at Mangalore before obtaining the judicial appointment.

century. Saraswat individuals played a vital part in the introduction.

Ullal Raghunathaya was the only son of Mangeshaya, the sharp-tongued *munsif* who had criticized young Pandurangashram Swami. Like other Bhanap government officers, Mangeshaya had encouraged his son to prepare for a similar career. In 1860 Raghunathaya was enrolled at the age of twenty for English studies in the Basel Mission school.[43] Although his parents were alert to the conversion danger, the educational process had more subtle effects. Raghunathaya's son-in-law, Gangolli Krishnarao, later recalled:

> To serious-thinking young men, to be told in school that the earth is round and at home to be taught that it is flat, to be told in school to sit along with boys of the Billava class and to be asked at home to bathe for the sin of coming into contact with them at school . . . was too much.[44]

Inconsistencies between school and home troubled many young students, but Raghunathaya's doubts were magnified by personal tragedy. His young wife died just as he was finishing his school course. Shaken, he entered a period of personal anguish and introspection. Had the missionaries recognized this and acted upon the knowledge, they might have had another convert. Raghunathaya read constantly in the mission library. There he came upon some tracts dealing with theological controversies then raging in Calcutta between Keshub Chunder Sen of the Brahmo Samaj and a Christian convert, the Reverend Lal Behari De. Those tracts led Raghunathaya to seek out the writings of Raja Ram Mohan Roy in the school library. Raghunathaya's notebook briefly recalled:

> 1861, Reading Room in Mission High School. Rev. Zeigler. The library contained works of Raja Ram Mohan Roy. Myself, Asugandi Subba Rao, and several others were regular members. All more or less had lost their faith in orthodoxy. Some had been slightly inclined towards Christianity. Raja Ram Mohan Roy's works, however, opened the eyes of most and attracted their minds. This was the first step.[45]

The second step was to subscribe to Keshub Chunder's journal. Soon Raghunathaya and several close Bhanap school friends joined in weekly meetings to discuss the Brahmo tenets.

However much inclined to reject orthodoxy the young men were, the fact was that conversion to Christianity meant a cataclysmic

43. *K. S.* 25, no. 4 (April 1941) :87.
44. *K. S.* 13, no. 7 (January 1930) :2.
45. *K. S.* 25, no. 4 (April 1941) :87–88.

disjunction. On the other hand, the simplified Brahmo *vedanta* ideals did not seem to pose a threat to family and caste duties—if only because no one in Mangalore had ever seen a Brahmo, much less become one.

In 1865 Raghunathaya joined the collector's office as an accountant at Rs. 15 per month. Because of his father's standing and his reputation as a bright young men, this subordinate appointment did not restrict his influence in caste affairs. He drew up and revised the forms of accounts for Shri Umamaheshwar temple and served on its reconstituted managing committee; he was among the leaders in the adoption of the so-called *vantiga shasana* in 1869 and was among the founders of the Saraswat school.[46] Like his father before him, Raghunathaya seemed destined to be one of the moving figures in Saraswat activities in Mangalore and beyond. As it turned out, he did exercise a strong influence in caste affairs, but not in the manner that could have been predicted in 1869. Ullal Raghunathaya took up the cause of religious and social reform.

Reform in nineteenth-century India has been carefully studied as a problem of intellectual history and cultural confrontation. The role of ideas, the conception of some thing called "society" and the perception of ways it should and could be improved, are widely known.[47] Social reform was primarily supported by members of higher castes who naturally proceeded against social evils which most directly impinged on their own lives and sensibilities. Looking back from the present day, it may be easy and fashionable to dismiss the social reform movement as "elitist" and ephemeral, but to the participants in the controverises at the time the issues seemed altogether vital, and the personal costs of participation could be exacting. For it developed that if one followed one's conscience and digressed markedly from what was considered to be *dharma*, the consequences could include fines, penances, and even the "social death" of excommunication from caste. In 1869 Mangalore, this was not yet well understood. It would be, soon enough.

Reform came to Mangalore with the formal arrival of the Brahmo Samaj in 1870. One of Ullal Raghunathaya's school friends was

46. "Madras Civil Establishments" [IOR: L/F/10/130/f. 90]; G. S. Hattiangdi, *Pandurang*, pp. 30–31; interview with Shri Sujir Sundarrao, Shirali, March 21, 1967; Ganapathi High School, *Diamond Jubilee Souvenir*, p. 2; *K. S.* 13, no. 4 (October 1929): 11.

47. Cf. Charles H. Heimsath, *Indian Nationalism and Hindu Social Reform* (Princeton: Princeton University Press, 1964).

Nireshvalya Arasappa, one of the few educated Billavas. He was working diligently to improve the status of his community. Perceiving no advantage in Hindu orthodoxy, Arasappa carried on lengthy negotiations with the Basel Mission. He thought that a mass conversion to Christianity might enable the Billavas to escape their low ritual and economic condition. The missionaries courted Arasappa, but upon realizing that he expected the Billavas to remain as a separate caste of Christians, they began to have doubts.[48]

Raghunathaya suggested that the Brahmo Samaj might provide a better alternative. In 1870 a telegram was sent to Keshub Chunder in Calcutta. If he would come to Mangalore, five thousand persons would embrace Brahmoism. As it happened, Keshub Chunder was about to go to England, and sent three other Bengali Brahmo "missionaries." These men and a representative of the theistic Prarthana Samaj of Bombay came down the coast by steamer, arriving at Mangalore in the awesome heat of late April 1870. A giant crowd awaited them on the shore. Perhaps the Bengalis should have stood more on hot-weather comfort than on the ceremonies and fashions of contemporary Calcutta, for when they arrived on shore in their western clothes, the majority of Billavas concluded that these were some form of Christians and departed in great haste.[49] Arasappa coaxed a few Billavas to attend a public meeting, but the Bengalis spoke in English and few in the audience comprehended the message. Raghunathaya and some Saraswat friends stepped in to serve as translators. As a result, a Brahmo Samaj chapter was established—but 19 not 5,000 had joined. Meeting in Arasappa's house, the congregation did not grow, and expired shortly after that gentleman's death in 1876.[50]

Part of the reason for the stagnation of the Brahmo Samaj was that most of the Saraswat adherents to Brahmo tenets were not entirely comfortable with the prospects of attending prayer meetings at the home of a Billava. Several of them did regularly go to Arasappa's, but most sought to avoid displeasing their elders. On June 11, 1870, they established a separate body, the *Upasana Sabha* (worship society). It accepted the Brahmo ideals and com-

48. B. E. M., *Thirteenth Annual Report* (Mangalore, 1870).

49. *K. S.* 25, no. 4 (April 1941) :88; H. Somappa, *A Brief History of the Mangalore Brahma Samaj*: *1870–1970* (Mangalore, n.d.), pp. 1–3; Sivanath Sastri, *History of the Brahmo Samaj*, 2 vols. (Calcutta, 1911–12), 2 :477.

50. *Bombay Gazette*, June 13, 1870, p. 3; *Bombay Guardian*, June 11, 1870, p. 113; H. Somappa, *Brief History*, p. 4.

menced weekly prayer sessions. To renounce the use of images in worship and to associate openly with Billavas was to court orthodox disapproval. Raghunathaya ignored this and was put out of caste in the autumn of 1871 by the express order of Pandurangashram Swami. Raghunathaya recorded the fact in his diary:

> 1st October 1871. Excommunication—imagine what effect His Holiness' Bulletin of excommunication had in affecting my private privileges or the interest of the Upasana . . . [which] is now well attended, and I train now my fellow laborers by giving them opportunities by turns to conduct the services. According to the Bulletin, none could have taken meal with me or with those who live in *samparkam* [association] with me; i.e., my parents, etc. What is the effect now? The present instance will illustrate. This day a large number of relations from paternal and maternal side had taken their dinner at mine. His Holiness is quite aware of this, as he lives in the temple which is one but the very next to my house.[51]

Raghunathaya was readmitted to caste through the exertions of his father, but continued actively in the Upasana Sabha, which ultimately renamed itself more correctly as the Mangalore chapter of the Brahmo Samaj.[52] The further history of religious reform will be examined below in Chapter 7.

This early encounter with reform revealed a fundamental problem. New learning and new behaviors that did not conform to orthodox patterns would nonetheless attract interest among the educated young men of the caste. Their small number was offset by their visibility. If orthodoxy responded with excommunication, however, and the taint were extended to all who had relations with the reformers, the consequences for a small caste could be momentous. Excommunication, the ultimate social sanction, appeared already in 1871 to have more impact when threatened than when applied. Most Saraswat citizens of Mangalore continued with the rest of their caste brethren to revere their *swami* and *maṭha*. Their religious practices had altered only in the additions and elaborations in ritual which their slowly growing prosperity had permitted. But a few men of a few families had encountered new, challenging values and beliefs. So long as the caste was predicated upon strict conformity to certain sanctioned principles of orthodox behavior,

51. Extract from diary of Ullal Raghunathaya, compiled from ms. notes of U. Manjappa, printed in Somappa, *Brief History*, p. 4.

52. "Sketch of Ullal Raghunathaya," *Subodh Patrika* (Bombay) Dec. 3, 1911, p. 3.

the germs of reform could threaten the corporate integrity of the Saraswats.

### *North Kanara: Rustic Alternatives in a New District*

Mangalore may not have been the most urbanized district town, but it appeared rather modern and progressive when compared with the rustic precincts of North Kanara. South Kanara district was eight square miles smaller in area than North Kanara, but it held over twice the population. The densities of population per square mile were 245.90 and 107.88 respectively, significant sections of each district's uplands lying in reserve forest. Densities were heavier along the coast, but comparison of the talukas of each district's headquarters town show that while Mangalore taluka's density in 1881 was 401.7 per square mile, the figure that year for Karwar was 169.9.[53] North Kanara was an underdeveloped tract at the time of its transfer to Bombay in 1862.

That transfer was itself the reflection of official desire to accelerate economic development in the Bombay Presidency's Karnataka districts. Kanara had been a slice of Madras territory through which passed roads from the cotton-growing tracts of Dharwar to the sea. English mercantile interests, anxious to develop a cotton supply in India, pushed for the development of new port facilities on the coast and improved roads leading thereto. Because it was believed that the Madras government would not pursue this development vigorously, the decision to transfer North Kanara was set.[54] Further pressure on cotton supply caused by the American civil war led to increased clamor for development of new roads and bridges from the cotton-growing areas of Dharwar to a new port facility on the west coast. A few years later, a railway was also proposed.

Development, but for whose benefit? That the citizens of North

53. *Bom. Gaz.* 15, *Kanara*, part 1 : 1–2; Madras District *Manuals* : *South Canara* 2 : 1–3. North Kanara had 3,910 sq. mi., with a population of 421,840 (107.7 per sq. mi.); South Kanara had 3,902 sq. mi., with a population of 959,514 (245.9 per sq. mi.).

54. Cf. Dwijendranath Tripathi, "Opportunism of Free Trade—The Sadasheogarh Harbour Project, 1855–1865," *Indian Economic and Social History Review* 5 (December 1968) : 389–406; and Peter Harnetty, "Indian and British Commercial Enterprise: The Case of the Manchester Cotton Company, 1860–1864," *ibid.*, 3 (September 1966) : 396–421.

Kanara might glean even marginal advantages from these projects is testimony to the depressed conditions of the district. For the literate, creation of a new district meant new openings in government offices. Expansion of the cotton trade might benefit local merchants. Construction of a new harbor offered temporary demand for labor, and a speculative market in land at the new port site seemed to promise the creation of fresh wealth. But the thrust of the projects themselves had little to do with North Kanara. Bombay officials continued to view the district itself as a scenic appendage best suited for reserve forests.

Saraswats had lived in the talukas which formed the southern part of North Kanara since the creation of their caste in the seventeenth and eighteenth centuries. They were not residents of the northern talukas where the new district headquarters town was ultimately located. Honavar, in the heart of Bhanap country, was passed over as choice for district town because of poor roads and a lack of trade. Sirsi, an above-*ghat* market town, was briefly considered. But the choice fell finally on a string of hamlets opposite the old fortress of Sadashivghar at the mouth of the Kalinadi. Anglo-Saxon tongues stumbled on "Sadashivghar," and the new town was called instead by the name of one of its sections, Karwar.[55]

The inhabitants of North Kanara were not enthused about transfer to Bombay. Some citizens of Honavar, upset at the downgrading of their town in the rise of Karwar, protested the entire proceeding. Others objected to the concomitant revision of all rules and procedures regarding excise, salt, and land revenue.[56]

Even as the Public Works engineers surveyed gradients for the new Karwar-Hubli road and drew up plats of the new district town, the Bombay government moved to introduce fundamentally revised procedures for land assessment and taxation, replacing the old Munro system with the standard Bombay survey settlement. The essential unit of revenue account had remained the estate or *varg* since Munro's time, although the basis of assessment had been modified.[57] The *varg* could be a consolidated landholding or a

55. MBRP, Oct. 6, 1860, no. 3247 [IOR: P/314/59/f. 59]; Jan. 4, 1862, no. 36; Oct. 27, 1862, no. 3893; Oct. 17, 1863, no. 3637 [IOR: Z/P/380/61].

56. Petition of Ramchunder Venkajee Oopony [Uponni] Bombay Revenue Proceedings [hereafter BRP] April 24, 1865, no. 1723 [IOR: P/380/61]; petition of Nadkarni Mangeshaya and other proprietors of salt manufacture in Nagarbyle, BRP, Aug. 12, 1863 [IOR: Z/P/3500/ff. 349–350].

57. Cf. MRO, SRSC: *The Land Assessment and the Landed Tenures of Canara* (Mangalore, 1853).

series of parcels united only by the scratchings in the *shanbhogs*' accounts. The Bombay settlement was based upon a field-by-field survey. It was introduced into North Kanara in 1864 in the talukas above the *ghats*. Careful survey soon revealed that the landlords of North Kanara had been adept at encroaching upon untaxed "wasteland."[58] The survey generated no substantial opposition until 1870, when it was introduced into the coastal taluka of Karwar. Survey brought reassessment and substantial increases in taxation. *Vargdars* took exception to the results, and refused to pay the first installments. Many suits were filed against the introduction of the new system. One test case went on appeal to the Bombay High Court, which ruled in 1875 against the landlords.[59]

Armed with this precedent, the Bombay government proceeded to resettle the rest of the district. Where the new assessment increased substantially, *vargdars* faced having to accept an unchangeable rent from their *mulgeni* tenants which was less than the new revenue demand. Although appeals were permitted, the balance of advantage in North Kanara's agrarian system slipped slightly from the *vargdars*, who now had to fear not only the loss of lands but also that former tenants might become landlords in their own right, thus reducing competition for land rentals.[60] No *vargdars* were cast into penury, but those, including Saraswats, who had depended exclusively on the income of their lands had to seek new sources of support.

Assessment increases were proportionately lower in Kumta and Honavar talukas, the site of most Bhanap landholdings.[61] Still, the principle was now fixed that revenue demands could be periodically

58. *Bom. Gaz.* 15, *Kanara*, part 2 : 177–180.

59. Vyakunta Bapuji *vs.* Government of Bombay, Bombay High Court Reports [hereafter *BHCR*] 12 (1875), Appendix. 1870 in Karwar was known as "the year of 4000 suits." Selections From the Records at Bombay Government [hereafter SRBG], n.s. 553: *Papers relating to Second Revised Survey Settlement of Karwar Taluka, Kanara District* (1913), p. 1.; SRBG, n.s. 158: *Correspondence Relative to the Revenue Survey and the Assessment of the Karwar Taluka of the Kanara Collectorate* (1883), pp. 2–18.

60. Maharashtra State Archives [hereafter M. S. A.], SRO: Administration Report for Kanara, Aug. 7, 1874, para. 6, R. D. 1874, Vol. 6; Administration Report for Kanara, July 28, 1875, para. 16, R. D. 1875, Vol. 5, pt. 2; *Native Opinon* (Bombay) 9 (June 30, 1872): 204; *Bombay Gazette*, Dec. 21, 1874, p. 3.

61. The increases in Karwar averaged 115 percent, in Ankola and Kumta, 36 percent, and in Honavar, which had been closest to the administrative offices under the old district, only 12 percent. *Bom. Gaz.* 15, *Kanara*, part 2 : 182. The Madras government subsequently revised the assessment of South Kanara on the basis of the North Kanara precedent.

revised. And the field-survey method inhibited traditional practices by which landlords had increased their estates. With each succeeding generation posing fresh risks of partition of property, a search for alternative occupations was imperative.

For Saraswats the obvious first choice for occupation would be in government service. The establishment of a new district administration gave immediate opportunity. A profile of the district staff in its early years reveals a predominance of Saraswats, Shenvis, and Christians. Their presence at Karwar was largely the product of migration, save for some Shenvi families who had lived in the area for centuries. Most of the Saraswats and Christians had moved to the town from old subordinate stations, Sirsi and Honavar. Because the higher grades of offices were tied to educational qualifications, most of the Saraswats in the superior ranks were migrants who had come north from Mangalore.[62]

The European officers of the Bombay services were apprehensive about this situation. The size of the bureaucracy inherited from Madras was thought to be on "a most unnecessarily lavish scale."[63] Their approach was to reduce the number of persons in service, while increasing the compensation of those retained.[64] There was also concern about "caste monopolies." Here it became apparent that there were a lot of Saraswat Brahmans in North Kanara service. The police superintendent pointed out that there were extensive "family connections," taking as an example a list of 54 persons who were alleged to be all relations of the *huzur sheristedar*, Mangeshrao.[65] The district collector, Mr. Shaw-Stewart, did not agree with the evaluation, since many of the relationships cited were very distant.

Mr. Shaw-Stewart was also dubious about the principle. He felt that demonstrated ability should be the first criterion for appointment, rather than reference to caste.[66] He tempered his idealism by the realistic judgment that competition between Saraswats and Shenvis would prevent any serious collusion or

62. Karwar Municipality, *Karwar Municipality Centenary Souvenir* (1964), p. 23.

63. BRP, June 26, 1862, no. 602 [IOR: P/380/45/ff. 721–727]; BRP (Abstracts), June 30, 1863, no. 2138 [IOR: Z/P/3500/f. 268].

64. "Bombay Civil Establishment, Imperial and Provincial on 1st April 1870" [IOR: L/F/10/149/ff. 106, 181–184, 458–467, 548, 561–562, 616–617, 645, 711–712].

65. BRP, Feb. 5, 1864 (Appendix to Abstract) [IOR : P/380/56/ff. 111–118].

66. *Ibid.*, M. J. Shaw Stewart to W. Hart, Oct. 19, 1863, para. 6.

corruption. Among the 148 stipendiary servants of the district and taluka office, 49 were Saraswats, 45 were Shenvis, 34 were other brahmans, and 13 were Christians.[67] The collector observed that there were relatively few people "fitted for employment in Government offices, whether Saraswut, Shenvee, or Native Christian," and within each group kinship ties were very intermingled. Family connections could hardly be avoided. Furthermore, "in carrying out the rule of selecting the best men for the work, the Saraswut Brahmins will have a great advantage. . . . Many of their sons are carefully educated at the German Mission School at Mangalore. With some notable exceptions, they are as superior in natural abilities to the Native Christians as in education to the Shenvee Brahmins."[68] Such perceptions may have been less than fully accurate, but in any event, Saraswats would benefit. Many young Bhanaps presented themselves at Karwar for employment. Those who could not be accepted had some success in taking clerical positions with the European cotton firms which had begun to open in anticipation of the improved harbor and transport facilities.

## *Education and Opportunity in a New Town*

Karwar's designation as district town necessitated transfer of all Saraswats who took up appointments. Not only was it a new town, it also lay well to the north of the traditional Bhanap frontier, the Gangavali River. If it was true that Karwar opened a fresh set of opportunities for members of the caste, there were also adjustments and expenses to be met. The migrants had to purchase housing or lands in a market inflated by the speculative boom.[69] Some government servants, who could not afford this cost, chose to reside in boarding hotels while their families stayed at ancestral homes in the south of the district. Once settled in Karwar, the caste began to build up the necessary institutions marking each site of major Bhanap residence. A local body of influential caste men was organized as a "ten," *hattu samastaru*. Participants included prominent officers, Udiavar Mangeshrao, the *daftardar*; Bhatkal Mangeshrao, the *huzur mamlatdar*, and Bijur Manjunathaya, the *munsif*. Staff and lawyers of the local court, Nadkarni Santapayya, Kalyanpur

67. *Ibid.*, para. 7.
68. *Ibid.*, para. 8.
69. *Bom. Gaz.* 15, *Kanara*, part 2 :26.

Gopalayya, Kaikini Vithalrao, and others were also counted in the body.[70] Through the "ten" the householders at Karwar linked themselves to Shri Chitrapur *Maṭha*. They then turned to the need for a separate temple for their own caste. Sufficient funds were collected to begin preliminary construction in 1868. The Karwar people were dependent upon salaries and fees, and many could give only small amounts each month. The temple was not finished until 1876, when Pandurangashram Swami visited Karwar for the full consecration of the deity.[71] A "ten," a temple, and a tour by the *swami* confirmed that Karwar's Bhanaps were now within the recognized range of Saraswat corporate activity.

Yet even in 1876 Bhanaps were moving out of North Kanara into new arenas of opportunity. This was a response to a paucity of educational facilities in the district and a limited range of employment opportunities. Schooling was a pressing need for persons in the Saraswats' position. Although an Anglo-vernacular school began in Karwar with English classes in 1864, there was not a full high school in the district until 1878.[72] Interest in education was restricted almost wholly to the castes and communities whose members competed for government employment. In 1875 the collector despaired:

> The children of Brahmins are only too numerous in our schools, and the education they receive at a very low cost partly unfits them for ordinary employment. They are ambitious of entering the Government Service, and when in it are ill content to remain for long in the lower grades.[73]

Education in North Kanara continued to be the preserve of a few literate castes and communities.[74]

North Kanara's school-attending population was proportionate in strength to other Bombay districts, but the chances for advancement to the higher levels of education were few. This backwardness was shared with the rest of the Bombay Karnatak. In 1866 there was still not one Kannada graduate of Bombay University. It was

70. H. Shankar Rau, *Chitrapur Saraswat Miscellany*, p. 77.

71. *Ibid.*

72. *Bom. Gaz.* 15, *Kanara*, part 2:211–215; Karwar Municipality, *Centenary Souvenir* pp. 95–98, 100–103.

73. M. S. A., SRO: Collector of Kanara to Rev. Commr., Southern Division, July 28, 1875, para. 60, R. D., 1875, Vol. 5, part 2, no. 2697. He hoped that a solution would be found through the opening of new jobs in private firms.

74. M. S. A., SRO: Administrative Report of Kanara, 1877–88, para. 60, R. D., 1878, Vol. 12, no. 1040.

observed that without a strong Anglo-Kannada high school, few graduates would appear; but if a solid program could be established, there would be an adequate supply of "Canarese undergraduates to the University, who may in a few years supplant the Marathas that now of necessity occupy all the important appointments in the south."[75] High schools did open later in the Karnatak, but the lack of these facilities in the time before 1878 compelled young Saraswat men to consider migration to more distant places in quest of schooling. The implications of this movement will be explored in Chapter 6.

In North Kanara itself, the options for service employment continued to be limited. As more and more willing candidates pressed forward to the matriculation examination, the educational standards required of government appointees rapidly inflated. The Bombay government revised the rules for admission of candidates for public service above menial levels up to a salary level of Rs. 50 per month. Only matriculates, or those holding certificates of equivalent attainment, would be considered. In 1866, the minimum age of admission was raised to eighteen years. None but those who were matriculates would be eligible for promotions to jobs paying over Rs. 30 and Rs. 20 in English and vernacular departments respectively until after three years' service.[76] Educational qualification was no longer an option. Nor was it guaranteed that success at school would ensure a good appointment.

One option open to young Bhanap students was to serve a few terms as master of a village school. Notoriously ill-paid, these positions were regarded as having no future prospects, since higher appointments would be reserved for university graduates. In 1885 it was suggested by an Indian subordinate that the masters' quality could be improved only by inducing more competent men to take the jobs. This was to be accomplished by reserving half of the *shanbhog* and *karkun* vacancies in the district establishment for men

75. *Census of India, 1871–72: Bombay* 2:74, table 7; *Report of the Director of Public Instruction, Bombay, 1864–65*, p. 126. Almost half a century later, the first such graduate, a prominent Saraswat, informed the Public Service Commission that "my province, Kanara, is perhaps in a more difficult position than any, because the people ... find it difficult to get employment as the Mahrattas go into all the districts." Oral evidence of Narayan G. Chandavarkar, Great Britain, Royal Commission on Public Service in India, *Minutes of Evidence, Bombay* (London, 1913), p. 300.

76. *Selections from Educational Records of Government of India* (Delhi, 1960) 1:268–69, "Note on State of Education in India 1865–66," para. 319.

who had served as schoolmasters. The collector feared, however, "that the bait would not be sufficiently tempting":

> The yearly vacancies among the *shanbhog*s are very few, not more than four or five, and I could not offer many *karkun*ships to trained masters, as there are always a number of matriculated [volunteers] in the different Revenue offices who are waiting for employment. Nor would it be a decided benefit to the Educational Department to take away its best men.[77]

The ready supply of volunteers who would willingly serve without pay in the hope of eventual employment indicates the competitive pressures of the district. If village schools were an unpalatable choice, schoolteaching in Karwar seemed to be a more satisfactory way station to success. In 1883, inspired by the success of the Saraswats' school at Mangalore, some Saraswats opened a private English school in Karwar. It obtained a good attendance, but ultimately failed when the majority of its teachers went off to take jobs in the revenue, excise, and forest departments.[78]

The only alternative "service" jobs which Bhanaps could obtain within North Kanara were to be found in the offices of the private cotton-trading firms. A few of these had opened at Karwar, but there were more at the older port town of Kumta, some forty miles down the coast. From the 1840s a trade in cotton had developed, growing into a major venture during the American Civil War.[79]

Even after the boom of the 1860s Kumta's trade was substantial; her narrow bazaar roads were congested with long trains of bullock carts and pack animals delivering the cotton to brokerage warehouses at the river. The presence of one Saraswat in a cotton firm office soon opened opportunities for others. An example was West's Patent Press, among whose chief employees were several Saraswats who subsequently emerged as entrepreneurs in the textile trade of the southern Deccan: Subrao Gopal Ubhayakar and the Sirur brothers, Ramkrishna Annappa and Narayan Annappa.[80]

The cotton trade faded away from North Kanara almost as

77. M. S. A., SRO: Collector of Kanara to Revenue Commissioner, S. D., Aug. 21, 1886, para. 60, R. D., 1887, Vol. 18, cons. 1585.

78. Karwar Municipality, *Centenary Souvenir*, p. 103.

79. MBRP, Nov. 23, 1843 [IOR: P/304/54 f. 18081]; Pharoah & Co., *Gazetteer of Southern India*, p. 554; *Bom. Gaz.* 15, *Kanara*, part 2:67–68, 326; *Native Opinion* (Bombay) 11 (Jan. 25, 1874) :56.

80. *K. S.* 5, no. 1 (January 1923) :8–9.; G. L. Chandavarkar, *Dattatraya Narayan Sirur* (n.p., 1950), pp. 2–4.

quickly as it had risen. Economic changes external to the district eliminated the need for the arduous and costly transshipment to the coast. The original railway project to link Karwar with Hubli was delayed and finally abandoned. Other railway lines, the Southern Mahratta and West of India Portuguese were opened in 1887 and 1888 respectively, diverting all of the Dharwar traffic.[81] By 1887 it was reported that the merchants and brokers of Kumta had begun shifting to other trading centers. The clerical Saraswats, faced with loss of livelihood, were compelled to follow suit accompanying their employers up over the *ghats* into Dharwar district. Ubhayakar, the Sirurs, and some 30 others found new opportunities when their former employer launched the Southern Maratha Spinning and Weaving Mills at Hubli in 1883.[82]

Other North Kanara Bhanaps found that the railway lines which had wiped out the old trade offered steady employment at Dharwar and Hubli, and in Goa at Mormagao. A Kashmiri Saraswat in the operating office of the Southern Mahratta Railway was credited with hiring many Saraswats in the clerical posts of the newly opened locomotive department at Hubli.[83] In Goa, Sadashivrao V. Harite, among the earliest students of the Karwar High School, completed his matriculation studies in time to answer a call for clerical staff on the West of India Portuguese line in 1882. He quickly rose to be head bookkeeper, in which capacity, it was said, he was instrumental in securing jobs for several Saraswat youths.[84] Economic necessity was again stretching the frontiers of the caste.

The four decades following the division of Kanara had seen on the one hand in Mangalore the rather considerable proliferation of urban institutions which made that town the first major arena of encounter for the Saraswats. That many did not have direct access to this arena was obvious even prior to the 1860s, but the partition

81. *Indu Prakash* (Bombay) March 28, 1881; *Bombay Chronicle*, March 27, 1881; Petition to Governor from Ramkrishna Parsu Pandit and 101 Other Rate Payers, n.d., in M. S. A., SRO: G. D., 1880, Vol. 49, no. 510; Report of First Assistant Collector to Collector, North Kanara, R. D., 1887, Vol. 19, Cons. 1585, part 2, para. 15: Kumta "must daily decline. Its death knell has been struck by the construction of the Southern Maratha and Marmugao railway which taps Dharwar."

82. It has not been possible to trace the papers of this enterprise. The capitalization of the firm under P. Chrystal was in fact aided by another Saraswat, Shamrao Vithal Kaikini, whose career will be discussed in the next chapter. V. L. Ugrankar, *A Brief Biographical Sketch of Shamrao Vithal Kaikini* (Bombay, 1911), p. 7.

83. R. V. Koppikar, "Saraswats in Hubli," *K. S.* 5, no. 1 (January 1923) :8–10.

84. Obituary of S. V. Harite, *K. S.* 22 (August 1938) :4–5.

and transfer of North Kanara served to accentuate the differential urbanization within the caste. Mangalore possessed more resources of modernity than any other place where Saraswats had settled to that time. Karwar and North Kanara, on the other hand, were backward, and, even after two decades of development, provided relatively limited opportunities which district inhabitants could exploit without further migration. The introduction of Bombay revenue procedures placed an additional pressure upon landed wealth in the north, creating further impetus to movement. In some instances this led to Dharwar and Hubli in the Bombay Karnatak. However, the enduring trend was toward the city of Bombay, and it is to the early phases of that encounter with urbanization that we shall turn in Chapter 6. While the evidence from both districts suggests that Saraswat families and individuals were prepared to adapt to new opportunities, there was yet another problem which the caste had to face. The administrative bisection of Kanara accentuated a spirit of separatism within the caste. It was expressed in the two stereotypes of *Badagis* (northerners) and *Tenkis* (southerners). The *Tenkis* were thought to be wise in the worldly ways of Mangalore. They were presumed to be polished, progressive, and wily. Their less advantageously situated northern cousins were rustic, but straightforward. One Bhanap recalled:

> Tenkis, we were told, were highly sophisticated, . . . their speech unctuous and their manners politeness itself, whatever the real thoughts and motives lurking in their well trained minds. Badagis, on the other hand, were supposed to be brusque, open in their manners and relationships, even with a hint of rustic simplicity, . . . which however was not to be taken at face value, as they had a way of working and doing things quietly.[85]

It was reported in later years that while a northerner father would have been only too happy to marry his daughter to a southerner boy with good prospects in government service or the law, he would be dubious about a match between his son and a southerner girl. *Tenki* girls were presumed to be too independent and likely to cause problems in any family. Of course on the other side of the coin, *Tenki* parents shuddered to think how hard their daughter would work if married into a backward *Badagi* family.[86]

These stereotypes reflected the fact that members of the caste

85. D. B. Chandavarkar, "A Bhanap Causerie," *K. S.* 28 (May 1944) : 108.
86. *K. S.* 14, no. 7 (June 1931) : 7.

had experienced differential access to the new influences of education, urbanism, and individualism. The traits of the individual were then ascribed collectively to the family; the traits of the family ascribed collectively to their town or village, which led ultimately to the generalization. The evolution of the distinction may have been indirectly caused by changes associated with British rule, but no colonial British ethnographer contributed to these ascriptive perceptions. In this instance, the subjects of the ascriptions appear to have been the sole authors of the stereotypes.

The resultant inhibition to exchanging brides posed a long-term menace to the continued integrity of the Saraswats as a single *jāti*. The *swami* of Shri Chitrapur *Maṭha* endeavored to bring both sides together through the inauguration of new observances and festivals at Shirali, but the menace was not eliminated until the threat of a fresh gulf had begun to appear among the Bhanaps, that of the mofussil against the cities.

# 6

## INTO THE CITY:

### *Early Saraswat Encounters with Urban Life, 1864–1900*

In 1860 almost every member of the Saraswat *jāti* lived within the borders of North and South Kanara. Forty years later, most still did. Small numbers, however, were to be found outside the home districts, in the growing urban centers of Bombay and Madras. At times during the intervening decades many others had spent time in the cities as students or employees. There they encountered problems of living in cosmopolitan centers at a great distance from their native districts. Such problems had not troubled the Saraswats since their ancestors' early migrations. Migration was clearly a part of the Saraswat heritage, but in those earlier travels the migrants had dropped all ties with those of their kin who had remained behind. The pattern of migration in the late nineteenth century was more one of circulation than of one-way movement. Improved communication meant that it was possible to maintain ties with the native place. But other modern developments, particularly the growth of secular interests, and the necessary personal behavioral adaptations required by city life, raised a cloud of misunderstanding between Bhanap city dwellers and their outwardly more orthodox rural cousins. A new challenge to the identity of the caste began to rise on the lines of a rural-urban dichotomy.

The advantageous circumstances enjoyed by many Saraswats in South and North Kanara districts generated wealth and prestige for some and at least a comfortable living for many. There were certain limitations in the situation. If it had been true that any Saraswat young man with some schooling could always find a place in the district administrative establishment during the 1860s, it did not remain so as the century progressed. The size of district administration did not increase. Young men of other castes and communities also began to press claims for employment in service which British officers did not ignore. With contraction of opportunity at the district level, some Bhanaps tried to qualify for the expanding provincial services which required education beyond that available in the home district. Although the majority of Saraswats hardly dared dream of the possibility, it is clear that, by the 1860s, he who had become a student in the university possessed advantages far beyond even those of the matriculate. And he who graduated held, in his B. A. degree, a key to a prosperous future. For educational advance, one had to leave the district.

The Indian educational system placed authority for the examination of secondary school students in the universities. To "graduate" from high school necessitated passing an entrance or "matriculation" test of the university. Until the 1880s those tests were administered only at the university in the presidency town—Calcutta, Bombay, or Madras. For a young scholar of Mangalore or Karwar, a journey to the metropolis was a necessary step in his education. Until the matriculation exams were expanded to district towns, thus enlarging the competition, success in that examination meant virtual certainty of a good appointment back in the home districts. However, success in the examinations was not easy. Some young men could not afford the costs. Financial weakness interrupted many Bhanap scholarly careers in the nineteenth century; poor marks on examinations ended some others. The locus of failure influenced what happened next. Most who "failed" in Madras returned to South Kanara for want of alternative employment. When similar misfortune struck their compatriots in Bombay, however, North Kanara offered fewer prospects than did the city itself. Clerical vacancies in private commercial firms offered a new opportunity. By the end of the century, migration for education was supplanted by migration for employment as the principal motivating force among the Saraswats.

### *Paths of Educational Migration: North Kanara and Bombay*

Depending upon their district of residence, young Bhanaps' quest for education took different paths to their respective presidency towns of Madras and Bombay. Students in South Kanara could find at Mangalore an established group of educational institutions where they could study up to the eve of the matriculation examination, and even begin preparation for an intermediate university certificate. In the northern district, students faced greater obstacles, until 1877 having to go out of the district even to study for the matriculation examination. The stereotyped contrasts of enterprising *Tenkis* and lethargic *Badagis* do not seem apt when efforts at obtaining education are taken into consideration. Some southerner families that had come to Karwar with the new district administration sent their sons back to Mangalore for schooling. This option was open also to any of the northerner families, but without relatives with whom a boy could stay in Mangalore it could be an expensive choice.

Apart from attempting private tuition, the other alternatives were to attend the government high schools at Belgaum and Ratnagiri or schools in Bombay city itself. Belgaum was difficult to reach, and the school's record was unenviable. Ratnagiri had a better reputation following its regeneration under R. G. Bhandarkar.[1] In 1872, five years after the first Bhanap boys had gone from Mangalore to the Madras matriculation examination, the first group of six young men went by boat from Karwar to Ratnagiri to prepare for the Bombay test. Leaving their wives and families at home, they studied at Ratnagiri for two years before proceeding to Bombay for the examination. The six migrants all passed, but only two could continue in higher studies; the others took up appointments in the educational and revenue departments in North Kanara.[2] This success was remarkable, when it is understood that the overall failure rate in the Bombay matriculation between 1860 and 1896 was approximately 75 percent; four times more students went through the high schools than were able to obtain adequate marks.[3] During the following decade, the examples of the early Bhanap scholars stimulated others to consider what blessings Bombay might offer.

1. *Report of the Director of Public Instruction, Bombay, 1864–65*, p. 126; S. N. Karnataki, *Gurūvarya Dokṭara Sār Ramakṛṣṇa Gopal Bhandarkara yāñce caritra* (Poona, 1927), pp. 56–57.

2. Interview with Vinayak M. Chickarmane, Gokarn, Feb. 12, 1971.

3. Ellen McDonald Gumperz, "English Education and Social Change in Late Nineteenth Century Bombay, 1858–1898" (Ph. D. diss., University of California, Berkeley, 1965), pp. 186, 290.

Ironically, the pioneer Saraswat migrant to Bombay did not go to the city for schooling, but rather in quest of employment. Shamrao Vithal Kaikini (1841–1905) was the son of Kaikini Vithalrao, a subordinate officer in the old assistant collector's office at Honavar in the days before the partition. Recognizing the value of English-language competence, the father arranged for private tutoring by knowledgeable colleagues, most notably Kerwar Narayanrao, the *sheristedar* of the district court.[4] Young Shamrao followed this tutorial arrangement even after passing the "mulki," or public-service qualifying test, in 1859. He found a clerical job in the revenue department, where he won the notice of the young English assistant collector, William Wedderburn. When the new district town at Karwar was established, the Kaikinis were among the Saraswats who packed up and moved there.[5]

Hearing stories of fabulous wealth and opportunity in the city from the Bombay traders who were setting up establishments at the new port, Shamrao gave up his job and at the age of twenty sailed alone to Bombay. He wanted to become a lawyer and began as a law clerk for S. N. Patkar, a prominent pleader. Unsatisfied with his progress in this position, the young man returned to Karwar and rejoined the collectorate staff. His brother Sheshgirirao was just starting a successful law practice in the Karwar court, and perhaps Shamrao would in time have joined this venture, but the path to Bombay was reopened. The introduction of Bombay administration to North Kanara involved imposition of new rules and procedures, including a new set of forest regulations. This set off a series of lawsuits which culminated in one case that went on appeal to the Bombay High Court in 1867. Sheshgirirao Kaikini solidified his reputation as the premier pleader of the district by taking the government's case at the district court. Shamrao was deputed to do the work of translating a mountain of documents, some authentic, some spurious, which had been presented in defense of the old forest privileges. When the appeal went to Bombay, Shamrao was recruited to come along.[6]

Shamrao was then appointed second Kannada translator to the

4. V. L. Ugrankar, *Shamrao Vithal Kaikini*, pp. 1–2.

5. *Ibid.*, p. 2; C. D. Maclean, *Manual of the Administration of Madras* 3:512.

6. Ugrankar, *Shamrao Vithal Kaikini*, pp. 3–4. Cf. advertisement calling for persons to undertake translation work, Kannada to English, for the Bombay High Court, at rate of Rs. 1 per folio of 90 words, in *Native Opinion* (Bombay), Oct. 17, 1869.

Bombay High Court. Assured of continuing employment, he sent back to North Kanara for his wife to join him. While carrying out his duties, he studied for the Bombay High Court pleaders' examination, which he passed successfully in 1871. Soon after, he realized his ambitions for a legal career and began a long practice on the appellate side of the Bombay High Court. "Being for many years the only Kanarese-knowing pleader at the High Court he was much in demand in the Appellate Courts of the Kanarese districts."[7] During this time he established a household in the Kandewadi neighborhood of the Girgaum section in Bombay. He began to assist kinsmen and the sons of caste fellows to come to the city for education, commencing in 1869 with his younger brother Manjunatha and his nephew Narayanrao Ganesh Chandavarkar. The nephew had lived with his mother's family at Honavar to attend school until the conversion of Ganeshrao in 1862, whereupon he was pulled out and tutored privately. Young Chandavakar's schooling was now accelerated through the assistance of his maternal uncle. Passing the matriculation examination in 1871, Narayanrao attended Elphinstone College, obtaining in 1876 the first University of Bombay B. A. degree won by a Bhanap.[8]

Shamrao Vithal also assisted others of the caste who came up to Bombay. When the first group of scholars arrived from Ratnagiri in 1874, they joined others who came directly to Bombay in establishing a rooming "club," a dormitory created in a room rented in a *chawl* near the Kaikini house in Kandewadi.[9]

## *Homesick in Bombay*

Clubbing together in this fashion could reduce the costs of a period of study in the city. It also lessened the traumas of leaving the familiar surroundings of home. Because of an already established practice in Kanara of young men going from village to town for schooling, students going to Bombay might be thought well condi-

7. *K. S.* 4, no. 3 (July 1922) :6, 8.

8. Ugrankar, *Shamrao Vithal Kaikini*, p. 9; V. V. Kalyanpurkar and S. N. Koppikar, "The Kanara Club, Bombay, 1874–1892," *K. S.* 5, no. 4 (October 1923) :9; D. G. Vaidya, *Nārāyaṇa Gaṇeśa Cañdavarkar* (Bombay, 1937), pp. 24–27; G. L. Chandavarkar, *A Wrestling Soul* (Bombay, 1955), p. 9.

9. Kalyanpurkar and Koppikar, "Kanara Club," p. 9. K. M. Panchanadikar and J. M. Panchanadikar, in "Process of Social Change in India under the Colonial and De-Colonial Era," *Sociological Bulletin* 14, no. 2 (September 1965) : 17, suggest that the dormitory club represents a characteristic early stage of urban entry.

tioned for separation. But most intradistrict migration brought students to homes of cousins or uncles, and in most cases involved moving from one house full of Bhanaps to another. Not so in going to Bombay. Most of the students had limited financial resources. It has been noted that "it was altogether impossible for ordinary parents in the mofussil ever to think of sending their children to the great cosmopolitan seat of the presidency unless they had some . . . kin living there who would be willing to provide for them the essential facilities of board and lodging."[10] Such was not available yet for Saraswats.

The migrants had to make adjustments to the city. Few could afford to buy new-style clothing or otherwise depart much from the patterns of Kanara. But their palates did have to make adjustments. The student club members were dependent upon local Maharashtra Brahman cooks, whose fare was sufficiently nourishing and pure, but a departure from the cuisine of home. Some culinary relief would come on weekends and holidays when Shamrao Vithal's wife would prepare the distinctive pickles and coconut chutneys so much a part of Bhanap cooking. Until the time when Saraswats had begun to settle in the city with their families on a permanent basis, the educational migrants depended on the club cook. Each meal reminded them that they had left their homes behind.

As membership increased, the "Kanara Club," as it was called, moved in 1877 into a larger room in a *chawl* in the adjoining Mugbhat neighborhood. Even after the government high school opened in Karwar in 1876–77, the hope for better preparation in city schools continued to stimulate the flow of educational migrants. As some Bhanaps could not afford to take up education immediately, they came to Bombay hoping to find employment which would pay the costs of returning to school later. These men also joined in the club arrangement. Men who either transferred in government service or were employees of private companies usually could not afford the expense of bringing their families to the city, and the advantages of inexpensive living and congenial companionship attracted them also to live in or near the club premises. Saraswat elders in North Kanara probably hoped that the presence of these nonstudents, some of them older, might ensure that a measure of decorum would be observed and that no "scandalous" behavior

10. G. C. Jambhekar, *Memoirs and Writings of Acharya Bal Gangadhar Shastri Jambhekar*, 3 vols. (Poona, 1950), 1:viii.

would occur. For example, Venkatrao Yennemadi, after formal education, underwent a probationary period in the Bombay Secetariat before being posted in a career line of the provincial revenue department. He could not afford to bring his family to the city and instead lived at the club, serving the members as an elder counselor.[11]

It was nonetheless assumed by many in rural North Kanara that those who resided in Bombay must surely come into some degree of questionable behavior. In fact, as noted above, economics if not conservatism meant that students were slow to adopt very many new fashions of the cosmopolitan style. *Dhotis* and old-fashioned coats with turban or cap were standard apparel. Few domestic rituals were appropriate to a club of students, but the young men were hesitant to deviate much from orthodox practice. They continued to have their heads shaved, save for the *shendi* tuft, and hesitated to patronize the public coffee and tea stalls.[12] The noted educator and lawyer Sundarrao Ramarao Dongerkery recalled his father's stories of how when he came to Bombay in the early 1880s—helped by his maternal uncle, Mulki Babanayya—to become a clerk in the Bombay, Baroda and Central India (B. B. & C. I.) Railway, he felt a thrill of excitement when he went once to a public restaurant and ate ordinary baker's bread.[13]

Generally it was difficult for college students to obtain inexpensive housing in Bombay. Kanara Club veterans recalled that average expenses, excluding books and fees, amounted to Rs. 15 per month. When the Russian orientalist I. P. Minayeff visited Bombay in 1880, he visited a student's residence in the Jambulwadi neighborhood. There four young men shared quarters at an expense of Rs. 18 per month. A "middle-class" student could spend Rs. 30 per month and "live decently"—including the college fee of Rs. 10. The foreign visitor's host was a GSB, Shivaram Sadashiv Nadkarni, but two of the other three students were of another caste. Nadkarni and his GSB colleague dined separately from their roommates, and would not permit their Russian guest even to enter the kitchen area.[14]

11. *K. S.* 9, no. 4 (April 1926) : 16; Kalyanpurkar and Koppikar, "Kanara Club," pp. 11–13.

12. *Ibid.*, pp. 12–13.

13. *K. S.* 28, no. 4 (April 1944) : 72–74. See also Kamala S. Dongerkery, *On the Wings of Time* (Bombay, 1968), p. 25; *K. S.* 15, no. 6 (December 1931) : 14–15.

14. I. P. Minayeff, *Travels and Diaries of India and Burma* (Calcutta, n.d.), p. 46; see also Kalyanpurkar and Koppikar, "Kanara Club," pp. 12–13.

If others could make such cooperative arrangements without strict regard to caste identities, why should the Kanara Club have continued to exist as an exclusively Saraswat institution? Not all Saraswat students stayed there. As some of them obtained admission to Elphinstone College they moved into its hostel, where their social field included young men of virtually all the high-ranking castes and communities of Western India. A much larger proportion of the Saraswat students, however, attended the college and high-school departments of the Free General Assembly's Institution—known later as the Wilson College. The reason was not predicated on caste prejudice, nor was there any particularly strong tie between the Bhanaps' outlook and the rigorous Protestantism of the Scottish missionaries. Rather, the school offered the dual attractions of academic excellence and lower fees—half those charged at Elphinstone College and substantially less than the costs of St. Xavier's.[15] Wilson College, however, had no hostel until the 1890s. The Kanara Club was nearby, and demand for space continued unabated as more Bhanaps attempted to advance in education at Bombay.

But convenience alone did not explain the matter. Many of the Bhanaps who did move into college hostels would spend a day or two at the Kanara Club each fortnight, as an antidote for homesickness. The special attention given to the students by Mrs. Kaikini was lost with her death, but this gap was filled when Bijur Narayanrao, a former club member, found suitable employment and brought his wife up from Kanara to join him. With the establishment of a household, the Saraswat students could look forward to familiar cuisine. A GSB cook was also obtained who learned the preparation of appropriate dishes. The club thus served as a cushion to the impact of urban life, an outpost of some mundane pleasures from a distant home. For Bhanaps it was a thing "of our own." Although specific figures are not available, the number of Saraswats coming to the city for study from both North and South Kanara had increased enough by 1885 to stimulate relocation again in larger quarters in Thakurdvar. Ultimately the membership divided into two groups, for considerations of space.[16]

The increase in migration may have been partly the result of improved transportation service along the coast, represented by

15. *Annual Report of the Director of Public Instruction, Bombay, 1885–86*, p. 9. Elphinstone charged Rs. 101 annually, St. Xavier's Rs. 84, and Wilson Rs. 51.

16. Kalyanpurkar and Koppikar, "Kanara Club," pp. 13–14.

the opening of the regular "Shepherds' Lines" services in 1887, connecting all important ports of North and South Kanara with Goa and Bombay. But the days of the club were numbered. In the 1890s the older college hostels expanded and a new one was erected at Wilson College when the new campus was opened at Chowpati Beach. At the same time a larger number of Saraswat men who were working in Bombay began to establish households, bringing wives and children to join them. Students could find accommodations with relatives or caste friends. In 1892 the Kanara Club was discontinued.[17]

## *Migration for Employment*

By 1880 a small cluster of Saraswat men had settled in Bombay as more or less permanent residents. Holding employment in government and private offices, they represented a new trend in the migration pattern of Bhanaps in Bombay. Initially the growth of this enclave was as much the product of failure as success in the city. As noted earlier, often more than half of the matriculation candidates did not obtain passing marks even if they had negotiated the initial English-language oral examination. Those who did pass often could not continue studies owing to domestic responsibilities and family crises. Whether the failure occurred in the examination hall or in the family purse, some would-be scholars were forced to halt their studies.

A few who had got beyond matriculation could find appointments back home in North Kanara. One such person was Gopalrao Subrao Koppikar. Born at Bhatkal in 1854, his chance for education had come when a well-to-do pleader at Kumta, Kulkarni Anantaya, arranged for the marriage of his daughter to Gopalrao. The young man then studied at Kumta and was aided by his father-in-law to complete the matriculation course. About 1873 he began college studies, but insufficient funds led him to give up. He returned to Kumta and read for the pleader's examination while teaching in a temporary vacancy. However, a clerical opening in the educational department appeared and Gopalrao became a government servant.

17. T. W. Venn, *Mangalore* (Cochin, 1945), p. 141; *Chitrapura Panachanga*, Appendix 2; J. M. Maclean, *A Guide to Bombay*, 29th ed. (Bombay, 1905), p. 291; Kalyanpurkar and Koppikar, "Kanara Club," p. 13.

His career was predominantly in teaching, retiring as an assistant master at the Karwar High School.[18]

To those without matriculation credentials, such a return to North Kanara offered little opportunity. For young men who had been students in Bombay, the only certain vacancies would be, as noted in Chapter 5, as village schoolmasters, hoping and waiting for a vacancy to occur in a government office.

On the other hand, in Bombay the post-American-Civil-War recession had passed. Once again the city was experiencing commercial growth and renewed prosperity. European-controlled mercantile firms, banks, and managing-agency houses operated very much like business "secretariats," a private reflection of the public bureaucracy. Unlike the government, the private companies were prepared to employ clerical personnel who were literate and skilled without possessing a matriculation certificate.[19] Private clerical service offered few prospects for much advancement, but offered the sedentary security and status of "quill-driving." After a few years it was usually possible to bring one's wife and family up to Bombay and rent a room in one of the middle-class *chawls* of Khetwadi or Girgaum.[20]

The growth of opportunity of this sort was far greater in Bombay than in Madras. The effect was to stimulate Saraswats from South Kanara to also turn to Bombay, even before competition for positions in Mangalore had become stiff. Two migrants who succeeded in finding suitable opportunities in Bombay were Venkatrao Anandrao Lajmi and Nagarmat Ramarao.

Venkatrao Anandrao Lajmi had grown up in Baindur, South

18. *K. S.* 19, no. 3 (March 1935) :8; Koppikar and Koppikar, *Bailaru Śri Lakṣminārāyaṇa* . . . , p. 63.

19. S. R. Dongerkery, *History of the University of Bombay* (Bombay, 1957), pp. 15–16, 170–71; *Gazetteer of Bombay City and Island*, 3 vols. (Bombay, 1909), 2 : 182–183, 161, and 1 : 274–450 *passim.*; "Rising in Life," *Native Opinion* 9 (Sept. 15, 1872) :292–293. Changes in occupational classifications between census projects make it difficult to enumerate the magnitude of this commercial clerical order; *Census of the Island of Bombay, . . . 1864*, p. 86, enumerated 36,257 "writers and accountants," but later census reports differentiated such jobs by reference to types of goods and services produced. *Census of India, 1871–2: Bombay Presidency*, part 2, pp. 197 and 201, counted only 10,579 "clerks and accountants," but separately listed commercial agents and their employees. Further changes in later census volumes' occupational data make generalization impossible.

20. *Native Opinion* 11 (Dec. 20, 1874) :803–804; *Indian Spectator*, Aug. 14, 1881; *Chitrapura Panachanga*, Appendix 2. There were 48 married men among the Saraswats in Bombay in 1896.

Kanara, a small town with only introductory educational facilities. In 1881, at the age of sixteen, he obtained a chance to renew his studies. His maternal uncle, Durgappa Krishnaya Kaikini, who held a clerical appointment in an office in Bombay, asked him to come to the city, promising support in his studies. Venkatrao studied for the matriculation at Wilson High School, then successfully passed the Previous, First B. A., and Final B. A. examinations, completing the last in 1887. The pressure of family responsibilities prevented him from continuing to his personal goal of legal studies and the LL. B, but with a B. A. degree he obtained an appointment as a clerk in the revenue department at the Bombay Secretariat. He remained in service for thirty years, rising to the position of senior superitendent before his retirement.[21]

Nagarmat Ramarao completed his secondary schooling at Mangalore, and proceeded to Madras to study for a university degree in 1878. In 1880 he passed the "First Arts" examination, but family crises made it impossible financially for him to continue. In 1880, the holder of the "First Arts" certificate could expect to find satisfactory employment—completion of two years of college still had elite standing. Ramarao found, however, that the only work he could find in Madras was a temporary staff position with the office of the commissioner of the 1881 census operations. He returned to Mangalore and in 1883 headed north. After working briefly in the office of the Southern Mahratta Railway at Poona, he went to Bombay. There he entered the service of one of the largest mercantile and managing-agency houses of the city, Killick, Nixon & Co. Commencing as a clerk in the shipping department at Rs. 50 per month, a most respectable wage, he remained with the firm until retirement, rising to be the head clerk of the shipping department.[22] It was not perhaps the dramatic mobility so often associated with the educated middle classes of India, but Ramarao was a respected member of his community and had the satisfaction of helping others to come to the city and indeed to find employment. Killick, Nixon was a haven of Bhanap employment well into the twentieth century.

The appearance of an overrepresentation of members of one caste in offices in Bombay was commented upon by an Indian I. C. S. (Indian Civil Service) officer: "When a single subcaste,

21. *K. S.* 4, no. 2 (April 1922) :41–42; *Chitrapura Panachanga*, p. 42.
22. *K. S.* 4, no. 2 (April 1922) :44.

e.g., Chitpavan or Saraswat, is massed together in an office in ministerial capacities immediately under the Collector or the Judge," a "caste monopoly" could occur. "But this phenomenon occurs equally in commercial offices in Bombay."[23] Targets for employment most often hit by Bhanaps included (besides Killick, Nixon) Thomas Cook & Sons, David Sassoon & Co., Cox & Co., and the general traffic manager's offices of the B. B. & C. I. and Great Indian Peninsular railways.[24]

### *Elite Status in Bombay?*

A handful of the Bhanap migrants obtained positions of status and wealth substantially in advance of their caste compatriots. The most visibly successful Saraswats in the city were Shamrao Vithal Kaikini and his nephew Narayanrao Ganesh Chandavarkar. Both were successful legal practitioners and well-known participants in the associations and activities of Bombay's cosmopolitan elite. It was in some measure their public achievements which stuck in popular memory as being representative of their caste. Indeed, in the early twentieth century, Saraswats in Bombay could identify themselves still as the "community of Shamrao Vithal."[25]

Shamrao Vithal had offered patronage and guidance to many fellow Bhanaps ever since they settled in the city in 1867. His circle of close friends went beyond the bounds of caste, however, to include such Bombay leaders as Doctor Bhau Daji Lad, Vishvanath Narayan Mandlik, Kashinath Trimbak Telang, and Mahadeo Chimnaji Apte. With Apte, he launched the Gayana Samaj, Bombay's first society for appreciation and revival of Indian classical music. They sponsored performances of noted musicians and of learned Sanskrit scholars.[26] Shamrao Vithal's honorary public roles included

23. Testimony of Govind Dinanath Madgavkar, I. C. S., in Great Britain, Royal Commission on Public Services in India, *Report* (London, 1913) 6:259.

24. Interviews with P. G. Sirur, Bombay, Dec. 4, 1966; G. S. Hattiangadi, Bombay, April 11, 1966; A. V. Gangolli, Seattle, Wash., Feb. 16, 1969; and R. N. Nayampalli, Santa Cruz, Bombay, Feb. 5, 1971. It is not known what incomes these employments generated. The first figures available, for 491 earning Saraswats in Bombay in 1912, showed that 112 earned less than Rs. 30 per month; 174 from Rs. 31 to 50; 143 from Rs. 51 to 100; 43 from Rs. 101 to 200; and 19 over Rs. 201. Kanara Saraswat Association, *Census of Kanara Saraswats in Bombay* (Bombay, 1912).

25. *K. S.* 4, no. 3 (July 1922):91.

26. Ugrankar, *Shamrao Vithal Kaikini*, pp. 4–6; one report, in *Native Opinion* 15 (Jan. 13, 1878):21, notes a function at the home of Sir Mangaldas Nathoobhoy,

service as justice of the peace, syndic of Bombay University, and honorary secretary of both the Bombay Vakil's Association and the Students' Literary and Scientific Society.

The nephew followed his uncle's path, and travelled even farther. While studying for his LL. B. degree, Chandavarkar took up the editorship of the influential Anglo-Marathi weekly, *Indu-Prakash*, and was subsequently active in the new Bombay Presidency Association, which deputed him to England as their official political spokesman in 1885. Later he served as president of the Indian National Congress and the Indian Social Conference, justice of the Bombay High Court, and vice-chancellor of the University of Bombay.[27] He led the Prarthana Samaj, Bombay's theistic society, and was an ardent champion of social reforms. These activities would ultimately complicate relations between the Bombay Bhanaps and their orthodox kin in Kanara.

Neither Shamrao Vithal Kaikini nor Narayanrao Ganesh Chandavarkar were "typical" Saraswats of late nineteenth-century Bombay, although most Bhanaps would welcome identification with men of such standing and achievement. Yet both men took pains to maintain links with their community. Shamrao Vithal endeavored to overcome apathy and suspicion to vitalize the ties between the Bombay Saraswats and Shri Chitrapur *Maṭha*, and organized a caste club in the 1890s. Chandavarkar, although a national figure, never lost touch with his caste. Some would suggest that his wife, Lakshmibai, made certain that social ties were maintained. Others might argue that the caste made certain that it did not lose touch with Chandavarkar instead. But on more than one occasion, Chandavarkar invoked the Saraswat identity. He once stated to a Saraswat gathering:

> We have all of us come to this place from our distant Kanara District. In one sense we are all foreigners in Bombay, and although I have always regarded that pride of country is far worthier than pride of community, yet I must say that we Saraswats, whether we come from North Kanara or South Kanara, have worthily upheld the honor and traditions of our great ancestors who came from the Panjab.[28]

---

a Gujarati leader, under invitations issued by V. N. Mandlik and Shamrao Vithal, for the purpose of displaying the intellectual attainments of Shastri Rangacharya of Coimbatore, who was the "master of forty subjects."

27. Cf. Vaidya, *Cañdavarkara*; Chandavarkar, *Wrestling Soul.*

28. *K. S.* 5, no. 1 (January 1923) :22–23.

This mention of the legacy of ancient migration may have reminded his audience that they shared a heritage with other castes of the Gaud Saraswat Brahman cluster who were also present in Bombay.

Coming into Bombay in the later decades of the nineteenth century, the Bhanaps were one of the last GSB sections to be represented in the city. Some Shenvis had been there since the seventeenth century.[29] These earliest settlers constituted a relatively small, stable community until well into the nineteenth century; in 1780 a census enumerated 409 "Shenvi Brahmins" in the island. These pioneers were divided into twelve lineages or families (*barghares*, twelve houses).[30] They established several temples and charitable properties which they managed exclusively, though they served any members of the Hindu community. Originally living in the Fort section of Bombay, they sifted first into the adjacent wards to the north and west of the Market, especially in streets and sections such as Lohar Chal, Popatwadi, Jambulwadi, and Kandewadi. As these areas were later preempted by Gujarati mercantile groups, the GSB moved northwest along the Palao Road (known later as Girgaum Road and still later as Jaganath Shankershet Road) into the neighborhoods of Thakurdvar and Girgaum.[31]

When the earliest Saraswat migrants came into Bombay after 1867, they moved into some of these areas where GSB were already present. Had there been a sustained interaction during the years since the Bhanaps' ancestors had left Goa, the recent migrants might have been absorbed within a broader GSB order in Bombay. However, several hundred years of separation, differing cultural environments, and acceptance of distinct lines of *swamis* served to perpetuate *jāti* boundaries among the various GSB sections.

29. Cf. Vāman Mañgeśa Dubhāśī, *Gauḍa Sārasvata Brāhmaṇa Jñātīcī Kamgiri* (Bombay, 1918), p. 24; V. R. Kerkar, "The Shenvis in Bombay," *Mahārāṣtra Sārasvata* 37, no. 2 (February 1948) : 32–41; Sir Charles Fawcett, *The First Century of British Justice in India* (Oxford, 1934), pp. 170n, 179; Malabari, *Bombay in the Making*, pp. 178, 379, 479; J. Gerson da Cunha, *Origin of Bombay* (Bombay, 1900), pp. 349–350.

30. Śarmā, *Bhūṣaṇa*, p. 317n, lists the families as Telang, Dalvi, Dhume, Lad, Sanjhgiri, Mulgaonkar, Deulkar, Bhende, Khote, Mandvikar, Wagle, and Amonkar, but not all families bearing these surnames were included; *Gazetteer of Bombay City and Island* 1 : 156–157.

31. Gerson da Cunha, *Origin*, pp. 60–61; K. Raghunathji, *Hindu Temples of Bombay*, No. 293, p. 352. G. W. Forrest, *Cities of India* (London, 1905), p. 35, contains a photo taken in this period in Girgaum which gives a good idea of the changing urban landscape. On one side of the road was a new five-story residential building, on the other an old-style Prabhu bungalow set in a garden.

Individual Saraswats who came into contact with the other members of the city's Indian elite met with their counterparts from other GSB sections. In a sense the Shenvis of Bombay were corporately an elite of the city; if Bhanaps were directly associated with this body, their own position within Bombay society might be more clearly defined. Shamrao Vithal was drawn into active support of the GSB community during a never-ending dispute over the brahmanical standing of the GSB in relation to Dravida Brahmans. Being a close friend of many GSB figures including Dr. Bhau Daji and Justice Telang, it was natural that Kaikini would interest himself in several public controversies over the ritual status of the GSB cluster. Allegations that GSB were not entitled to fully carry out all brahmanical duties were not new; in the 1870s they received more publicity, however, because of press coverage.[32] Shamrao Vithal took an interest, but most Bhanaps did not. Perhaps as struggling clerks and students, whether or not they were entitled to teach the Veda was not an altogether pressing issue.

The marginality of the Bhanaps to these controversies reflected their general relations with other GSB groups. In 1896 a controversy among GSB developed concerning management of the community's temples and charities in Bombay. A lawsuit was begun over the question of whether or not the rights of management were vested only in the families and connections of the *barghares*. The Bombay High Court was presented with the thorny issue of defining "who was a member of the GSB community of Bombay." Upon examination of the evidence, Justice Badruddin Tyabji found that during the nineteenth century members of every caste and subsection of the GSB caste cluster had been resident in the city and had participated in caste meetings and subscriptions. He therefore held that, on the basis of that precedent, the old dominant local interests could not press claims for exclusive rights. He hastened to add that he was ruling only on issues of temple and charity management:

> So far as the internal caste or religious affairs are concerned, I must leave the community to itself and it may for that purpose split or subdivide itself into as many sections or castes as it pleases. This court has no right or jurisdiction to compel any section to intermarry or to interdine with any other sections. I am only dealing here with the

32. "Printed extracts from Suit No. 43 of 1896, Bombay High Court, Original Side," in papers of the office of the Trustees of the Temples, Charitable Institutions and Funds of the Goud Saraswat Brahman Community of Bombay, Bhuleshvar, Bombay 3.

> management of the temples, charitable institutions, and funds which admittedly belong not to any particular section but to the whole of the [GSB] or Shenvi community of Bombay, and it is in this connection . . . only that I am considering whether the outside sections which are admittedly [GSB] . . . can be considered as forming a part of the Shenvi community of Bombay so as to be entitled to attend and vote at meetings not of any particular sections but of the whole.[33]

This decision led to the writing of a new temple trust charter that made all GSB eligible to participate. This would include the Bhanaps. However, this made little difference to most of them, for along with other recent arrivals, when compared to the older Bombay residents, they did

> not hold very high or respectable positions. They mostly belong to humbler classes and are employed as clerks or servants or peons &c., but of course there are very eminent exceptions. It is not to be wondered at therefore that they would not trouble themselves about caste affairs or caste meetings.[34]

Justice Tyabji's insight goes some distance to explain the slow and incomplete accommodation of the Saraswats with what, by rights, should have been their natural alliance with a wider GSB community. Expansive consciousness of wider communities was primarily a luxury to be afforded only by the well-to-do. Tyabji's explanation of lack of Saraswat participation in GSB meetings may also explain an equally retarded development of institutions for their own *jāti* in Bombay.

### *Urban Saraswats and Their Caste*

Migration had continued to bring Bhanaps to Bombay. By 1896, 226 Saraswats resided in 53 households in the city, making it perhaps the tenth most populous center of the caste.[35] But unlike

33. Vasudeo Gopal Bhandarkar and others *vs.* Shamrao Narayan Laud and others, Judgment, Feb. 11, 1898, Tyabji, J. "True Copy", in *ibid.*

34. *Ibid.* One result was the creation of several other trusts for scholarships open to all GSB students, which would benefit Bhanaps directly. Cf. Government of Bombay, *Directory of Public Trusts* (1954); F. K. Dadachanji, *Hindu Charities in Bombay* (Bombay, 1919).

35. *Chitrapura Panachanga*, Appendix 2 : 146 males and 80 females. The uncertainty regarding the rank order of Bombay's community is because the 1896 census did not have reports for Puttur, South Kanara, or Kumta, North Kanara, either of which would probably have been larger then the Bombay cluster at the time; both still had over 300 Bhanaps each a generation later. H. Shankar Rau, *Chitrapur Saraswat Directory, 1933* (Bombay), pp. 20–21.

other centers of the caste, Bombay had not seen the growth of those integrative social and religious institutions which had come up after the move into Karwar in 1862. Because many of the Saraswats present in the city at a given time were either students or persons subject to transfer in government service, the permanently settled population was quite small. The Saraswat population was maintained largely by circulation rather than unidirectional movement. Many who were established in the city were earning no more than Rs. 30 per month and were remitting a portion of that to their kin back in Kanara. Those who were very well established, a Shamrao Vithal or Narayan Chandavarkar, were patrons of cosmopolitan and, while willing to donate to the welfare of their own caste, were unable to bear solely the expenses of a new temple exclusively for the Saraswats. There also was no Saraswat priest recognized by the *maṭha* to carry out *purohit* duties.

In 1889 Nadkarni Subbarao asked the *maṭha* to arrange for a priest to be sent to Bombay to serve the householders of the city. He obtained the Bombay Bhanap's consent to form a "ten" or *sabha*, as it was then coming to be called, and to pay *vantiga* in the amount of 2 percent of annual income. They would support a caste *purohit* by a cash payment of Rs. 15 per month plus enough business in ritual work to earn Rs. 40 to Rs. 50 in fees and gifts.[36] It was thought that the best arrangement could be made if the priest also knew how to keep accounts for an eating house (*khanaval*)—perhaps reference to the boarding arrangements of the Kanara Club. The proposal was not acted on. Pandurangashram Swami doubted if the Bombay population could generate enough work and wondered if *vantiga* would ever be received. In response to the proposal that the Bombay people should establish a "ten," he suggested that the time was not ripe for a *sabha*. There was little evidence of sustained collective leadership of caste members in the city. If the *swami* wished to send a message, he said he could write to Shamrao Vithal. Hence the Bombay householders should make the first move:

> It is not now necessary to have a local *sabha* in Bombay. Let us consider it after consent to pay *vantiga*. No letter is received from Bombay *gṛhasthas* [householders]; only after a reply will Swamiji issue orders.[37]

36. R. S. C. M., letter no. 32 dated Virodhi Samvatsara, Pushya Bahula 13 [1889 A. D.].

37. R. S. C. M., letter no. 121 dated Magha Shukla 15 [A. D. 1888]; cf. letter no. 32 dated Virodhi Samvatsara, Pushya Bahula 13 [A. D. 1889].

Several years would pass before a recognized "ten" would function in the city. The difficulty lay in the circumstances of the Saraswats in Bombay. Unlike at Karwar or Mangalore, a very real break had occurred in leadership. In the Kanaras, several generations of influential men and their families had dominated local caste affairs, utilizing resources accumulated from employment and landed estates. Until the 1890s the majority of Bombay Bhanaps were of the younger generation, anxious to rise within the modest constraints of clerical service. The wealthy elite members of the caste devoted many of their resources to cosmopolitan causes, although support and sympathy could be given to caste fellows. Even Chandavarkar, by now a noted spokesman against caste in the social reform movement, recognized special ties. His wife Lakshmibai always kept close contact with her more humble relations, even when the Chandavarkars moved into a mansion on Peddar Road after his elevation to the bench of the High Court. Chandavarkar himself said:

> I assure you that I have never forgotten that Saraswats blood runs in my veins. . . . One thing stands before me as giving a golden character to my past career, and it is the days of my youth . . . when I had Saraswat parents and Saraswat grandparents, and above all when I was brought into contact with certain Saraswat persons.[38]

Shamrao Vithal tried without success to organize a "ten" or *sabha* to open ties with Shri Chitrapur *Maṭha*. He worried too that there was no organization that would focus the interests of Bombay Bhanaps. After the closure of the Kanara Club, he, Kundapur Anandarao, and others launched the Chitrapur Sangha in April 1892 "to develop cultural and social life and bring into being a community spirit."[39] A room was rented in Bhalachandra's Building near the Grant Road railway station. There all Saraswats could

38. *K. S.* 5, no. 2 (July 1923) :2. Lakshmibai was the younger sister of Ramakrishnarao and Narayanrao Sirur. She was married to Chandavarkar in 1875 at the age of 12. She remained with her family until her husband completed his LL. B. and had launched his legal career, joining him in 1881. Rao Bahadur R. N. Nayampalli recalled going as a boy with his aunt, who was Lakshmibai's niece, to the Peddar Road mansion, and of the wonder and consternation he felt upon seeing the carpeted floors and English-style bath. Interview, Santa Cruz, Bombay, Feb. 5, 1971. Cf. Chandavarkar, *Wrestling Soul*, pp. 59–64.

39. *Chitrapura Panachanga*, p. 41. According to R. A. Lajmi, who migrated to Bombay in 1894, most local people were not enthusiastic about paying *vantiga*, or any other dues. Interview, March 18, 1971.

gather evenings and weekends for relaxation and discussions. But Shamrao Vithal hoped that it would do more. Stimulated perhaps by the examples of the Pathare Prabhu Social Samaj founded in 1888, and the Brahman Sabha organized a year later, Shamrao Vithal suggested that the new organization could also serve as an instrument for advancing the caste's material interests.

A first step was to be publication of an annual almanac which included information about the *maṭha* and members of the caste. The first such volume appeared in 1896, incorporating a novel attempt at a caste census.[40] The Chitrapur Sangha seemed destined to become a major integrative mechanism among the Bhanap migrants in Bombay. But 1896 also saw another first in Bombay: the outbreak of plague.

How the plague reached Bombay was never known, although it was assumed to have come from southern China or the Persian Gulf. Its causes also were not known in 1896. Although preventive vaccine was developed soon after, popular resistance to vaccination and remedial sanitary improvements permitted the disease to spread and remain epidemic for over a decade.[41] Between September 1896 and the following June, the plague claimed 11,412 victims among the citizens of Bombay. Many who were not afficted evacuated the city. Wives and children returned to rural homes; those who remained knew fear. Apprehensions arose not merely from the epidemic and its grim consequence, but also from the possible inconveniences of detention in isolation camps and dislocation of all domestic arrangements. With evacuation of families, "permanent" migrants returned to the style of life of their predecessors, hanging on in the city only to hold their jobs and support their kin that had returned to Kanara. The ratio of births per thousand population dropped from 19.33 in 1896 to 11.36 a year later.[42] Because Saraswats were prepared to accept the preventive measures, a fair number of them stayed on and avoided the disease. But the

40. *Chitrapura Panachanga*, pp. 2–9. Cf. V. R. Gulvaṇe, *Brāhmaṇā Sabhecī Gelī Sāṭha Varṣe* [The Past Sixty Years of the Brahman Sabha] (Bombay, 1949), pp. 8–30; S. N. M. Trilokekar, *The Pathare Prabhu Social Club Golden Jubilee Celebration Souvenir* (Bombay, 1938), pp. 8–16.

41. *Gazetteer of Bombay City and Island* 3:174–177; L. W. Michael, *The History of the Municipal Corporation of the City of Bombay* (Bombay, 1902), pp. 187–249.

42. M. S. A., SRO, G. D., vol. 477 of 1898 (Plague), comp. 560, examines the social dislocations caused by the plague and the preventive measures.

dislocations were too great to keep up the club. The Chitrapur Sangha atrophied and died, itself a victim of the plague.[43]

### *Alternative Migration: Dharwar and Hubli*

Saraswat urbanization was not restricted solely to Bombay. Between 1880 and 1900 small colonies of Bhanaps were established at Hubli, Dharwar, and Madras. The recruitment of Saraswats to serve under private cotton-trading firms at Kumta and Karwar led directly to the creation of a small nucleus at Hubli. Hubli was a major market town of Dharwar district, some 80 miles northeast of Karwar. In the late eighties of the nineteenth century it was becoming the center of the cotton trade in the Karnatak.[44]

Among the earliest Saraswat migrants was Subrao Gopal Ubhayakar, whose European employer, P. Chrystal, sent him as a cashier to Gadag in 1878, promoting him a year later to be business manager of the West's Patent Press in Hubli. Soon thereafter Narayanrao Annappa Sirur also came to Hubli to develop a new industrial enterprise in partnership with Chrystal, the Southern Maratha Spinning and Weaving Mills, which began operation in 1883.[45] The central fact behind this shift of focus in the cotton trade was the construction of the Southern Mahratta Railway connecting Hubli to Poona and Bombay. As noted in the previous chapter, the construction of a locomotive shop at Hubli opened a number of clerical vancies which were taken up by young Saraswats. From 1888 until 1908, when the main locomotive shop was shifted to Madras in the merger of the Southern Mahratta with the Madras Railway, the offices of the railway and cotton mill were equally important sources of Bhanap income. The Sirur and Ubhayakar families went on to develop an extensive commercial network that dominated the cotton trade of southern Bombay and Mysore state, which had the effect of planting small Bhanap enclaves in towns such as Gadag, Ranebennur, and Devanagere.[46]

43. Some well-to-do Bombay Hindus began building suburban homes as retreats for the plague season. Chandavarkar, *Wrestling Soul*, pp. 62–63. Caste fellows frequently would spend visits at the Chandavarkars' estate in the then distant village of Borivili. Shamrao Vithal shifted his residence to suburban Santa Cruz, yet plague caused his death in 1905. *K. S.* 4, no. 3 (July 1922) :68.

44. *Bom Gaz.* 22, *Dharwar* :341–346, 354, 359–365, 729–761.

45. *K. S.* 5, no. 1 (January 1923) :8.

46. G. L. Chandavarkar, *Dattatraya Narayan Sirur* (n.p., 1950), pp. 4–26. Shamrao Vithal served as Chairman of P. Chrystal & Co. and played a part in

With no major educational institutions to attract students, the Bhanap population of Hubli was more settled. By 1896, 201 Saraswats resided in the town. Six years earlier Narayanrao Sirur had taken a lead in organizing a local *sabha.* He also cooperated with a Saraswat pleader from Karwar, Narayan Ananta Vinekar, and the taluka *mamlatdar* to purchase a tract of land in Hubli where house plots were allocated to be sold to members of the caste. At the new site a *dharmshala* was erected; it later was expanded to be a Shiva-Krishna temple. In 1896 the young Bhanaps who worked for the railway urged the need for some meeting place. A room in the *dharmshala* was given over, along with the personal library of a deceased Saraswat government servant, Raghavendra Subrao Nagarkar. The "Nagarkar Library" was given its own building in 1899 through a subscription drive among Saraswats in Hubli and elsewhere.[47] Although not all Bhanaps of Hubli lived in the neighborhood of the housing plot, temple, and library, the caste nontheless had a focus for its corporate activities in the town, linking government servants, lawyers, mercantile entrepreneurs, and railway clerks in sustained social intercourse.

Saraswats entering neighboring Dharwar during the same period came as government servants. It was the headquarters of the district. In 1888, the Southern Mahratta Railway set up its administrative headquarters there, causing a fresh invasion of Bhanap "quill-drivers." As in Hubli, the settlement became clustered. Most resided in what was known as the Mission Compound area, which was proximate to government offices. A "ten" was established, but no caste temple was built. Saraswats relied upon domestic priestly services of other brahmans until 1900. For major rituals they remitted funds to temples in their old villages of Kanara.[48] With creation of a high school in Dharwar, some students began circulating to the town as well, but the growth of the educational establishment there awaited developments in the twentieth century.

## *The Other Metropolis: Saraswats in Madras*

Madras had attracted Saraswats from South Kanara, primarily for education and examination, from 1865 onward. As such, the

obtaining the managing agency of the Maharaja of Mysore Spinning and Weaving Mills at Bangalore for the Sirurs in 1904.

47. *K. S.* 9 (April 1925) :9; *Chitrapura Panachanga*, Appendix 2.

48. *K. S.* 13, nos. 10–12 (April-June 1930) :15; K. S. 19, no. 8 (August 1935) :12; obituary of Vedamurti Ramakrishna Mangesh Bhat Kadle, who did similar work at Hubli.

educational migrants would not necessarily remain long in the city. From 1867 to 1880 every Bhanap matriculate candidate from South Kanara—including those who had no desire nor means to actually enter the university—had to go to Madras for the test. The journey was accomplished by taking a steamer or the leisurely combination of bullock carts and ferry boats 130 miles down the coast to Calicut. Opposite that town was Beypore, described as a "miserable spot," which for over a quarter-century served as west-coast terminus of the Madras Railway. The rail journey from Beypore to Madras, which was four times the distance from Manga- to Beypore, took only one-tenth the time.[49] The journey was expensive but not arduous. And with each passing year a few more Mangalore boys would set out to test their knowledge and fortunes in the examination hall. Matriculation certificates would open positions for them back home. Some continued to read in the university's syllabus for advanced certificates and degrees, either at Mangalore or Madras. A few enrolled at the Presidency College.

The first successful Saraswat graduate was Ullal Baburao, who obtained the Bachelor of Law degree in 1869 and returned to launch a law practice at Mangalore, ultimately accepting appointment as *munsif* (judge) at Kundapur. He was followed by several successful B. A. candidates, Kalle Ramarao in 1872 and in 1875 Kundapur Krishnarao and Sujir Raghunathaya. In the next decade at least 15 Bhanaps passed the Madras B. A., three continuing on to add the B. L. diploma.[50] Some of the graduates did enter terms in preparation for a legal career, but in the 1870s and 1880s this qualification was usually regarded as "only a stepping-stone to Government preferment as *munsif*s or deputy collectors in the mofussil."[51]

Indeed, at least 25 Saraswat graduates joined the Madras provincial services and took up gazetted posts scattered throughout southern India. Since these officers' salaries were in the range from Rs. 250 to Rs. 750 per month, they could afford to bring their families with them. Thus at any given time after 1880, isolated Saraswat households, consisting usually of one earning male and his dependents, could be found in such places as Vishakapatnam, Cocanada,

49. Maclean, *Manual of Administration* 1 :426n, 434n.

50. *Chitrapura Panachanga*, pp. 42–45.

51. H. Narayan Rao, "The Late Rao Bahadur Savur Mangesh Rao, B. A.," in H. Shankar Rau, *Chitrapur Saraswat Miscellany*, p. 123.

Cuddapah, Bellary, Erode, Kumbakonem, Tinnevelly, and Coimbatore. Being subject to transfer, these migrant Bhanaps remained on the move in the circulating society of government service. Such mobility could not contribute to establishment of permanent Saraswat colonies.[52]

The higher level of education available in South Kanara enabled more Saraswats to successfully complete examinations and higher degrees in Madras than did their counterparts of North Kanara in Bombay. But when financial straits or examination failure did occur, the city of Madras did not offer the same level of alternative employment prospects.

Although a great administrative and educational center, Madras was commercially and industrially retarded.[53] The lack of clerical vacancies in private firms meant that if no berth could be found in public service, a young Bhanap would have to look elsewhere. Nagarmat Ramarao, it will be recalled, had left the city after the only employment offered was temporary work with the census office. Dongerkery Ramarao similarly failed to find steady employment in Madras and turned to Bombay instead.[54]

Saraswats who settled in Madras were those whose education could qualify them for the professions or positions in advanced public service. Kilpadi Rama Rao, who rose in the Abkari department to be a deputy collector, was said at the time of his death to have been "the first among Mangaloreans who rose to a high official position in the Presidency town."[55] Several Bhanaps made advances in educational appointments at Madras. Savur Mangeshrao climbed from an assistant master's job in Mangalore, after his B. A. in 1876, to a place on the faculty of the Presidency College nine years later. He served also as Kannada translator to the University of Madras. From there he obtained the post of Kannada translator to the Government. Panje Mangeshrao, Kilpadi Krishnarao, Benegal Ramarao, and Nirodi Bhavanishankarrao similarly distinguished themselves in Madras appointments involving study

52. *Chitrapura Panachanga*, Appendix 2.

53. C. S. Srinivasachari, *History of the City of Madras* (Madras, 1939), p. 289; Anil Seal, *Emergence of Indian Nationalism* (Cambridge, 1968), pp. 101–102; Eugene F. Irschik, *Politics and Social Conflict in South India* (Berkeley and Los Angeles 1969), pp. 22–23.

54. *K. S.* 4, no. 2 (April 1922) : 44; *K. S.* 15, no. 6 (December 1931) : 14–15.

55. *The Hindu*, June 9, 1892, p. 3.

and teaching of Kannada.[56] Medical doctors, engineers, and a few persons employed in business rounded out the early Bhanap colony at Madras. Apart from their dependents, all other Saraswats in the city were students enrolled in the several colleges.

Although a number of Bhanap households clustered in the Vepary, Kilpauk, and Pursavakam neighborhoods, others were scattered throughout the city. Students at Presidency College and Madras Christian College lived in hostels, but some resided with friends and relatives. The home of Kilpadi Krishnarao was likened to a *carvanserai* of itinerant Bhanaps.[57] The Madras Saraswats did not yet have the service of a caste priest, although one had been requested as early as 1889. Apart from domestic observances, their ritual life was conducted in the public Shaivite and Vaishnava temples of the city.

Madras continued to attract Saraswats whose educational attainments enabled them to enjoy a measure of wealth and prestige. The slow overall economic development of the city meant that for many years Madras could not attract as broad a cross-section of the caste as had clustered in Bombay.

The early urban migration of Saraswats emerged from several motivations, primary of which was a quest for education and employment. In each new urban settlement the patterns of migrants' work, lives, and institutions varied. Once a Bhanap set out to better his prospects, however, the final end of mobility could not be forecast. Stretching lines of communication between home districts and cities might be expected to diminish close ties and connections which had held the caste together. Pandurangashram Swami at the *maṭha* was endeavoring in the same period to create additional linkages between caste and *maṭha* and to advance the community interest through innovations in religious life. But this attempt coincided with an urban-based movement among some Saraswats for what they called social reforms. The collision of these two forces, both of them mixtures of pragmatism and ideology, placed a fresh burden upon the integrative ties of the caste, and at the time appeared to threaten its continued existence.

56. H. Shankar Rau, *Miscellany*, pp. 123–124; interview with Molehalli Sanjivarao, Madras, Jan. 26, 1971; interview with G. R. Shirale, Madras, Jan. 26, 1971.

57. Interviews with Molehalli Sanjivarao, Madras, Jan. 26, 1971; Dattatraya Savoor, Madras, Jan. 27, 1971, G. R. Shirale, Madras, Jan. 26, 1971; Ramarao G. Philar, Bangalore, Jan. 29, 1971, Mangesh Vishveshvar Nadkarni, Madras, Jan. 27, 1971.

# 7

# RELIGION AND REFORM:

## *Crises of Caste Integration, 1870–1915*

As MEMBERS of the Saraswat caste pursued new education and occupations both in the Kanaras and in new urban arenas, their *swamis* were cultivating devotion to the *maṭha* and to *dharma* among their disciples. Institutional elaboration of religious life formed a counterpoint to the social and economic changes in the life of the *jāti*. Pandurangashram Swami, *guru* to the Bhanaps for over fifty years, gave particular emphasis to the desirability of all his disciples' conforming in their behavior to a rigorous concept of brahmanical purity. As acceptance of this abstract standard was an obligation for those who would be disciples of Shri Chitrapur *Maṭha*, and as adherence to the *maṭha* and *guruparampara* were distinctive markers of Saraswat identity and coherence, it followed that the integrative force of the *maṭha* upon the caste would depend upon the willingness of Saraswats to accept and conform to the *swami*'s standard. But that standard, which emphasized orthodoxy as an ideology, was coincident in time with another ideology, that of social reform.

### *Promoting* Dharma

As related earlier, the Saraswats ploughed many of their newly earned resources into expressions of religious action during the nineteenth century. By endowing temples, new rituals, and rest houses, they elaborated the religious life within their caste while reinforcing their brahmanical status. Shrimat Krishnashram Swami (1839–1864) and Shrimat Pandurangashram Swami (1864–1915) built upon this foundation, giving shape and meaning to the position of the *maṭha* in the life of the community. The overall effect of these activities was to publicize and enforce what may be termed the ideology of brahmanical purity, of thought and deed. Most Saraswats followed *laukika* (secular) occupations and seem to have left full and careful study of *veda*s and *shastra*s to their *swami*s and the more intellectual among the priestly families of the caste. Both Krishnashram Swami and Pandurangashram Swami urged that more young men of the caste study Sanskrit and then use it to develop a strong, disciplined understanding of *advaita* philosophy as well as acts of prayer and ritual. To the extent that these efforts prompted a view of *dharma* as an objective "thing", an ideology against which practice could be measured, social and religious customs of the caste ceased to be only a "way of life" that was practiced unreflectively. This was not "revivalism" or "revitalization" of religion, but an attempt to bring behavioral practice into conformity with existing standards which Pandurangashram Swami believed were being ignored. The roots of these developments lay in the life of the *maṭha* during the middle of the nineteenth century.

Although many of the promises made by the laity in connection with the selection of Krishnashram Swami as *shishya* in 1835 included assurances of regular support for the *maṭha* thereafter, *vantiga* payments did not subsequently flow into the *maṭha* with regularity. Krishnashram Swami found it necessary to transmit special appeals in order to maintain the institution.[1] During his 25 year reign, he toured repeatedly among the places of Bhanap residence in Kanara urging his followers to support the *maṭha* and to observe the *smarta* traditions associated with it. He ordered that Vaishnava sectarian markings on the person should be discontinued by any who used them, but he did not interfere with yearly observances of the Krishna Jayanti festival which remained popular among Bhanaps.[2]

Just as he and his predecessors had patronized and encouraged the construction of new temples throughout Kanara, Krishnashram

1. Records of Shri Chitrapur *Maṭha* [hereafter R. S. C. M.], letter to Gokarn householders Manki Janardayya, Manki Lakshmaya, Karkala Annapaya, Honavar Bhanappa, *et al.*, from Shrimat Krishnashram Swamiji, dated Plavana Samvatsara, Kartika Bahula 13 A. D. 1847]; letter to Mangalore householders from Shrimat Krishnashram Swami, dated Plavanga Samvatsara, Margashirsha, Bahula 13 [A D 1847].

2. R. S. C. M., letter to Mallapur householders, dated Pingal Samvatsara, Phalgun Shuddha 4 [A. D. 1858]; interview with Sujir Sundar Rao, Shirali, Feb. 18, 1971.

Swami also undertook to enhance the spiritual prestige of the community through elaboration of rituals at the *maṭha*. During the late 1850's several disciples suggested that he inaugurate an annual car festival (*maharahotseva*) typical of the important temples of South India, including the great Krishna temple at Udipi.[3] This wish was also advanced by Pandurangashram Swami, the *shishya* who had been adopted in 1857.[4] Apart from the enhancement of sanctity, such a festival could draw together the Bhanap families who after 1859 were residing in two distinct districts.

Krishnashram Swami requested that all disciples pay *vantiga* and donate necessary materials for the new festival.[5] Ritual specialists from other religious centers were consulted so that the festival could be arranged in strict accordance with the prevalent *agamokta-vidhi* system of southern India. The inaugural observance commenced April 14, 1862, and lasted for eight days. Shri Bhavanishankar, the deity of the *maṭha*, was first taken out in procession to nearby hamlets and temples. On the full-moon day, the image was placed in a large wooden "car" (*ratha*) and drawn by devotees across the open area in front of the *maṭha*. Each evening the image was carried in a palanquin through the village. There followed a drama, singing of devotional hymns, and a sermon. Dinners were given for all caste members, as well as special feeding of the poor. The festival closed with a sermon by the *swami* himself.[6] Although planned within the Hindu calendar, the festival also neatly coincided with the opening of the hot-weather holidays of the British raj, when schools and courts closed. Thus a great many Bhanaps could come to Shirali, renewing ties of loyalty to the *maṭha*, paying *vantiga*, and restoring social ties with members of the caste from other towns and villages. The car festival was Krishnashram Swami's final legacy to his disciples, for he passed away into *mahasamadhi* in 1864. His other legacy was his *shishya*, Pandurangashram Swami.

When Krishnashram Swami chose a *shishya* in 1857, as in his own case 22 years earlier, an individual who was not directly related to

3. *K. S.* 10, no. 5 (July 1927) : 17; *Bom. Gaz.* 15, *Kanara*, part 1 : 121–123, surveys car festivals in North Kanara district.

4. G. S. Hattiangdi, *Pandurang, Pandurang*, pp. 42–43.

5. R. S. C. M., file of correspondence for Raudri Samvatsara [A. D. 1860–61], e.g., letter from Krishnashram Swamiji to Nadkarni Mahabaleshwarayya, dated Raudri Samvatsara, Shravana, Bahula 14 [A. D. 1860], requesting timber for construction of the temple car.

6. *K. S.* 10, no. 5 (July 1927) : 17; *K. S.* 13, no. 9 (March 1930) : 5.

the Shukla Bhat family was selected. In fact the candidate was Nagar Kalappa, the *swami*'s nephew.[7] There were further parallels. The decision to adopt had been made at the instance of Mangalore householders who put Kalappa's name forward. And when other names had been suggested, Kalappa was confirmed when reference was made to the oracle of Shrimat Ananteshwar temple at Vithal.[8] Two of Kalappa's attributes, intelligence and a strong will, had figured in the *guru*'s choice. Although when he succeeded Krishnashram Swami in 1864 he was only sixteen, young Pandurangashram Swami asserted himself rapidly in manner that was to be characterstic of his reign.

The new *swami* took steps to assure that his own studies could continue. He recruited eminent shastric scholars from various centers of South India. He also acted to realize his predecessor's desire that more young Saraswats take up priestly occupations, and classes for training priests were established at the *maṭha*. It was hoped that Bhanap priests could be provided in those towns or villages where caste members were currently dependent upon priests from other brahman castes.[9] Pandurangashram Swami continued this endeavor throughout his career. One of those who studied at Shirali, Vedamurti Aldangadi Lakshman Bhat, recalled that the *swami* himself taught classes in grammar one hour daily and sometimes observed the scholars' progress in the study of the *Ṛgveda*.[10] The scholarly concern was visible also in Pandurangashram Swami's leadership of the Saraswat *jāti*. He continually endeavored to stress the intellectual and textual forms of brahmanical tradition as against local or customary practices. By so doing the *swami* was attempting profound reform, to reinforce his conception of

7. Technically it is incorrect to refer to this as a kinship relation, since when Krishnashram was adopted as *shishyaswami* in 1835 he became a *sannyasin* without kin, protected only by Shri Bhavanishankar. Nagar Kalappa was the son of Nagar Santappa, the younger brother of Parameshwara prior to his adoption as *shishya* in 1835. Kalappa was not born until 1847.

8. Hattiangdi, *Pandurang*, pp. 9–13.

9. *Ibid.*, pp. 17–19; R. S. C. M., letter to Pandurangashram Swamiji from Mallapur Venkatesha Bhat, son of Ganapathy Bhat; Nagar Santapayya's son Rama; Murdeshvar Krishna Bhat's son Shanta Bhat; and Mallapur Mangesh Bhat's brother Shankara, dated Kshaya Samvatsara, Ashadh Bahula 2 [A. D. 1866].

10. Interview with Ved. Aldangadi Lakshman Bhat, aged 96, at Ullal, South Kanara, Feb. 20, 1971. He remembered with some awe the character of the *swami*, "sat shak Pandurang" ["he was literally Pandurang (Vishnu) himself to be seen"].

orthodoxy by a process of accretion whereby daily Saraswat life would be informed by the tradition of *dharmaṣhastra*. This did not mean that Saraswats were previously not following brahmanical norms. Rather it was a matter of changing emphasis, of ever increasing the sanskritic component in the corporate affairs and practices of the caste.

This meant some subtractions also from the religious life of the Bhanaps. Although both he and his *guru* had been confirmed by the spirit-medium oracle of the temple at Vithal, Pandurangashram chose not to confirm a successor when this position fell vacant, preferring to let this unbrahmanical custom lapse in spite of the considerable revenues it had brought the temple.[11] Later he also declared that Saraswats should avoid participation in, or support of, any festive celebrations which contained "lewd and vulgar" displays, such as were common in the observance of Holi.[12]

There were more additions to the sacred repertoire than subtractions, however. Several innovations were introduced at the *maṭha* to enhance its prestige. Within a year of assuming his duties, Pandurangashram Swami began the system of *sadavarta* or daily subsistence for itinerant ascetics and pilgrims. By relocating and renovating small privately managed temples at Shirali, the environs of the *maṭha* were brought up to the standard of a *kshetra*, a place worthy of pilgrimage. The construction of the Shivaganga Sarovar, a ritually correct tank (pool) adjacent to the *maṭha* further strengthened this holy claim.[13] Some secular innovations were also provided. An annual market was inaugurated in conjunction with the car festival.[14] The success of this measure led to the establishment in 1897 of a weekly market, held Sunday mornings on the road in front of the *maṭha*. During its early years, the number of visitors was increased by Pandurangashram Swami's habit of sitting in the Gopalkrishna temple adjacent to the bazaar to grant audiences.[15]

This constructive work was not without critics who feared that

11. Interview with S. D. Kombrabail, Bantwal, March 25, 1967; interview with K. Shankarrao, Vithal, March 25, 1967; interview with Yellore Babu Rao, Mangalore, March 24, 1967.

12. *Indian Social Reformer* [heareafter *I. S. R.*] 10 (March 18, 1900) :225. It was reported that Bhanaps at Mangalore subsequently observed Holi without the traditional "obscenities." *I. S. R.* 11 March 31, 1901) :241.

13. Hattiangdi, *Pandurang*, p. 53.

14. SRBG, n.s. 556, *Papers relating to the First Revision of Revenue Assessments: Honavar Taluka* (Bombay, 1918), pp. 4, 33.

15. *Ibid.*, p. 33; Hattiangdi, *Pandurang*, p. 54.

monies given for the *maṭha* were being misspent or wasted. In fact, the *swami* proved to be a shrewd overseer of the institution's resources. Between 1864 and 1909, income from rice lands deeded to the *maṭha* had quadrupled, the amount of rice had tripled, and the annual yield of coconuts had risen from 2,000 to 12,000.[16] But expenditures had also increased substantially. More than Rs. 100,000 was invested in repairs and construction at the Chitrapur *maṭha* and the three other *maṭha* buildings at Mangalore, Mallapur, and Gokarn. The redevelopment of Shirali, including street lighting, a market building, and a school raised expenses. A rest house was erected on an adjoining hill for use during the car-festival palanquin procession. It was justified as being convenient for "the very important and big people of our community." In short, such expenditures were not only necessary for the *maṭha*, but "essential for the prestige of the community."[17]

Investment of *maṭha* income in permanent structures and facilities did not yield a material return. Much of the annual *vantiga* was dedicated to covering costs of rituals performed on behalf of the donor or members of his family. As personal incomes rose, presumably *vantiga* would rise also. But even under the *vantiga shasana* of 1869, local *sabha*s or "tens" found it difficult to collect more than what had been paid on earlier occasions. Pandurangashram Swami perceived that the *maṭha* would be caught between the fixed commitments of reconstruction, an increasing demand for performance of rituals, and an inelastic *vantiga* collection. In 1888 he convened a new *mahasabha* (great assembly) of men from various local *sabha*s to develop a consensus among caste elders on several issues. One idea discussed at this time was a one-time special collection to amass a fund which could be capitalized; the yield from this investment might be sufficient to cover the annual costs of ritual. The *swami* issued a proclamation on this in 1894. During the next few years Rs. 2025 was paid in, but thereafter the plan fell into abeyance in the backwash of a prolonged and bitter controversy over social reform. A similar capitalization plan was begun by at least one Bhanap temple, with modestly successful results.[18]

Pandurangashram Swami demonstrated little reluctance to

16. Review of *maṭha* finances in *Proceedings of Mahasabha held at Sri Chitrapur Maṭha, Shirali, . . . Soumya Samvatsara, Vaishaka Bahula 1–6* [A. D. 1909], para. 45 [translated with assistance of Mrs. Radha J. Sujir, Bangalore].

17. *Ibid.*, paras. 45, 47, 50.

18. Hattiangdi, *Pandurang*, pp. 31–32; *Umamaheshvara Devasthana Varadi Shaka*

employ technological innovations in his promotion of *dharma*. When the Southern Mahratta Railway had completed its line through Hubli from Poona, he determined that rail travel would facilitate pilgrimage to more distant shrines of Hinduism. To explore the possibility on behalf of his flock, he decided to make a *Kashi yatra*, a pilgrimage to Benares. The costs of such a tour with a party of 45 came to Rs. 13,405, of which Rs. 2,225 went for rail fare.[19] Accompanied by priests of the *maṭha* and a few laymen, the *swami* went to Hubli, then proceeded by rail to Allahabad (Prayag), and then on to Benares. Although he took time en route to visit clusters of Saraswat settlement at Hubli, Dharwar, Gadag, and Bijapur, he did not include Bombay city in his tour, even though existing rail connections involved a change of train at Kalyan, only about thirty miles northeast of the city.[20] The absence of a functioning local *sabha* and organized Bhanap community in Bombay may have been the reason for this omission. Yet it symbolized an emerging antipathy and suspicion between rural and urban segments of the *jāti*.

While at Benares, Pandurangashram Swami had rituals done for many members of the caste who had commissioned him for the purpose. He also appointed individual priests as *kshetra purohits* to whom later Bhanap pilgrims could turn when on pilgrimage in the future. The *swami* attended several gatherings of *pandits*. Discussion topics included *veda*, Panini's grammar, *nyaya shastra*, and *Mimamsa*. An account of the tour relates that he brought one of these discussions to a brilliant climax "when he asked a profound question relating to the *Shrutis*. None of those present could answer it satisfactorily."[21] Sanskrit verses were composed in honor of Pandurangashram Swami. Clearly the standing of the Saraswats and their *guru* had been enhanced.

Upon his triumphal return from the pilgrimage, Pandurangashram Swami commemorated the event by inaugurating additional regular rituals at the *maṭha*.[22] He then made a tour of South Kanara

*1803–30* (Kannada) [Umamaheshwara Temple Report, 1881–1909)] (Mangalore, 1910), p. 5. [Translated with assistance of Shri H. V. Nagaraja Rao.]

19. Personal communication from Shri Sujir Sundar Rao, Shirali, Feb. 14, 1971, based on examination of *maṭha* accounts.

20. Hattiangdi, *Pandurang*, pp. 130–131.

21. *Ibid.*, p. 21.

22. R. S. C. M., circular letter no. 121, Pandurangashram Swami at Karwar to local *sabhas* dated Sarvajitu Samvatsara, Magha Shukla 15 [A. D. 1889]. *Ramanavami utsava* was added and additional *maharudras* were performed.

and at Mangalore, in December 1888, convened the first *mahasabha*, drawing together delegates from the local *sabhas* to discuss finances of the *maṭha* and the question of permission of widow marriage in the caste. The *swami* published a treatise on the latter issue. He subsequently wrote and published two additional works—one systematically setting forth the prayers and rituals appropriate to each deity and holiday, and the other giving the Sanskrit text with a verbatim Kannada translation of the Saraswats' hymns and prayers of morning, evening, and special occasions, preceded by an introductory discourse on *advaita* philosophy.[23] He thus attempted to ensure that his disciples could employ their burgeoning literacy toward perfection of their brahmanical heritage. Pandurangashram Swami revealed a sense of his audience when he expounded the the need for Bhanaps not to become totally enmeshed in worldly attainments:

> We who are born into this world of action strive to seek happiness by various means. No one desires misery. This is, of course, generally within your experience. That is why you engage yourselves in the study of English and other subjects as a means of attaining happiness. And if one sees your incessant efforts, notwithstanding the various difficulties encountered during the period of study, it is quite obvious that you are full of desire to obtain happiness. Now how many kinds of happiness are there and what are the main modes of achieving them? This is usually not understood either during childhood days or in later years.[24]

The *swami* then elaborated upon the differences between everlasting and transient happiness and how, though the latter could be obtained through spiritual and secular work, the former was to be realized only through full performance of brahmanical duties and full knowledge of the universal and eternal *Brahman*, the underlying essence of the universe.

## *Enforcing* Jāti Dharma

Pandurangashram Swami was prepared to innovate on behalf of his conception of *dharma*. He also employed his role as spiritual preceptor of the Saraswats to reinforce orthodox thought and practice. And here the caste elders played a major part. While final authority concerning individual transgressions against *jāti*

23. *Devatarchana-vidhi* (Shirali, n.d. [1892?]); *Sandyavandanava* (n.p., 1896).
24. Introduction to *ibid.*, translation provided by G. S. Hattiangdi.

*dharma* lay with the *guru*, he normally only took cognizance of issues which were brought to his attention by the laity.

If a local *sabha* received a report—usually through gossip—of some act of commission or omission, it would investigate and, if satisfied of the gravity of the offense, would announce a ban on social association (*samparka*) with the accused. The matter would then be referred to the *swami* for his orders confirming the punishment and setting a penance *(prayaschitta)* for expiation of the sinner.[25] *Prayaschittas* varied in line with the nature of the violation. They included paying fines, shaving off the moustache—a particularly embarassing public sign—carrying out sacrifices, and possibly a pilgrimage to some sacred shrine. The bulk of cases recorded at the *maṭha* were minor and prosaic—complaints of minor acts of omission such as nonpayment of *vantiga* or failure to fully perform rituals. Accusations of acts of commission included public drunkenness, gambling, or philandering. Accusation did not mean automatic guilt, for Pandurangashram Swami was prepared to dismiss cases in which he felt the evidence was insufficient.[26]

If the decision was confirmed, however, the *maṭha* would issue a bulletin (*riyas*) to the original local *sabha*, with copies to other local *sabhas* throughout North and South Kanara.[27] When the penance had been done, the *maṭha* was informed, and in turn notified the population of the caste that the former sinner was now eligible to be admitted once again into full *samparka*, social association.[28]

In this, as in most other matters of *maṭha* management, Pandurangashram Swami endeavored to maintain his independence of action. Yet he was dependent upon the elders of the caste not only for maintaining a watch upon activities of his disciples, but also for enforcing the sanctions. The 1869 *vantiga shasana*, which had been aimed at bringing order to the collection of *maṭha* income, reflected

25. Based on examination of correspondence files at Shri Chitrapur *Maṭha* for 1839, 1847, 1854, 1857, 1860, 1866, 1871, 1882–3, 1888, and 1892.

26. R. S. C. M., letter no. 477 from Pandurangashram Swami to Bankikodla *Sabha*, dated Khara Samvatsara, Bhadrupad Shuddha 4 [A. D. 1891]. In this instance the *swami* was prepared to override the testimony of several witnesses accepted by the *sabha*.

27. In some instances the circulation of the bulletin or *riyasa* would be only to villages in the vicinity of the offender's village. R. S. C. M., letter from Shri Chitrapur *Maṭha* to Khambadkone-Bijur local *sabha*, dated Subhanu Samvatsara, Ashadh Shuddha 11 [A. D. 1883].

28. R. S. C. M., circular letter no. 474, from Shri Chitrapur *Maṭha* to local *sabhas*, dated Khera Samvatsara, Shravana Krishna 13 [A. D. 1891].

in both its creation and provisions the dependence of the *maṭha* upon the influential men of the caste. Pandurangashram Swami was a *sannyasin* who accepted the burden of spiritual guidance for the entire *jāti*. Technically he was fully independent, but practically he was dependent upon the good will and support of his disciples. His endeavors to bring these disciples to follow his own exacting standards collided with efforts of some individual Saraswats to introduce social reforms into their caste and Hindu society generally.

### *Resisting Social Reforms*

Social reform proponents identified a broad spectrum of institutions and relations within Indian society which they perceived as "evils" when compared to an abstract standard combining western precepts of Christian ethics, secular humanism, and the traditions of classical Hinduism. Although the disabilities of untouchables and low castes were included in social-reform concerns, the thrust of the movement during the late nineteenth century was directed toward "adjusting the ideas and behavior of high-caste educated men and their families."[29] Narayan Chandavarkar, the best-known spokesman for social reform among the Saraswats, rationalized the high-caste emphasis: "the customs and institutions with which the social reformer proposes to deal are common to the higher classes of Hindu society, from which the lower castes take their standard."[30] Since Indian social reformers were experimenting in new modes and methods of public-opinion formation, it followed that they *said* a great deal more than they *did*. Thus the movement can properly be viewed as a chapter in modern India's intellectual history. But some acted upon their ideas, and by attempting to practice what they had preached produced unforeseen consequences for themselves, their families, and their castes.

Reform and dissent came to Mangalore in religious guise in 1870, discussed above in Chapter 5. It was the first corporate encounter with reform among the Saraswats. The threat of excommunication had discouraged potential members in the Brahmo Samaj, and a separate Upasana Sabha had attracted quiet support

29. C. Heimsath, *Indian Nationalism and Hindu Social Reform*, p. 5. Cf. remarks on R. G. Bhandarkar and reform in D. D. Kosambi, *Myth and Reality*, p. 38.

30. Narayan G. Chandavarkar, *Speeches and Writings of Sir Narayan G. Chandavarkar* (Bombay, 1911), p. 54.

from a few Bhanap families. But even Ullal Raghunathaya, the original leader of the movement, had been readmitted to the caste. A fresh religious-reform controversy broke out when a few young students and older men among the caste became interested in the Arya Samaj. One of these enthusiasts was a rather remarkable police inspector, Gulvadi Venkatrao. A graduate of the Basel Mission School, he had begun as a clerk in the district police office in 1864, but was later appointed as an inspector. An avid student of literature—he read through Shakespeare each year—Venkatrao was the author of one of the first true novels in Kannada, *Indirabai*. Having studied Hindi in the course of his police work, he was able to read Swami Dayananda Saraswati's *Satyarth Prakash* in its original language. In 1888 he brought out an Arya Samaj journal in Kannada at Mangalore, *Mitrodaya*.[31]

By this time Pandurangashram Swami had returned from Benares and was visiting Mangalore. He studied the Arya teachings and declared them to be contrary to the *dharma* of the Saraswats. Most of the members dropped by the wayside. *Mitrodaya* ceased publication in the face of orthodox opposition. Gulvadi Venkatrao, instead of retreating, pushed on to explore another religious system. Beginning by reading R. C. Dutt's *Civilization in Ancient India* and then Max Müller's "Sacred Books of the East" volumes, the Bhanap ex-Arya police inspector became a Buddhist and in 1900 was received into the faith by Anagarika Dharmapal at Madras. Several Saraswat priests at Mangalore, including Mangalore Rama Bhat and Gulvadi Narayan Bhat, actively espoused the Arya Samaj cause, the latter being ultimately excommunicated for having taught the *Ṛg veda* to some non-brahman Hindus.[32]

One Bhanap lawyer, Kudmul Rangarao, was prepared to work directly for improvement of the condition of the district's untouchable population. He organized the Depressed Classes Mission in 1887. Although he was boycotted for this work by members of service castes, barbers and washermen, he was not excommunicated from his own caste. In fact he received much sympathetic support from younger Saraswats. Five years later he was put out of caste, but the excommunication resulted from his having dined with

31. *K. S.* 24, no. 4 (April 1940) :93–95.

32. *Ibid.*, p. 95; interviews with Gollerkeri Somashekarrao, Mangalore, Feb. 21, 1971; Nayampalli Ramarao, Mangalore, Feb. 20, 1971; A. K. Nadkarni, Mangalore, March 23, 1967 and Feb. 21, 1971.

Ullal Raghunathaya—who had himself been excommunicated for failure to use orthodox forms in the funeral ceremonies of his mother.[33]

These early encounters with reform appear not to have greatly disturbed the corporate life of the Saraswats. Apart from Mangalore, no other towns in South or North Kanara manifested such interest. And when Pandurangashram Swami came to Mangalore, the local householders showed him all due respect. But it was during his visit in 1888 that the *swami* convened the first *mahasabha*, at which another social-reform issue surfaced—the question of permitting second marriages for young girls of the caste who had been widowed.[34]

As with other brahman castes, Saraswat practice allowed a woman only one marriage. Aside from a few legends associated with the Nadkarni and Kulkarni families, there is little evidence to suggest that widowed Saraswat women cast themselves upon their husbands' funeral pyres.[35] Yet the widow's life was led in twilight—head shaven, wearing the red *sari*, serving as a drone in the joint household. The only respectable alternative was to turn to a life of religious meditation and devotion. One of Kanara's best-known woman saints, Jognani, had been a Bhanap widow in the seventeenth century. More immediately, Nadghar Shanti Bai (1860–1902), after being widowed during the 1890s, was famous among Saraswat inhabitants of the west coast as a devotee of Shri Vithoba and Shri Dattatraya.[36] But these instances were rather exceptional, and in both cases the individuals were mature women. Social reformers were concerned especially with the plight of widows who were still very young, whose husband had died even before consummation of the marriage. Such "virgin widows" were expected to keep the same observances as mature widows.

The plight of such persons provided the first real social-reform issue to confront the Saraswat *jāti*. In 1884 some Saraswats living at Madras became active in a widow-marriage group and solicited the cooperation of their kin in South Kanara, who in turn asked Pandurangashram Swami's advice. He circulated a bulletin to

33. *K. S.* 12, no. 1 (July 1928) :23–26; *I. S. R.* 6 (Aug. 23, 1896) :400.

34. R. S. C. M., letter no. 318 from Chitrapur *Maṭha* to Kashi Bhau Bhatta Purohita, dated Sarvadharvi Samvatsara, Ashvidha, Krishan 4 [A. D. 1888].

35. On Nadkarni and Kulkarni traditions, see S. S. Talmaki, *Saraswat Families* 2 :3–4, 33.

36. H. Shankar Rau, *Miscellany*, pp. 95–97, 102–106.

all local *sabha*s and other devotees, asking their opinions. A few, notably Shamrao Vithal Kaikini in Bombay and Gulvadi Venkatrao, president of the Puttur local *sabha*, supported the reform. But most asked the *swami* to guide them.[37] The correspondence and Pandurangashram Swami's replies were themselves published by by him in a small book with a big title, *Vidhavodhvāhacikīshumata bhanjanam*, "The breaking into pieces of the opinion of one who wants to do widow marriage."[38]

The enquiry of the South Kanara Saraswats is illuminating, for they appeared to be much moved by the condition complained of and sought guidance from the *swami* before any widow marriage actually occurred. They said that the Madras Bhanaps had quoted *dharamashastra* and observed that "those Madras men are well educated." But if the *swami* showed widow marriage was wrong, "then these people will not venture in such things."[39] The local *sabha* at Kundapur went to the extent of citing a case in *Moore's Indian Appeals* to suggest that perhaps the Madras men would not be doing wrong, but the *swami* was adamant—there were not enough instances in the *shastra*s to permit Saraswats to participate in or support widow marriage.[40]

Later an unsympathetic Bhanap complained that the *swami* had substituted convoluted language for sound argument: "For my part, I had to go through a good deal of linguistic exercise before I could read it with tolerable facility."[41] Yet Pandurangashram Swami's arguments reflected much more than willful opposition to change. He pointed out that the worst problems arose when young girls were married to older men who then died in a few years. Girls should always be married before their first menses, but poor families often could not find suitable young men because of the growing evil of dowry—for which there was no shastric injunction. Pandurangashram Swami stated:

> This system of dowry now has a new amendment. That is, one who has passed middle-school examination demands Rs. 500; a matriculate,

37. The Madras reformers also published their cause in a Kannada weekly, *Kannada Suvarte*, then published in Bombay. It seems to have had a wide circulation among Bhanaps in Bombay and North Kanara. *K. S.* 24, no. 4 (April 1940) :93, 95.

38. Published in Bombay, Shake 1810 [A. D. 1888]. [This work, hereafter cited as *Vidhavodhvāha*, was translated with the assistance of Shri H. V. Nagaraja Rao.]

39. Letter of M. Shiva Rao of Manjeshvar to Pandurangashram Swami, Tarana Samvatsara, Magha Bahula 14 [A. D. 1885], in *Vidhavodhvāha*, pp. 102–103.

40. *Ibid.*, p. 169.

41. *I. S. R.* 9 (July 16, 1899) :362.

> Rs. 800, and a graduate B. A., Rs. 1000. There is great pressure on fathers of girls that they should pay all the expenses incurred in the process of educating the groom, who wants to go off to Bombay or Madras. Since to get a young educated groom is difficult and expensive, fathers give their daughters to older widowers ... [which led to young widows].[42]

Pandurangashram Swami improved upon the moral by suggesting that problems also arose from his disciples' lust for an English education to qualify for government jobs. Students whose parents had extracted a dowry would leave their wives at home and go on to school, where they overworked themselves, took up bad habits of smoking, and weakened their constitution so that even girls who married younger grooms faced an uncertain future.[43]

The *swami* was by no means opposed to education. For example, he authorized a loan to Damble Narayanrao, a poorly paid medical compounder at the Mangalore civil hospital, so that his son who had passed his matriculation could go to Madras for further study. Also, the priests at the *maṭha* regularly performed rituals to assist students. In response to a request from Manki Mangeshayya at Madras, "*sevas* to give him *vidya*" [worship for knowledge] were offered to Shri Bhavanishankar "so that he might pass in his examination."[44]

After publishing his treatise, the *swami* convened the *mahasabha* at Mangalore. The delegates were unwilling to express any opinion they thought might anger their *guru*; most were not prepared to express opposition to his rulings. Yet the Madras Bhanaps, who had still not had a chance to perform a widow marriage, affirmed their belief in the correctness of the reform. And in Bombay, Shamrao Vithal Kaikini published a brief pamphlet refuting the *swami*'s arguments. It seemed that the urban Saraswats were straining at the tether.[45]

42. *Vidhavodhvāha*, p. 172. The *swami*'s figures on dowry were confirmed in similar reports in the reform press. *I. S. R.* 9 (May 14, 1899) :285. By 1924 inflation had worked its mischief—a matriculate demanded Rs. 1000 and a B. A. Rs. 3000 or more. *K. S.* 6, no. 3 (July-September 1924) :9.

43. *Vidhavodhvāha*, pp. 173–176.

44. R. S. C. M., letter no. 461, Pandurangashram Swami to Shukla Narayan Bhat, Mangalore, dated Khara Samvatsara, Shravana Krishna 9 [A. D. 1891]; letter no. 512 from Shri Chitrapur *Matha* to Manki Mangeshayya, dated Khara Samvatsara, Ashividh, Shuddha 9 [A. D. 1891].

45. Hattiangdi, *Pandurang*, pp. 30–35; S. L. Ugrankar, *Shamrao Vithal Kaikini*, p. 3–4.

However, the distance between urban and rural Bhanaps as a whole was more apparent than it was real. City residence may have been suspect in the eyes of the rural householder. Well-to-do and visible individuals like Shamrao Vithal of Narayan Chandavarkar were known to have interests in "cosmopolitan clubs," theistic societies, and social reform. But since similar beliefs were present at least in Mangalore, there was no logical connection to city life. More humble Bhanaps in Bombay were suspected of being lax in ritual observances while living in the city. It was firmly believed that people who went to Bombay carried on with a scandalous disregard for propriety by patronizing Irani tea stalls and eating bread baked by persons unknown.[46] But as we have seen, the extent of rejection of orthodox behavior in the city was limited, if only because of expense. Suspicions may also have stemmed from the lack of caste *purohit*s in either Bombay or Madras. Pandurangashram Swami had declined to appoint priests to these places, for he thought there would be insufficient call upon their services, since city dwellers would continue to have recourse to their village or family shrines during visits to Kanara in the hot-weather holidays.[47] Since rural families hardly ever hesitated if one of their promising sons could be sent off to the city for education or employment, it appears that much of the antipathy was grounded in envy of the comfortable salaries that many urban Saraswats earned—comfortable at least by the standards of rural North Kanara. In any event, fresh controversies over social reform soon surfaced among the Bhanaps, to further strain relations within the caste.

## *The Sea-Voyage Controversy*

"Before the question of sea-voyage was raised in our community, very few of its members even knew of such a movement as Social Reform."[48] This recollection of one Saraswat may have overstated the ignorance of Bhanaps concerning reform during the period before 1890, but he did not underestimate the force and impact of the controversy once it was raised. Until 1885 the Saraswats had

46. Interviews with G. S. Hattiangdi, Bombay, Feb. 21, 1966; P. G. Sirur, Bombay, Sept. 14, 1966; Sujir Sundarrao, Shirali, March 10, 1967; R. A. Lajmi, Bombay, March 18, 1971.

47. R. S. C. M., letter no. 32 from Shri Chitrapur *Matha* to Nadkarni Subrao of Karwar, dated Virodhi Samvatsara, Pushya Bahula 13 [A. D. 1889].

48. *I. S. R.* 9 (Aug. 13, 1899) :394.

observed the shastric prohibition against brahmans' going "across the black waters" to lands where they could not preserve their ritual purity and might encounter irrevocable pollution. But in many instances the presumed sin could be removed upon return through taking of a penance or *prayaschitta*.[49] The number of Indians who traveled to Europe was minuscule, but sustained by a growing interest among the educated in qualifying for the bar, the Indian Civil Service, or the medical profession.[50] The question of "sea-voyage" had been raised and settled much earlier in Bengal, but in rustic Kanara the issue did not come to a head until 1896.

Narayan Chandavarkar—so often the "first" among his caste fellows in various achievements—was also their pioneer voyager, going to England in 1885 as political representative of the Bombay Presidency Association.[51] When he returned to Bombay he encountered no response from the local Bhanaps other than admiration. The question of travel to England was by no means settled, however. In 1886 the British Indian Association petitioned London to offer simultaneous I. C. S. examinations in India, in order to reduce the expenses of Indians who wished to compete. It was pointed out that the trip also meant "the loss of social position in all but small minority who break with Indian society from personal motives and are unable to faithfully reflect its sentiments by reason of their isolation."[52] The combined effects of presumed ritual pollution and cultural alienation among the "England-returned" troubled thoughtful observers. A Marathi weekly editorialized:

> It is exceedingly painful to observe that with their advantage in knowledge they grow indifferent and callous to the natural ties of affection and love. A change in the brain brings also a change in the heart. It is the fault of the man and no defect in the education imparted to them. They forsake their native habits . . . and transform themselves into *saheb loks*. . . . A change of costume and modes of life is not a *sine qua* of civilization. Our England-visiting people . . . are not content with a change of dress and habits, but are often found to treat with contempt not only the people of India in general, but even their friends and relatives.[53]

49. Cf. P. V. Kane, *History of Dharmashastra*, 5 vols. (Poona, 1930–1962), 3:933–938.

50. *I. S. R.* 10 (Jan. 28, Feb. 18, and Feb. 25, 1900):175, 199, and 207, lists names of 286 Indians then in the west; in 1893, the number had been 302.

51. Chandavarkar, *Speeches and Writings*, pp. 46–47.

52. Quoted in B. B. Misra, *Indian Middle Classes* (London, 1961), pp. 376–377.

53. Quoted in *Bombay Gazette*, Oct. 6, 1869, p. 3.

Chandavarkar and other Bhanaps who went to England later did nothing to merit such criticism. They evinced no contempt for their homeland. Chandavarkar's own strong and disciplined personality, coupled with western ideas, had led him to conclude that there were positive advantages in going to England. It would be fine, he thought, if I. C. S. examinations could be simultaneous, but the successful Indian candidates ought then go to England for two years so as to obtain what he saw as the primal British virtues: "Pluck, enterprise, and moral courage."[54]

Chandavarkar recalled in 1901 that when he had returned from England in 1885, "I was received by my caste and my family. I was treated as if I had never violated any of the rules of the caste." He had reported as much in testimony before the Indian Public Service Commission in 1887. Asked if his caste had any objection to going to England, he replied that there was none. He had experienced no difficulties: "Caste friends came to me and mix[ed] with me freely."[55] Nor had he had to undergo any purifying rites.

When the commissioners later took testimony at Madras, they found that one witness, Mundkur Srinivas Rao, was of Chandavarkar's caste, and explored the question further. Would the caste object to a visit to England by a member? Mundkur thought the caste "would have some objection." What about Chandavarkar? Had he actually been readmitted to caste? Mundkur's reply was indirect, but significant: "He has never been to this part of the country." Chandavarkar had not been excommunicated. But if he were, would he not suffer any disadvantage? Again the witness responded, "Not unless he came to this part of the country."[56]

In other words, if a Saraswat were to go to England, the questions of being in or out of caste were not answered by what happened in Bombay, but rather what would transpire when the presumed sinner returned home to Kanara.

Chandavarkar's residence in Bombay and his affluent independence meant that the issue of his "sin" would not be pursued unless it was taken up by others bent upon forcing a showdown, or until such time as he might become socially dependent upon the caste, e.g., when it would be necessary to find marriage partners for his children. It is clear that Pandurangashram Swami was

54. Indian Public Service Commission, *Proceedings* (1887) 4:230.
55. *Ibid.*,p. 229; Chandavarkar, *Speeches and Writings*, pp. 108–109.
56. Indian Public Service Commission, *Proceedings* 4:229; 5, part 2:333.

disinclined to take any notice of the visit to England, and so long as the *matha* was not pressed for definitive pronouncements, the issue could lie dormant. At the second *mahasabha*, held at Shirali in December 1894, the *swami* was interested in advancing the *vantiga* capitalization plan for stabilizing *matha* finances. But a query about sea-voyage was put to him, and he had to move. He issued an order that Saraswats should avoid social contact (*samparka*) with "England-returned" men pending determination of the severity of the "sin." Local *sabhas* were queried; so were other GSB *swamis*. A consensus leaned toward a view that such "England-returned" persons could be readmitted upon taking a penance. No further action was taken, however. Chandavarkar did not petition for relief, nor did he appear to suffer any disabilities.[57]

Other young Bhanaps, Kaval Vithal Rao, Manki Raghavendrarao, and Labhadaya Ramamohanrao, were in Britain already, as students. When Kaval Vithal Rao returned to India, he visited Madras in June 1896. He was feted at a dinner attended by over 40 Bhanaps. A list of guests, subsequently prepared for the *swami*, revealed 42 individuals, almost all of whom were well educated government servants, educators, lawyers, or doctors. They were not merely the elite of the Madras Bhanaps, they constituted almost the whole representation of the caste residing in the city.[58] The *swami* wrote to Madras upon hearing of the dinner, and asked for information about the matter. The Madras Saraswats followed a procedure whereby no one could accuse another, and no one need testify against himself. Not surprisingly this legal strategy meant that the response to the *swami* was that nothing untoward had happened in Madras. At the same time, the case was publicized in a Madras weekly, the *Indian Social Reformer*.[59]

57. *I. S. R.* 7 (Sept. 6, 1896) :6–7; 8 (Feb. 6, 1898) :183.

58. R. S. C. M., report from Madras to Pandurangashram Swami on those in Madras having *samparka* with Kaval Vithal Rao [n.d., prob. October 1896].

59. *I. S. R.* 7 (6 September, 1896) 5; Hattiangadi Narayanrao was on the editorial staff of the *Indian Social Reformer* and N. G. Chandavarkar served as the paper's Bombay correspondent. It ultimately shifted to Bombay. Coverage of the social reform questions among the Saraswats appears to have been increased as a result of H. Narayanrao's presence on the staff. The coverage increased Bhanap readership, but did not always please it. Shamrao Vithal objected vigorously to some critical remark in the paper on the *swami* in 1896. The detailed attention which the caste received even extended to reports of minor infractions by unknown common people., *I. S. R.* 11 (18 August 1901) 403; It represented an imperfect means of communicating items of interest, an experience which contributed later

When Vithal Rao went on to Mangalore, the caste members there split over whether or not it would be proper to have social relations, *samparka*, with him. And at Karwar one member of the local *sabha* urged that "England-returned" men be kept out of the caste absolutely, even if they applied for readmission.[60] Most, however, were inclined to try some compromise along lines suggested in a pamphlet published by Shamrao Vithal at Bombay. He urged that England-returned men should apply to the local *sabha* for readmission and a penance. When this was done and the penance completed, the readmission would be final. The penance could consist of a fine or piligrimage to some prescribed holy site.[61]

Shamrao Vithal's nephew, Chandavarkar, objected to this compromise, for he considered that he had committed no sin. In a letter to a friend at Karwar he asked, "Of what use is a *prayaschitta* if, instead of leading to sincere penitence and preventing the commission, it only becomes a promoter and abetter of sin?"[62] This was a critical point. For if rites of penance became routine, how could a "sinner" feel obliged to avoid repetition of the "sin"? In this, ironically, Chandavarkar's position was close to that of Pandurang-ashram Swami, on both moral and constitutional grounds. Both men saw the greatest good obtaining when an individual was consistent in his professed values and his accomplished deeds. The rest of the Bhanaps did not quite agree, for although no one would say so, uncompromising idealism could hardly serve as a basis for holding a caste together and preserving its social relations.

The publicity given the matter in the *Indian Social Reformer* muddied the waters. One Saraswat letter-writer launched a general attack upon all "orthodoxy" and, warming to his subject, suggested that if the Bhanaps wanted to really accomplish something, they should excommunicate Pandurangashram Swami and set up Narayan Chandavarkar as the head of the caste.[63]

Accounts of this advice were quickly passed on to the *swami*. His response was to issue a proclamation on October 22, 1896, in which he volunteered to become a true *sannyasin*, leaving the *maṭha*

to the thrust for the creation of a separate caste journal. *I. S. R.* 11 (30 June, 1901) 345; K. S. 4 no. 2 (April, 1922), 37.

60. *I. S. R.* 14 (Feb. 7, 1914) :281

61. Ugrankar, *Shamrao Vithal*, pp. 7, 10–11; *K. S.* 13, no. 3 (September 1929) :2.

62. D. G. Vaidya, *Cañdavarkara*, pp. 208n.

63. *I. S. R.* 7 (Sept. 6, 1896) :6–8.

and letting the disciples manage it as they pleased. Many, perhaps most, Saraswats had been somewhat indifferent to the sea-voyage issue, but now it appeared that some "reformers" were bent not merely on enabling "England-returned" men to reenter the caste, but also on undermining the very fundamental spiritual and social institution of the caste.[64]

Emotion rather than intellect was in the ascendant. The caste became polarized, but not between the educated and noneducated. One Saraswat graduate asserted that Pandurangashram Swami was "the very embodiment of learning and good sense." One recent Madras B. A., Bijur Shankarnarayanrao, said that to assert that there was no need to control interdining would open the possibility of indiscriminate interdining with even non-Hindus, which would destroy "the root of all caste distinctions." Moreover, the Saraswats were a small caste and could not take such steps and expect not to lose the hard-won acceptance and admiration of other castes.[65]

In Bombay, Shamrao Vithal called what may have been the last meeting of the Chitrapur Sangha on November 16, 1896, to discuss the readmission question and the matter of a *mahasabha* that was to be held in Shirali a month later. Greatest attention was given to the need for the *swami* to adopt a *shishya*, should he be serious about retiring. The value of a *guru* as a medium through whom all could obtain *moksha* was strongly emphasized. The members sent a petition to the *swami* urging adoption of a *shishya*, preservation of the *maṭha*, and readmission of the "England-returned" if they had lived in accord with brahmanical practice while abroad. The club members also promised to commence paying their two-percent *vantiga*.[66]

The same afternoon in Mangalore, a meeting of "the educated section of the Saraswat community" gathered in the Ganapathi temple school to discuss the "sea-voyage" question. It was placed in the perspective of national growth—the Bengalis and Panjabis had overcome opposition and were going abroad to help acquire the basis for modernizing India. But patriotism was not enough for many in the audience. They were afraid that their beloved *swami* might leave them.[67] On the other hand, almost the whole of Manga-

64. *I. S.R.* 8 (Feb. 6, 1898) : 183–184.
65. *I. S. R.* 7 (Nov. 15, 1896) : 86; 7 (Oct. 18, 1896) : 54.
66. *Bombay Gazette* Nov. 18, 1896, p. 3; *I. S. R.* 7 (Dec. 6, 1896) : 97.
67. *I. S. R.* 7 (Dec. 6, 1896) : 104–105; 7 (Dec. 13, 1896) : 114–115.

lore's Bhanap elite had dined with Kaval Vithal Rao or with someone who had done so. The prohibition against *samparka* was vexing. Public dinners at the caste temple had been suspended and an annual caste feast was given up, out of uncertainity as to who was and who was not under the ban. Except for a handful of persons excommunicated earlier in connection with Ullal Raghunathaya's activities, most Mangalore householders appear to have wished the subject would simply be resolved without delay.[68]

When the *mahasabha* finally convened in December 1896, only a handful of the delegates took up the need to readmit the "England-returned." Perhaps overawed by Pandurangashram Swami, the majority reversed their earlier advice, said no readmission could even be considered, and gave the *swami* full authority to deal with the matter.[69] Pandurangashram Swami took his disciples at their word and ordered final excommunication (*bahishkar*) for those who had gone to England, and penances for any who had been in *samparka* with them. It was this which seemed to endanger the unity of the caste. Since "England-returned" men would probably take up positions in cities and not the mofussil, a special burden would be laid upon Bhanaps at Madras and Bombay and upon their kin back in the Kanaras who might have ties with the "sinners."

Chandavarkar's social dependence was fast approaching. His daughter had attained the ideal age of marriage—twelve—and had been betrothed to Dattatraya, son of merchant of Hubli, Narayanrao A. Sirur, whose sister was Chandavarkar's wife. Sirur's elder brother, a strong devotee of the *swami*, nonetheless urged that the ceremony be carried out, if only for the family's honor of meeting its promises. The wedding in 1898, relinking two Bhanap families, attracted a mammoth gathering, even though the plague forced its relocation from Bombay to Hubli.[70] After the festivities the price had to be paid. All who attended, including the officiating priest, were ordered to take penance. A correspondent of the *Indian Social Reformer* said bravely:

> In spite of the fulminations of this great Shankaracharya, interdining between the sinners and the saved goes on . . . to an extent which

68. *I. S. R.* 7 (Dec. 27, 1896) : 129; *The Hindu*, Dec. 26, 1896, p. 6; interviews with Nayampalli Rama Rao, Mangalore, Feb. 20, 1971; A. K. Nadkarni, Mangalore, Feb. 21, 1971; Pandit Shiva Rao, Mangalore, Feb. 21, 1971.

69. *K. S.* 13, no. 3 (September 1929) : 2; *I. S. R.* 7 (Jan. 3, 1897) : 134.

70. *I. S. R.* 8 (July 3, 1898) : 350–351. G. L. Chandavarkar, *Wrestling Soul*, places this event in 1899, but the report referred to suggests this is incorrect.

> causes very little inconvenience to the former, especially in the large towns. If orthodox priests do not officiate at ceremonies, there are wiser men to profit by their aloofness, for where there is money, there are priests.[71]

The Saraswats of Hubli knew it was not so simple. No sooner was the wedding over than an anonymous complaint to the *swami* brought an order for the local *sabha* to investigate the matter. Its meetings filled every evening. None dared miss for fear of being accused and excommunicated. And in fact the Hubli *sabha* was being asked to investigate itself, for almost all in the town's Bhanap community had had *samparka* with someone who had been at the wedding. And then, too, some had travelled elsewhere. One bemused Bhanap thought, "the infection of *samparka*, like the plague infection, does not remain in one place."[72] The Hubli case resolved nothing and compounded uncertainty.

The reform-minded Saraswats were generally dissatisfied with the management of the *maṭha* as well as the immediate controversy. There was a saying current among the younger Bhanap graduates that "We shall never be saved until we have an M. A. at the head of the *maṭha*."[73] If more and more persons were excommunicated, perhaps the caste would be confined "to the *Swami* and a few favored *Bhats*." The income would suffer, "but the *maṭha* had property enough to feed the *Swami* and the *Bhats*."[74] This sarcastic humor stimulated a response. In a collection of short stories based upon themes of the Saraswats' problems, one author parodied a "typical reformer," one Narayan Sharma of Mangalore, who was "shaving, cropped [haircut], western dressed, and one year at Madras Christian College." The hero explains: "I am a brahman but I didn't know any hymns, so I began to think I was a reformer. I gave lectures to the reform groups, but I wasn't regular member—why waste money?"[75]

The reformers were not justified in assuming that everyone in the caste was prepared to undergo excommunication. In fact, many were doing their penance. In February 1898 it was reported that Pandurangashram Swami was on his way to Mangalore, and on

71. *I. S. R.* 9 (July 16, 1899) :357.
72. *I. S. R.* 8 (July 3, 1898) :351.
73. *I. S. R.*10(June 10, 1900) :322; Hattiangdi, *Pandurang*, p. 38.
74. *I. S. R.* 11 (June 30, 1901) :348.
75. Gulvadi Annaji Rao, *Rohini* (Mangalore, 1906), p. 2. [Translation assistance by Shri Shankar Shetty.]

March 1st a mass all-Mangalore Saraswat *prayaschitta* was administered during a twelve-hour ceremony. Each family paid one rupee as a fine, and only a few who were already out of favor with the *maṭha* refrained.[76] The risk of the *swami*'s displeasure was seen as too great for most Bhanaps.

A person in Chandavarkar's position might have another option—to remove himself and his family from the caste altogether. This would mean having to seek matrimonial alliances elsewhere. The *Indian Social Reformer* suggested that such persons should look to persons belonging to "closely allied communities speaking the same language and observing very nearly the same manners and customs" for new marriage prospects. The problem of orthodox rites could be solved by performing the wedding under the rites of the theistic Prarthana Samaj. But the real issue was not one of rituals. The Prarthana Samaj simply did not offer the equivalent potential kin which the caste provided.[77] When the sanctions of caste were invoked, they lay against not merely the offending individual, but also his family. When Chandavarkar's son reached the age for his thread investiture (*upanayan*) in 1901, there were no theistic rites available. Traditional ceremonies were performed by the boy's maternal uncle. This demonstrated the dilemma of a reformer. If the reformers or theists of Bombay formed a community of which the boy could become a member, the father might inflict no serious injury on him by detaching him from his original caste. But failing that, what was the father's duty?[78] Some accommodation seemed necessary.

For most Saraswats who found themselves under the ban, but who required performance of a ritual, it was reported that an expedient compromise was available. "The contaminated man, if he has to perform a ceremony which might be pronounced invalid if performed under defilement, pays down a few rupees and admits to a penance" lasting for one day.[79]

Of course, as Ullal Raghunathaya had proven in Mangalore, excommunication did not necessarily cut off all relations beyond the world of ritual. On the eve of the sea-voyage controversy,

76. *I. S. R.* 8 (Feb. 13, 1898) : 188; 8 (March 13, 1898) : 224–225.

77. *I. S. R.* 9 (July 16, 1899) : 357; Heimsath, *Social Reform*, p. 105.

78. *I. S. R.* 11 (June 16, 1901) : 329; *Subodh Patrika* (Bombay) 29 (June 30, 1901) : 1.

79. *I. S. R.* 10 (June 10, 1900) : 322.

Narayan Chandavarkar told a social reform meeting in Madras:

> It is supposed that an excommunicated man, by formally ceasing to be a member of his caste, ceases to exercise any influence over it and thereby frustrates his own object. Now we have heard this argument a number of times . . . but we have not heard of a single reform of importance effected by those who affect their caste by giving way to its prejudices.[80]

He added that "no reformer wishes to separate from his people, but because people separate from him by proclaiming the ban of excommunication against him, it is not to be supposed that the separation causes a destruction of his personality and the influence of his example."

Chandavarkar's analysis was supported by his experiences during a visit to Mangalore in 1900. He received an enthusiastic welcome from most of the younger Saraswats. He addressed a local social reform association in the hall of the new GSB-sponsored Canara High School and later talked to a large gathering of Bhanaps within the very precincts of the Shri Umamaheshwar Temple. He urged his hearers to not be reformers only so far as "you do not lose caste dinners and you are not put to any inconvenience."[81]

Pandurangashram Swami was growing impatient with his disciples. He circulated a set of five questions to be answered by each loyal member of the community. The questions were broad and general, and seemed to reflect confidence in the traditional patterns of the *maṭha*. No doubt he expected that these queries would remind the Bhanaps of their ancestral heritage:

1. Why was this *samsthana* established? If its continuance is desired, why?
2. What are the duties to be hereafter discharged by the head of this institution?
3. If some practices of the community hitherto observed are to be given up by reference to the requirements of the times, how much is to be retained?
4. Explain fully what is meant by saying that the government of the caste must be regulated in accordance with the needs of the times.
5. What is the kind of relation that ought to subsist between the head of the *maṭha* and his disciples?[82]

The *Indian Social Reformer* suggested in response to the fifth question

80. Chandavarkar, *Speeches and Writings*, p. 67.
81. *Ibid.*, p. 79; *I. S. R.* 10 (Jan. 14, 1900) : 153.
82. *Ibid.*, pp. 323–324.

that in excommunication the community, and not the *swami*, should have the final word. Turning the argument full circle, it suggested that every member of the caste, whether accepting the *swami*'s views or not, ought to contribute to the *maṭha*. In so doing they would be paying their dues, for in a sense the caste was "in the nature of a club." If the caste adopted practices inconsistent with their *guru*'s principles, then it was up to him to decide whether or not he ought to continue as their preceptor.[83] It is striking how close this was to the position of Pandurangashram Swami.

As a *sannyasin*, the *swami* was in a position to detach himself and leave, however improbable that might seem. In fact he threatened an equivalent act by refusing to select a *shishya* who could be his successor. Of course the spiritual lineage could be continued by action of the caste, as had happened in the eighteenth century. But under the circumstances of declining support for the *maṭha* and the alienation of substantial numbers of Saraswats, it was not clear after 1900 that sufficient support could be mustered from the much-reduced ranks of the faithful.

In 1902 Pandurangashram Swami again convened a *mahasabha* at Mangalore. Although the delegates raised the question of adoption of a *shishya*, the sea-voyage question also arose. The president, Nayampalli Shivarao, endeavored to point out the practical problems which a ban on sea travel to England would entail, in the light of the need of Saraswats "to make up for lost ground by taking to fresh fields." In the best traditions of the bar, he also asked if mass threats of excommunication did not risk a charge of libel. When a North Kanara delegate interjected that he thought not, Shivarao "coolly replied that if the Northerners had entire satisfaction about their own investigations about their kith and kin in Bombay and elsewhere, they were at perfect liberty to bring their question to a final decision," but the Mangaloreans did not feel they had conclusive information from Madras and would not make a hasty judgment.[84]

An example of the problems involved came up the following year. One of the persons alleged to have dined in Madras with Kaval Vithal Rao, Dr. Hattikudur Narsingrao, was about to have his daughter married. He applied to the local *sabha* of Karkala for a penance, and that body passed the favorable recommendation of

83. *Ibid.*, p. 324.
84. *I. S. R.* 12 (April 20, 1902) :274.

a small fine on to Pandurangashram Swami. He took no notice nor action. So Dr. Narsingrao went to Shirali itself for a *prayaschitta*, prostrated himself, and offered to pay any fine. The *swami* was adamant. So the "sinner" went to Mangalore and applied to the local *sabha* there to decide whether or not he could be in caste. They decided that he was not guilty, gave him permission to celebrate his daughter's marriage, and took part in those ceremonies. This alerted the *swami* that Mangalore was no longer "loyal," and a number of prestigious Saraswats, including Shivarao's son Nayampalli Subbarao, were excommunicated unilaterally.[85]

The effectiveness of excommunications and resulting social boycotts were most effective in mofussil towns and villages, working far greater hardships than could occur in Bombay, Madras, or even Mangalore. The letter and not the spirit of the law was often observed in families where one or two men were under the ban. When Dr. Krishnarao Nadkarni and his father Mangeshrao were both excommunicated, they took their meals outside the kitchen on the verandah. Ultimately Mangeshrao did take a *prayaschitta*, after much pressure from very close friends who had managed to avoid excommunication even as they had aided the reform movement: Kabad Ramarao, Bharadvaj Shivarao, and Dhareshwar Ananthaya. In Mangalore, several reform-minded priests continued to serve as *purohit*s to outcasted families.[86]

On the other hand, in villages the ban could be ugly. Extreme anguish was caused to one excommunicant when his father died and his fellow Saraswats refused to perform the traditional service of carrying the corpse to the burning ground, and he had instead had to employ some low-caste men to do the job.[87]

The *swami* angrily sent out a series of eight further questions which were supposed to be answered by all disciples of the *maṭha*. The responses of one reformer demonstrate that heat rather than light was generated. The *swami* again asked, "With what object

85. *I. S. R.* 14 (Feb. 7, 1904) :280–281.

86. Interview with A. K. Nadkarni, Mangalore, Feb. 21, 1971. Kabad Ramarao had presided at reform meetings; Bharadvaj Shivarao was a supporter of the Brahmo Samaj, Upasana Sabha; and Dhareshwar Ananthaya had close ties with the reformers, marrying his daughter, Kamaladevi, to the son of an excommunicant, Nayampalli Subba Rao. She was subsequently widowed and married a second time to a Bengali poet. She became a well-known figure in the nationalist movement and in the mobilization for women's rights in India.

87. This case was reported by a Saraswat residing in Poona who requested anonymity; the event in question occurred in 1909.

was the Shri Samsthana founded in our community of Gaud Saraswats by our ancestors?" The reformer, known to the reading public only as "A Saraswat," replied:

> Since Hindu society was split into innumerable castes . . . and the Brahman declared superior to all human beings, most people naturally became possessed with a keen desire to secure the status of Brahman. There was however a rule that none could claim to the status . . . without being a [disciple] . . . of some *guru maṭha*; and this proved an obstacle in the way of the Saraswats, who therefore founded the Chitrapur *Matha* and became its disciples in the fond hope that they would thenceforth be recognized as Brahmans.[88]

This was not an answer that Pandurangashram Swami expected, nor was it wholly correct. An orthodox response, given by Baindur Narayanrao, president of the *mahasabha* convened in 1907, was succinct: "Our people required guidance in their behavior and to be shown the correct path along with worldly and spiritual improvement."[89]

Reform enthusiasts were frequently portrayed as proponents for change facing an unchanging, conservative orthodoxy; but as we have seen, the *swami* had introduced new elements into the religious world of the Saraswats. Also, while many orthodox persons credited the reformers with adopting European ways, the reformers could reply, "The truth is that we are all in the throes of a revolution, and no sect or party . . . is left untouched by the spirit of change."[90]

One Bhanap from Bombay attended the car festival at Shirali in 1899. He reported that he had been surprised to find many changes. "The *Bhats* [priests] vied with each other in the use of European articles of dress, and outshone the visitors from such places as Mangalore and Karwar." The old rough-hewn image of Krishna had been replaced by one of fine marble. The band in attendance played an English tune. Photographs had been taken of Pandurangashram Swami and were for sale to the faithful. And now when the *swami* went on tours, his arrival in a town was greeted not merely with the traditional prostrations and *padapuja* (worship of his feet), but also with welcoming addresses in the fashion of the official tours of the English governors. It was thought by some that this

88. *I. S. R.* 13 (March 15, 1903):267.

89. Proceedings of the Mahasabha held at Shirali, Shaka 1829, Plavanga Samvatsara, Nija Chaitra, Bahula 6 to Vishaka Shuddha 4 [May 3–16, 1907]. [Translated from Kannada by Ramarao G. Philar, Bangalore.]

90. *I. S. R.* 10 (Jan. 14, 1900):158.

all meant that Pandurangashram Swami was trying to stay ahead of all other *gurus*; had he been instead a lay householder with children, he probably would have sent them to England for study in order to better the family's prospects.

A small caste could not sustain these disputes and preserve its unity. The British census commissioner reported in 1911 that the Saraswats were divided between the "Londonwalas" and "non-Londonwalas."[91] Perhaps the *jāti* was breaking up. For several years it did appear that the Bhanaps who were out of favor with the *maṭha* might attempt to develop some alternative social ties. One opportunity was presented in the form of a movement among members of the various castes of the GSB cluster to unite all into a single new caste. The *swami* was certain that in this new organization lay the seeds of only further deviations from *dharma*. A *mahasabha* was called in 1912, and the delegates dutifully ratified the *swami*'s opinion that Bhanaps ought not to participate in the GSB unification movement. The rationale was that since other GSB *swami*s had not enforced such rigorous standards for their devotees as had Pandurangashram Swami, association with those devotees would necessarily compromise the Saraswat purity.[92] As it developed, this new organization, the Samyukta Gauḍa Sārasvata Brāhmaṇa Pariṣad (united GSB Conference), did little more than meet, pass resolutions, and enjoy intercaste diners, but it captured the imagination of many educated Bhanaps, including some who had stood by the *swami* on the sea-voyage question. Thus the new prohibition on membership in the "*parishad*" drove a fresh wedge between caste and *maṭha*.[93]

The most visible result at Shirali was the decline in the annual *vantiga* tithes collection. The collections in the 1890s appear to have been around Rs. 15,000 annually, but in 1909 they were only Rs. 11,248, falling the next year to Rs. 9,520. Receipts rose in 1911–12, but the impact of the *mahasabha* declaration on the GSB

91. *Census of India, 1911* 7, *Bombay*, part 1, Report: 204. Similar divisions were reported among other South Indian brahman castes. M. N. Srinivas, *Marriage and Family in Mysore* (Bombay, 1942), pp. 29–30.

92. A fuller examination of the unification movement is Frank F. Conlon, "Caste by Association: The Gauda Saraswata Brahmana Unification Movement," *Journal of Asian Studies* 33 (May 1974): 351–366.

93. "An Open Letter to Followers of Chitrapur *Maṭha*," pp. 46–53 in *Karvar yethila pañcavya Samyukta Gauḍasārasvata Brāhmaṇa Pariṣad Hakīgata* (Bombay, 1915).

*parishad* was ruinous; *vantiga* fell in 1912–13 to Rs. 7,742.[94] The distrust and misunderstanding between the *swami* and *maṭha* and the increasingly urbanized Saraswat population boded ill for the caste's future. To be sure, perhaps only 500 persons out of nearly 10,000 might be actually excommunicated at any time. But the families and friends of these would number substantially more. Further, as many of these were members of families that had earlier been strong supporters of Shri Chitrapur *Maṭha*, the basis for maintaining the elaborated *maṭha* program diminished.

Pandurangashram Swami was inclined to let the *guruparampara* expire with him. Eight times *mahasabhas* requested that he adopt a a *shishya*, and eight times he refused. The laity grew apprehensive that as the *swami* grew older he might become ill and never turn away from his resolve. At the various *mahasabhas* the loyal supporters agreed to obtain letters from each Saraswat local *sabha*, signed by the heads of all families, pledging support to the *maṭha* and praying that the *swami* select a disciple to be his successor.[95] Such mobilization efforts had limited success even in the towns of North Kanara which were reputedly the heartlands of orthodoxy. The *swami* detected on the letters signatures of persons who were already excommunicated, and he questioned the validity of such persons' loyalty oaths. He observed that in spite of resolutions, many of the disciples were not improving their conduct:

> In every town, that which is against *jāti*, *pankti*, *dharma*, and *maṭha* is growing. Nobody made any efforts with heart and soul to rectify this, no one is doing it, and it does not seem that they will do it in the future. All our aspirations that the people will be good are completely vain. Well, I don't care![96]

Nothing, it seemed, could change Pandurangashram Swami's mind. Given the weakened financial condition of the *maṭha* and the lack of sympathy for its mission among a substantial proportion of the Saraswat population, what chance would a new, young *shishyaswami* have? In 1915, however, only a few days before he

94. Accounts of Shri Chitrapur *Matha*, quoted in Hattiangdi, *Pandurang*, p. 31.

95. R S C M, "Pledge given by devotees of the *maṭha* on their own behalf and their families, including minors, voluntarily and with a sincere and everlasting assurance to His Holiness Shrimat Pandurangashram Swamiji, on Shalivahana Shaka 1835, Pramadi Samvatsara Jyeshta, Krishna 12" [May 3, 1913].

96. R. S. C. M., letter no. 254, dated Pramadhi Samvatsara, Phalguna Bahula 7 [printed paper in records of Shri Umamaheshwar Temple, Mangalore]. [Translated with the assistance of Shri Bellare Dinkar Shrinivasrao, Mangalore.]

passed away, Pandurangashram Swami was persuaded—most assert by divine inspiration—to select a son of one of the *maṭha* priests to be his successor. The *shishya* was designated Anandashram Swami. Nine days later, on June 14, 1915, the old swami attained *mahasamadhi* and a young, untrained boy of twelve was left to face the difficult task of being spiritual preceptor to the Saraswats.[97] The decline of the *maṭha* might be yet arrested, but the place of the institution in the life of the caste and the role of the *swami* therein would require dramatic reorientation and reconstruction. The corporate existence of the caste itself, with members now scattered in distant and alien cities, would also require fresh initiatives and enterprise.

What had happened in Pandurangashram Swami's reign should not be seen only as a revolt against tradition by some highly urbanized reformers. It would be more accurate to state that all Saraswats, including the *swami*, were experiencing changed conditions and were endeavoring to adjust to the opportunities and requirements of the times. Many of the *swami*'s reforms were departures from what had been Saraswat practice in the previous century. What distinguished these reforms from those of the "social reformers" was their reference to a different set of standards and priorities. The reformers, for their part, similarly aimed at an abstract model derived more from western experience. But only a few very independent members of the caste could afford to fully break their emotional ties to traditional behavior. Most caste members fell between the two ideological models of *swami* and reformer.

Because of the penances and excommunications, the suspicion of the city-dwellers' polluting environment, and perhaps the Bombayites' urbane amusement or exasperation at aspects of life in Kanara, a more fundamental alienation was occurring along the lines of an urban-rural split within the *jāti*. The territorial boundaries of the Bhanaps were stretching to what seemed a breaking point.

97. Hattiangdi, *Fifty Years of Bliss*, pp. 3–11.

# 8

# CONCENTRATION AND DISPERSAL:

## *Saraswat Urbanization, 1900–1932*

MIGRATION and urbanization dominated individual and corporate Saraswat life during the first third of the twentieth century. The urban Saraswats grew in numbers and influence to the extent that, by 1932, the caste's strength was based on its members living in cities and large towns. This was in no small part due to their creation and promotion of new voluntary associations open only to Bhanaps, offering a generous assortment of banking, housing, educational, and social services. Although outwardly defined by caste—only Saraswats could be members—these organizations appeared to supplant the venerable Chitrapur *maṭha* in defining the caste itself. For the new bodies ignored the excommunications (*bahishkar*) over sea-voyage and the unification *parishad*, and embraced any and all whose ancestors were Saraswats. It remained an open issue whether or not the *maṭha* and its *swami* could ever be restored to their former premier position at the top and central point in the hierarchy of Bhanap integrative institutions. During this period, participants in the new caste associations began self-consciously to explore and articulate what they took to be suitable ideals of behavior and belief for themselves. Every caste, it appeared, should have its culture.

### *Limitations of Opportunity in North and South Kanara*

Between the years 1896 and 1932, when Bhanaps conducted censuses of their caste, the shape of the community was altered. More persons came to reside in more urban places. The old "home districts" of

North and South Kanara experienced absolute population decline among the caste members. In 1896 North Kanara contained 3,697 Bhanaps; in 1932 there were 3,163. South Kanara's count fell from 4,549 to 4,001.[1] The decline in population did not connote an automatic decline in the position of the Saraswat caste and its members within either district. Many Bhanaps continued to enjoy their standing in each district's elite. What was clearer was that the Saraswats of Kanara could not command influence within their *jāti* as had been the case in the late nineteenth century.

Government service continued to attract Saraswats, but the lower levels of district administration became increasingly the object of intense competition by young men of many castes. This did not mean that opportunity for Saraswats suddenly dried up, for the Saraswat successes in higher education between about 1890 and 1910 qualified many for gazetted appointments of high pay and status in the Madras and Bombay provincial services. Under the Madras government alone, 46 Bhanaps held gazetted posts in 1933.[2] Saraswats continued to be prominent in both Kanara's administrations. While members of other castes were publicly critical of this situation, and British officers were prepared to recognize non-Brahman claims to public office, as late as 1924 it could be reported that almost all offices at one South Kanara taluka town were held by Bhanaps.[3] In North Kanara, seniority and education kept a heavy representation of Saraswats in government offices, but the lower echelons could no longer be seen to belong to any single caste or community. Saraswats themselves thought that opportunities were growing more scarce in North Kanara, further swelling the flow of migration out of the district to distant urban centers, notably Bombay, where employment prospects were thought to be good.[4]

Even those who could find official appointments in either district would usually be presented with the chance of transfer in service to

1. Calculated from *Chitrapura Panachanga*, Appendix 2 and H. Shankar Rau, *Chitrapur Saraswat Directory*, pp. 11–21. The decline was actually slightly greater, since the 1896 census did not include data from Kumta and Sirsi in North Kanara, and Basrur, Hattiangadi, Hemmady, and Puttur in South Kanara.

2. Calculated from Government of Madras, *History of Services of Gazetted and Other Officers in the Civil Department* . . . (Madras, 1933).

3. *K. S.* 6, no. 2 (April 1924) : 17, re Udipi, where all major posts save *munsif* were held by Bhanaps.

4. Interview with Venkat Subrao Nadkarni, Poona, Dec. 7, 1966.

posts outside. Vinayak Mangesh Chickermane (b. July 15, 1878) was one such person. He had studied three years at a Kannada primary school at Gokarn, then went at age nine to live with a cousin at Kumta, Bhavanishankar M. Chickermane, a prominent pleader who fed and housed about a dozen Bhanap students from other places in the district who attended the local Anglo-vernacular school.[5] In 1894 young Vinayak went to Karwar to attend the high school, but as there were no relatives there at the time, he lived in a small boarding hotel. He could not afford college, and because the matriculation examination was no longer also a qualifying test for government service, he took the new School Final examination instead and in 1899 joined the postal department, advancing to the post of signaller in the Karwar telegraph office in 1902. Subsequent promotions carried him outside the district to other towns in the southern Bombay Presidency. In 1917, during the First World War, he was selected for field service at the Government of India's enclave in Aden. After two years there, he returned to India as a postal inspector in Dharwar, Bijapur, and North Kanara districts, retiring in 1933.

The telegraph service was a new field of opportunity in government employment to which Saraswats were quick to respond. But even those who began careers in a rural district like North Kanara were more likely to experience geographical mobility through transfers than their fathers, who had served in the more traditional revenue or forest departments, had been. Mobility was becoming a way of life even for those who did not head off to find their fortunes in Bombay.

Finishing high school could no longer guarantee upward mobility in employment, however. Well-educated government servants in the mofussil could find themselves ensnared in the upper levels of a district bureaucracy with no prospects for promotion, because higher ranks now required university degrees. In 1922 a survey of Saraswats residing at Karwar revealed that of 151 wage-earners, 104 were in government service. All 151 were literate, and 127 were literate in English. Yet their salaries were low in relation to educational attainment—approximately half earned less than Rs. 50 per month. Only 14 of the Karwar sample were university graduates.[6]

5. Interview with Vinayak Mangesh Chickermane, Gokarn, Feb. 12–13, 1971.
6. *K. S.* 4, no. 4 (October 1922) : 119–120.

Saraswat individuals continued to be represented in the local self-governments and public affairs of both Kanaras. Eminent pleaders and retired government officers routinely filled municipal and district board seats. In South Kanara, Nayampalli Subbarao was elected to the Madras Legislative Council. A retired subordinate judge, Sujir Raghunathaya, became the first nonofficial to be president of the Mangalore taluka board, and for a time led the Puttur Landholder's Association, a landlord protective group.[7] In North Kanara, Karwar's slowly developing municipal politics saw continued representation of Bhanaps. The presidency of the municipality was held by Dattatraya Krishna Upponi (1886–1901), Shivaram Subrao Nagarkatte (1909–10), Rao Bahadur R. R. Gangolli (1910–19), Divan Bahadur V. D. Yennemadi (1919–22), Manjunath Vithal Kaikini (1923–25 and 1929–31), and Rao Bahadur Manjunath Gopal Chandavarkar (1934–38).[8] The significance of these achievements for the caste cannot, however, be said, to have been great. Bhanaps of North and South Kanara could draw satisfaction from the attainments of their caste fellows, but such positions reflected the elite standing of members of the caste in both districts, without assuring any positive reinforcement for further benefits. Such positions would be more noticeable in later years when Saraswats no longer seemed automatically the heirs of status and power.

The rural economy in both Kanara districts during the early twentieth century did little to arrest the decline of Saraswat interests in landholding. The rigidity of forest restrictions and the introduction of a revised survey settlement in 1902 in South Kanara, and between 1913 and 1918 in North Kanara, reduced the profitability of landed estates. *Vargdars* found themselves with assessments in excess of their tenants' fixed rents, and resented the new uneconomic rates. Because of the increasing efficiency of the survey, old modes of encroachment could not be brought into play. A Bhanap landholder in the Mangalore taluka reported that on land that earlier had been paying Rs. 30, the assessment was now Rs. 130. He added with some exaggeration: "All the *vargdars* here are

7. *Swadeshabhimani* (Mangalore) of March 6, 1914, in *Madras Native Newspaper Reports* [hereafter *Madras N. N. Rept.*], 1914, p. 348; of April 21, 1911, in *ibid., 1911*, p. 624.

8. Karwar Municipality, *Centenary Souvenir*, pp. 58–62.

ruined. God help us!"[9] In fact, the actual working of the revenue demand did not bankrupt landlords. But it clearly reduced the profitability of landholding and further stimulated Bhanap families still residing in the countryside to seek additional or alternative occupations in the towns and cities. A symbolic, but telling, point was that the *shanbhog* positions which had been the backbone of the Bhanap presence in Kanara were being given up gradually; by the late 1930s there were few Saraswat *shanbhogs* left.

## *Urban Migration*

Urbanization was not a new phenomenon among the Saraswats. Within the Kanaras some members of the *jāti* had resided in the district headquarters as government servants since the mid-nineteenth century. In 1896 the urban share of the caste's enumerated population was high: 3,279 out of 9,736, or about 34 percent.[10] Mangalore, with 1,693, and Karwar, with 680, accounted for 72 percent of the urban dwellers. Four other places outside Kanara—Bombay, 226; Hubli, 201; Dharwar, 146; and Madras, 134—supplied another 21.5 percent; the remainder were scattered in 17 other towns and cities. Thirty-six years later, another caste census gave evidence of a fundamental trend toward urban residence among the Saraswats. Out of an enumerated total of 14,703 persons, 7,769 (over 52 percent) were residing in urban centers in 1932.[11] Bombay and its suburbs, with 2,631 persons, now contained just over a third of all urban Saraswats. Bangalore's Bhanap population had dramatically risen from 14 in 1896 to 707 in 1932; with Hubli (504), Dharwar (626), Poona (229), and Madras (465), this accounted for almost another 30 percent of the urban caste members. The rest were located in 49 other towns and cities scattered between Trichinopoly and Calcutta, Karachi and Rangoon.

The 1932 census also revealed that, with few exceptions, the caste's population in North and South Kanara villages and towns

9. *West Coast Spectator* (Cochin [Gokarn Subbarao, editor]), Dec. 17, 1902, in *Madras N. N. Rept., 1902*, p. 444. Cf. *Swadeshamitram* (Madras), Nov. 30, 1905, in *ibid., 1905*, pp. 440–441; *Sattyadeepika* (Mangalore), Dec. 29, 1905, in *ibid., 1906*, p. 33; *Swadeshabhimani* (Mangalore) of Sept. 24, 1909, in *ibid., 1909*, p. 764; of Sept. 20, 1912, in *ibid., 1912*, p. 425.

10. Calculated from *Chitrapura Panachanga*, Appendix 2.

11. Calculated from H. Shankar Rau, *Directory*, pp. 11–19.

had declined absolutely, by just under 15 percent and 12 percent respectively.[12]

The quantitative results of migration produced several long-term trends within the caste. Urbanization had, in effect, two meanings: on the one hand, increasing concentration; on the other, greater dispersal. The proportion of the caste's population residing in relatively few urban centers, most especially Bombay, was outstripping any previously known aggregation. By 1922 there were more Saraswats living in Bombay than had lived in any one place at any time in the past. On the other hand, urbanization also meant dispersal of single families or of a few individuals in other urban places. If Bombay had a greater concentration than ever before, it was also true that never before had so many Saraswats lived in relative isolation. When Bhanaps had resided in Kanara villages, there too had sometimes been only one or two households present. But numerical comparisons apart, the village residents' lives contrasted with those of isolated urban residents in distant places like Patna or Lahore. The villagers were frequently members of an extended joint-family based upon landholdings, surrounded by familiar language and culture and secure in the status of caste and kin identity as members of the district elite. The Saraswat living in distant Patna or Lahore faced differences in local culture and language, an economic dependence upon employment, and a lack of "natural" linkages to others of the locality.

Because only scattered evidence remains concerning patterns of migration, conclusions with regard to motivation and duration must be made cautiously. It can be noted, though, that the migration was not unilineal, and migrants to the isolated urban centers frequently migrated again, usually as a result of transfers in service. No single-direction flow from village to city can be seen. Rather, it appears that Saraswats migrated to the more distant places after periods of residence in Bombay or Madras. In most instances these moves were in pursuit of employment opportunities or requirements; and with advances in public or private service, further movement was almost always certain.

While during the 1920s a substantial Bhanap population developed in the metropolis of Calcutta, the numbers might be

12. *Ibid.*, p. 20. It should be noted that the Bhanap population of a few Kanara towns grew during the period—e.g., Kundapur, up 32%; Gokarn, up 53.4%. No single cause could be found to explain these exceptions to the overall pattern.

misleading, since relatively few of the persons enumerated on one occasion would be still resident in the city a decade later. The Calcutta Bhanap population grew slowly and unsteadily from about 1907. In 1922 there were 66 persons (38 males, 28 females) in 12 households. Eighteen families were represented, but "more often than not, the earning member is alone or clubs with somebody else while his family remains in Kanara."[13] The instability of the population can be seen in that, during 1922 alone, 14 earning members had come to the city while 6 had left.[14]

The migratory experience touched almost every family and household in the caste during the early twentieth century. Of the 4,243 Saraswats who were 36 or older in 1932, only 811, approximately 19 percent, had remained at the same place of residence for 36 years; more than 80 percent of those surviving from 1896 to 1932 had changed their location at least once.[15] The Bhanaps had been a caste on the move.

## *Bombay*

Bombay city was the most important single target of Saraswat migration in the early twentieth century. Following the plague disruptions, the size of the Bhanap community there grew rapidly. By 1912, 1,252 Saraswats lived in Bombay.[16] A decade later their numbers had risen to 2,167 and by 1932 to 2,631.[17] The actual number of migrations required to build this population is not recorded. Of the 226 persons counted in the 1896 census, only 95 remained in Bombay at the 1912 enumeration, and 61 a decade later. Of the 1,252 Bhanaps tallied in 1912, 688 were still in the city in 1922.[18]

Although not all who migrated to Bombay stayed on as permanent residents, those who were employed in the city were bringing their wives and families to live with them as early as 1896. This increased the likelihood that families would remain in the city, creating a foundation for a permanent community. Table 2 illustrates the

13. *K. S.* 4, no. 3 (July 1922) : 84–85.

14. *K. S.* 4, no. 1 (January 1922) : 19; no. 2 (April 1922) : 51; no. 3 (July 1922) : 82–83; no. 4 (October 1922) : 126.

15. H. Shankar Rau, *Directory*, pp. 37–38, 23. Cf. K. C. Zachariah, *Migrants in Greater Bombay* (Bombay, 1968), pp. 48, 338–339.

16. Kanara Saraswat Association, *Census of Kanara Saraswats in Bombay*, p. 21.

17. *K. S.* 4, no. 4 (October 1922) : 107–108; H. Shankar Rau, *Directory*, p. 22.

18. *K. S.* 4, no. 4 (October 1922) : 108.

TABLE 2

SARASWAT HOUSEHOLDS, POPULATION, AND SEX RATIO IN BOMBAY CITY, 1896–1932

| | *Saraswat Brahmans in Bombay city* | | | | | | *All Saraswat Brahmans* | | |
|---|---|---|---|---|---|---|---|---|---|
| *Year* | *Households* *No.* | *Male* *No.* | *Male* % | *Female* *No.* | *Female* % | *Total* *No.* | *Total* *No.* | *Male* % | *Female* % |
| 1896 | 53 | 146 | 64.6 | 80 | 35.4 | 226 | 9,736 | 51.7 | 48.3 |
| 1912 | 344 | 765 | 61.1 | 487 | 38.9 | 1,252 | n.a. | n.a. | n.a. |
| 1922 | 454 | 1,202 | 55.5 | 965 | 44.5 | 2,167 | n.a. | n.a. | n.a. |
| 1932 | 522 | 1,414 | 53.7 | 1217 | 46.3 | 2,631 | 14,763 | 52.4 | 47.6 |

SOURCES: Chitrapur Sangha, *Chitrapura Panachanga* (Bombay, 1896), Appendix II; Kanara Saraswat Association, *Census of Kanara Saraswats in Bombay City* (Bombay, 1912), p. 21; *Kanara Saraswat* 4, no. 4 (October 1922) : 109–110; H. Shankar Rau, *Chitrapur Saraswat Directory* (Bombay, 1933), pp. 22, 42.

changing sex ratio within the Bhanaps of Bombay and the growth in number of households between 1896 and 1932.

Housing for this growing Bhanap population in Bombay was located largely in rental properties. A few well-to-do families could afford to own homes in the Girgaum neighborhood during the late nineteenth century, but most could not. The construction of blocks of flats on the sites of former coconut gardens drastically altered the urban landscape along the Girgaum Road, but in the wake of this building came a steady advance of persons seeking better dwellings than had been available in the Lohar Chal, Dhobi Talao, and Kalbadevi neighborhoods adjacent to the Fort. High-caste Maharashtrian Hindus predominated in the advance north and west into Girgaum. This area was where Bhanaps had begun to live while students at the old Wilson College; after completing their education, many chose to remain in the same neighborhood. If one Saraswat found satisfactory rental quarters in a flat or *chawl*, and further vacancies became available, others from the caste would be alerted to the opportunity. The result was a series of small residential concentrations.[19] After the closure of the Kanara Club, young men coming to the city for the first time sought accommodation temporarily with relatives or friends from Kanara. Some of the young migrants, however, rented rooms and obtained their meals at an almost legendary boarding establishment, Sakhubai's Khanaval, where a brahman widow offered two vegetarian meals daily for Rs. 8 per month. During the first two decades of the century, the establishment was a popular meeting place of Bhanap office workers.[20] With the creation of more permanent households and the launching of a caste social club, recourse to the eating house declined.

In little more than half a century from the arrival of the first Saraswat settler, Bombay had become the single most populous center of the caste. In his introduction to the report on the 1922

19. The term "*chawl*" had multiple meanings in Bombay. Those built for public employees or factory workers were blocks of buildings containing rows of single-room tenements entered from a common hall or verandah, provided with common privies and washrooms. This working-class imputation eroded in Girgaum, where some *chawls* were two rooms instead of one. Some were quite well lighted, clean and ventilated, others were "grossly insanitary." *Census of India 1921* 9, *Cities of Bombay Presidency*, part 1, Report (Bombay, 1922), part B: viii-ix.

20. See map 3 for locations of Bhanap residence. Interviews with Mr. and Mrs. Anant Gangolli, Vile Parle, March 21, 1971; Rao Bahadur R. N. Nayampalli, Santa Cruz, Feb. 5, 1971.

caste census, Shripad S. Talmaki observed that "one outstanding fact brought prominently to notice . . . [was] that an ever-increasing number of people in the community, consisting mostly of youths, [were] being sent out to Bombay every year." What was more, "almost every family in the community" was represented.[21] The circumstances of this concentration were notable in that a substantial majority of the Bhanap Bombay population resided within an approximately two-square-mile area where the Girgaum, Gamdevi, and Tardeo neighborhoods met, centering near the Grant Road station of the Bombay, Baroda, and Central India Railway.[22] At no time in the previous history of the caste had so many Bhanaps lived in one place. Map 3 illustrates this area of Bombay city circa 1920, displaying residential locations of two or more Saraswat households.

### *Middle-Class Occupational Orientations*

The occupational preference of the majority of the Saraswats in Bombay favored the urban incarnation of what had been their fathers' specialty in Kanara—clerical employment in "service." Whether in government offices or private firms, the predominance of this preference remained marked throughout the first three decades of the twentieth century, as shown in Table. 3. Clerical vacancies were plentiful in Bombay until the closing year of the First World War, when a contraction of opportunities occurred. Until that time young Bhanaps came to Bombay with every assurance of finding a suitable job, frequently exploiting a connection of family or friendship in the process.[23] The promise of easily obtained employment led some young Saraswats in the Kanaras to curtail their education and board the first available steamer to Bombay. "In fact, the chances of securing positions in trading and banking concerns were so many and so tempting that several youths did not even care to receive higher education, though it

21. *K. S.* 4, no. 4 (October 1922) 112.

22. Based on analysis of residential data and census tracts in Kanara Saraswat Association, *Census of Kanara Saraswats in Bombay*, p. 3; Kanara Saraswat Association, *Sixth Annual Report* (Bombay, 1917), p. 18; Kanara Saraswat Association, *Triennial Directory* (Bombay, 1920), pp. 1–2.

23. *K. S.* 6, no. 1 (January 1924) :23; interviews with R. A. Lajmi, Bombay, March 18, 1971; G. S. Hattiangdi, April 10, 1966; R. N. Nayampalli, Feb. 5, 1971; P. G. Sirur, Jan. 2, 1971; Anant Gangolli, Vile Parle, March 21, 1971.

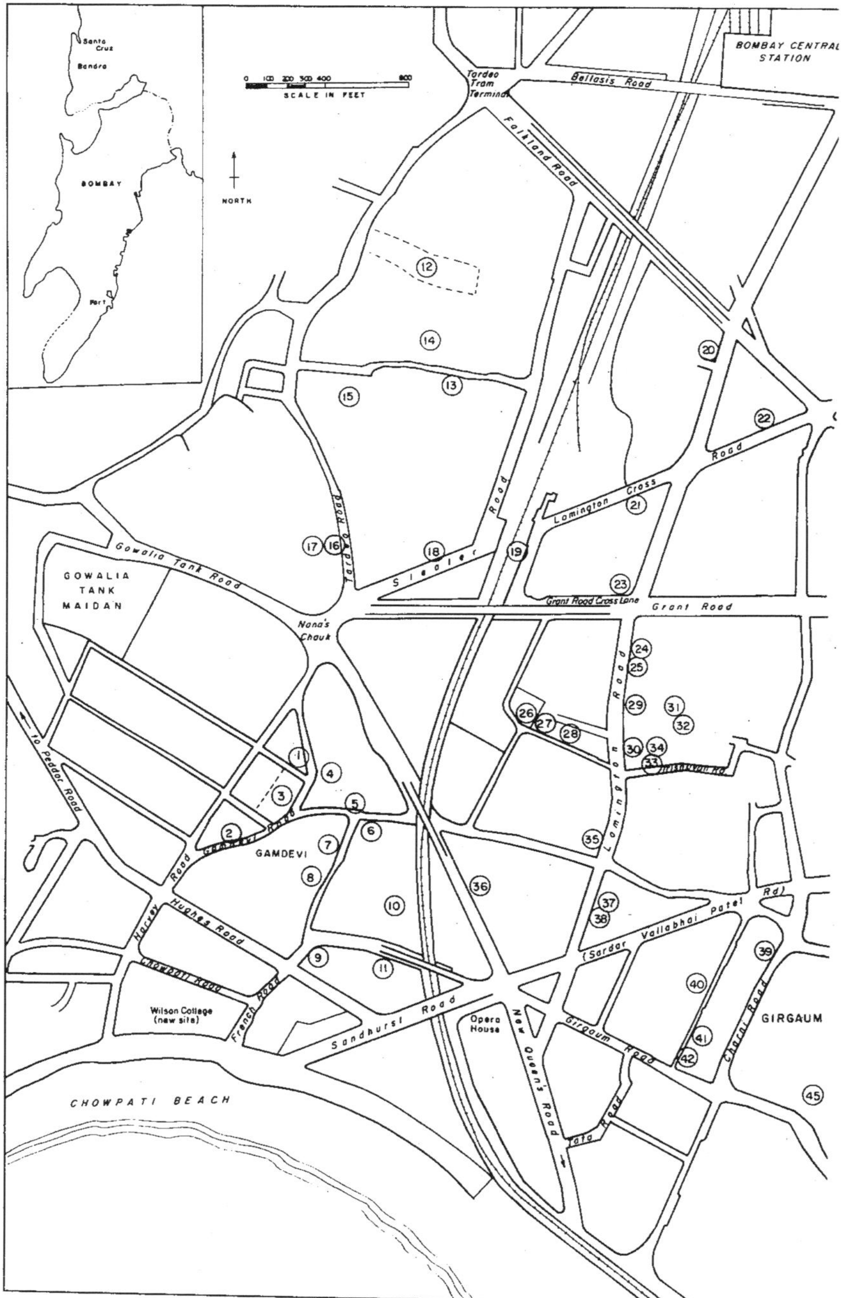


Map 3. Bombay city, c. 1920, showing the primary residential sites of Saraswats between 1912 and 1922, based on caste censuses and directories.

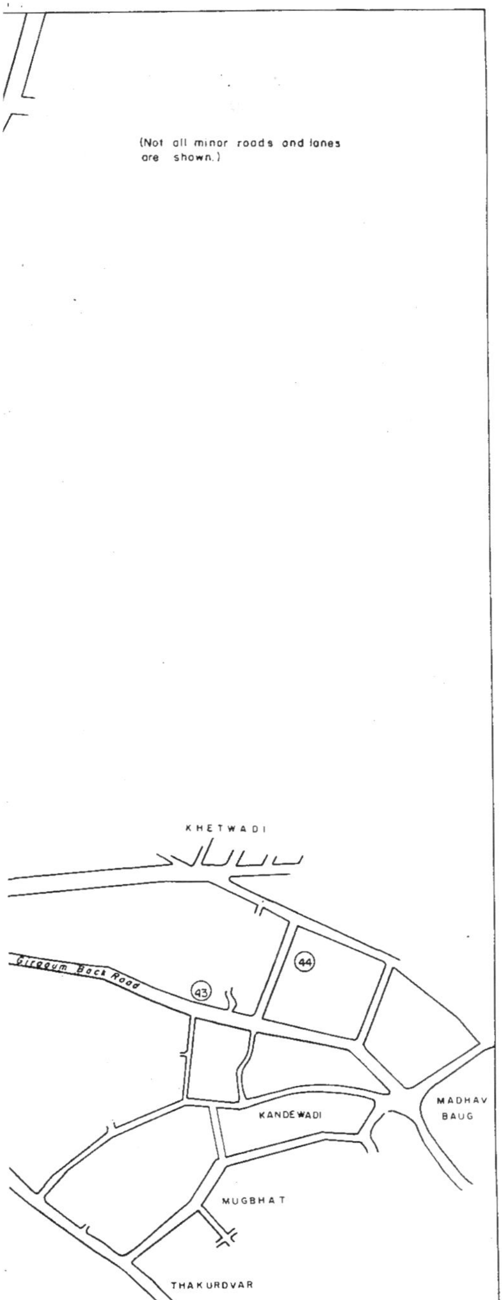
(Not all minor roads and lanes are shown.)
KHETWADI
Girgaum Back Road
44
43
MADHAV BAUG
KANDEWADI
MUGBHAT
THAKURDVAR

### Key to Map 3

1. Ramji Bhagvan Bldg. (now Kapoli Nivas)
2. Mantri Bldgs.
3. Saraswat Co-operative Society Plot
4. Dadoba Jaganath Religious Trust Bldg.
5. Goregaonkar Chandrabhagabai Bldg.
6. Goregaonkar Wadi
7. Billimoria Bldg. (now J. K. Bldg.)
8. Victoria Mill Chawl
9. Parmanand ("Boti") Chawl
10. Haji Cassum's Wadi
11. Raman Nivas
12. Site of Talmakiwadi Co-op Society
13. Memon Bldg.
14. Tukaram Javji Bldg. (now Dattatreya)
15. Bhagirathibai Bldgs.
16. Irani Bldgs.
17. Lakduwala Chawls
18. Bhalchandra's Bldg.
19. Grant Road Station (B. B. & C. I. Ry.)
20. Motivala Bldg.
21. Parvati Mansions
22. Dongre Bldg.
23. Pannalal Terrace
24. Brelvi Bldg.
25. Aabid House (1912)
26. Anandashram Co-op Colony Plot
27. Hanuman Bldg.
28. Old Hanuman Bldg.
29. Topivala's Lakshmi Bldg. (Now Rajesh)
30. Hanuman Terrace
31. Dr. Gidh's House
32. Sharada Bldg. (Topivala)
33. Shethe Bldgs.
34. Ganpat Moroba's Tara Temple Lane
35. Tribhuwan Terraces
36. Navalkar Bldgs.
37. Prabhakar's Chawl—Sakhubai's Khanawala
38. Welinkar Bungalow
39. Prarthana Samaj
40. Ravte Bldgs.
41. Soman Bldgs.
42. Contractor's Bldgs.
43. Bhaskar Shivaram's Chawl
44. Wilson High School (Old College Site)
45. Morarji's Chawl

TABLE 3

OCCUPATIONS OF SARASWAT MALE EARNING MEMBERS IN BOMBAY AND SUBURBS, 1912–1932

| *Category* | *1912 No.* | *1912 %* | *1922 No.* | *1922 %* | *1932 No.* | *1932 %* |
|---|---|---|---|---|---|---|
| Service | | | | | | |
| Government and Railways | 109 | 22.5 | 159 | 21.0 | 186 | 23.9 |
| Mercantile (including Professional firms) | 330 | 68.0 | 527 | 69.8 | 467 | 60.1 |
| Miscellaneous (including Domestic) | 9 | 1.8 | 2 | 0.3 | 14 | 1.8 |
| Service Subtotal | 448 | 92.4 | 688 | 91.1 | 667 | 85.8 |
| Professions | | | | | | |
| Law | 5 | 1.0 | 3 | 0.4 | 8 | 1.0 |
| Medicine | 5 | 1.0 | 9 | 1.2 | 15 | 1.9 |
| Journalist, Artist | 4 | 0.8 | 6 | 0.8 | 8 | 1.0 |
| Engineer | 0 | — | 0 | — | 1 | 0.1 |
| Education (in private schools)* | 2 | 0.4 | 3 | 0.4 | 8 | 1.0 |
| Religious | 3 | 0.6 | 4 | 0.5 | 11 | 1.4 |
| Professions Subtotal | 19 | 3.9 | 25. | 3.3 | 51 | 6.5 |
| Business, Manufacturing, Management | 18 | 3.7 | 42 | 5.6 | 51 | 6.5 |
| Land and Investments | 0 | — | 0 | — | 8 | 1.0 |
| Total for all Occupations** | 485 | 100.0 | 755 | 100.0 | 777 | 100.0 |

SOURCES: Kanara Saraswat Association, *Census of Kanara Saraswat in Bombay City* (Bombay, 1912), p. 24; *Kanara Saraswat* 4, no. 4 (October 1922): 108–109; H. Shankar Rau, *Chitrapur Saraswat Directory* (Bombay, 1933), pp. 47–48.

NOTES: *Persons employed as teachers in government and municipal schools were enumerated under "Service-Government and Railways.

**Female earning members, mostly recipients of pensions or landed property income, numbered 6 in 1912, 11 in 1922, and 18 in 1932.

was within their reach, in order that they might take the shortest cut to fortune."[24]

The "fortunes" thus realized were by no means princely; they grew still less so during the general inflation of the war years. Table 4 provides a profile of monthly income reported by Saraswats in Bombay city. The general rise in income was offset by inflation and the fact that the postwar recession which constricted the commercial life of Bombay dried up fresh vacancies in service occupations. A new word was imprinted in the Saraswat lexicon: "retrenchment." Although accurate figures on retrenchments are unavailable, it is thought that as many as 100 Bhanaps had been laid off by 1922. Some migrated elsewhere in search of jobs or returned to their family homes in North or South Kanara.[25] Those who stayed on in the city eked out meager livings in low-paying positions, contributing to an increase in the number and proportion

TABLE 4

MONTHLY INCOME REPORTED BY SARASWAT BRAHMANS IN BOMBAY CITY, 1912–1932*

| *Income range per month* | 1912 *No.* | 1912 % | 1922 *No.* | 1922 % | 1932 *No.* | 1932 % |
|---|---|---|---|---|---|---|
| Up to Rs. 30 | 112 | 22.8 | 16 | 2.0 | 40 | 5.0 |
| Rs. 31 to 50 | 174 | 35.4 | 28 | 3.6 | 92 | 11.6 |
| Rs. 51 to 100 | 143 | 29.1 | 279 | 36.4 | 273 | 34.3 |
| Rs. 101 to 200 | 43 | 8.7 | 319 | 41.6 | 254 | 31.9 |
| Rs. 201 to 500 } | | | | | 113 | 14.2 } |
| Rs. 501 to 1000 } | 19 | 3.8 | 124 | 16.1 | 18 | 2.3 } 17 |
| Rs. 1001 and up } | | | | | 5 | 0.6 } |
| Total for all income ranges* | 491 | 100.0 | 766 | 100.0 | 795 | 100.0 |

SOURCES: Kanara Saraswat Association, *Census of Kanara Saraswats in Bombay City* (Bombay, 1912), p. 24; *Kanara Saraswat* 4, no. 4 (October 1922): 108–109; H. Shankar Rau, *Chitrapur Saraswat Directory* (Bombay, 1933), pp. 53–54.

NOTE: *Incomes were reported for all income receivers without differentiation as to sex. These figures include women earning members, while figures in Table 3 refer only to men.

24. S. R. Dongerkery, "Unemployment Among Us," *K. S.* 10, no. 1 (July 1926): 10–11.

25. *K. S.* 6, no. 1 (January 1924): 23. Cf. Bombay Labour Office, *Report on an Enquiry Into Middle-Class Unemployment in the Bombay Presidency* (Bombay, 1927).

of Bhanap earners receiving under Rs. 51 per month.[26] These shifts in economic opportunity and well-being were by no means limited uniquely to the experience of the Saraswats. But to the extent that the members of the caste were increasingly dependent upon urban "service" employment, such circumstances would be reflected in the evolution of corporate caste activities in the city.[27]

Many Bombay Bhanaps were caught in an economic dilemma characteristic of many members of the urban middle class in India. Dependent almost entirely upon relatively stable wage earnings, they nonetheless faced a general rise in the cost of necessities at a time when they were also developing rising expectations with regard to their material comfort and well-being. It was the latter element which usually caused Saraswat expenditures to outpace earnings, leading ultimately to indebtedness and in some cases real poverty.[28] Indebtedness, while not epidemic, was widespread enough to cause concern. This was particularly true when young Bhanap householders would borrow a modest amount from one of the Pathan street-corner moneylenders, who charged "four *annas* interest," meaning four *annas* per rupee per month—about 300 percent per annum.[29] Concern among the better-established Saraswats of the city over the economic situation of their compatriots led to creation of several cooperative caste institutions which grew to be vital new integrative mechanisms.

### *Voluntary Associations*

Unlike other sites of new Saraswat residence, Bombay did not soon possess a caste temple or other religious shrine. A local *sabha* of Shri Chitrapur *Maṭha* was only briefly active in the 1890s before lapsing for more than a decade. This absence of institutional replication, as explained in Chapters 6 and 7, had two basic causes. Many urban Bhanaps had few financial resources to dedicate to local

26. See Table 4. The Bombay Labour Office placed Rs. 50 as the lowest scale of pay considered "middle class," but coupled this to education through Fourth standard in English. *Ibid.*, p. 2.

27. Cf. Maureen L. P. Patterson, "Changing Patterns of Occupations Among Chitpavan Brahmans," *Indian Economic and Social History Review* 7 (September 1970):375–396; an average derived from 34 Chitpavan family histories showed a rather lower percentage of "service," 55.5%.

28. Interview with A. R. Savoor, Bombay, March 22, 1971; H. Shankar Rau, "Family Budgets," in *Miscellany*, pp. 15–31; Bombay Labour Office, *Report on an Enquiry Into Middle-Class Family Budgets in Bombay City* (Bombay, 1928).

29. H. Shankar Rau, *Miscellany*, p. 28.

shrines after remitting earnings to families still in the Kanaras. Also, the rise of antipathy between rural orthodox supporters of Pandurangashram Swami and the urban "social reformers" had scarred relations between Bombay and the *maṭha*. Although Shamrao Vithal and Kundapur Anandarao had envisioned the Chitrapur Sangha as a link to the *maṭha*, the plague dislocations brought the organization to an early demise. It was not replaced for over a decade. Yet the idea of a caste-based organization seemed to Shamrao Vithal and others to possess merit. Further, such voluntary associations were being organized successfully by other Hindu neighbors of the Bhanaps in Bombay. The technique was available, and the Saraswats were not long in adopting it.

Voluntary associations in India with membership restricted to a single caste have been examined widely as adaptive phenomena by which castes play new roles in a changing society and economy.[30] The idea of special interest groups recruiting exclusively from one caste and then propelling their members toward "modernity" has been explored by social scientists for over a decade. While a full analysis of associational pursuits among the Saraswats must be reserved for a later study, certain general and specific aspects of the phenomenon should be explored. Not all Saraswat endeavors to first launch and then pilot various voluntary organizations were fully successful, but most did serve the instrumentalities for which they had been conceived with overall efficiency, conferring collective benefits upon their members.

Thus they qualify as successful measures of a caste adapting to urban conditions. But because the new voluntary associations ignored divisions between Saraswats who were in or out of favor with the *maṭha*, they were in effect defining the caste rather than being defined by it. In so doing they offered means for reintegration of the Saraswat community.

### *The Beginnings of Cooperative Action: Credit*

The Indian Cooperative Credit Societies Act of 1904 was an official effort to enable the introduction of cooperative credit

30. Cf. L. I. and S. H. Rudolph, "The Political Role of India's Caste Associations," *Pacific Affairs* 28 (1955):235–253; R. S. Khare, *The Changing Brahmans: Associations and Elites Among the Kanya-Kubjas of North India* (Chicago, 1970); Vilas A. Sangave, "Changing Pattern of Caste Organisation in Kolhapur," *Sociological Bulletin* 11 (1962); Rajini Kothari and Rushikesh Maru, "Caste and Secularism in India," *Journal of Asian Studies* 25 (1965):33–50.

societies among the peasants of India. Although predominantly agrarian in character, the act also foresaw creation of urban credit societies.[31] A provision of the legislation permitted such bodies to be organized by members of a single caste or community. Since a few Saraswats, including Raghavendra L. Udyavar, were employed in the offices of the Registrar of Cooperative Societies, and several others, most notably Shripad Subrao Talmaki, were interested in popularizing the principles of cooperation, it was no cause for surprise when members of the caste circulated a proposal to launch a cooperative credit society of and for Bhanaps.[32] Talmaki, joined by Kundapur Anandarao and Sumitra A. Hattiangadi, saw such a society as a means "to improving the moral and material well-being of the community and ameliorating its economical condition." The society was registered in December 1906 with 88 members. It was named the Shamrao Vithal Cooperative Credit Society, honoring the pioneer Saraswat settler in Bombay, who had died the previous year. In restricting participation to "members of the community of Shamrao Vithal," the organizers avoided the question of whether or not excommunicant Bhanaps were any more or less members of the caste. Membership was obtained through purchase of shares, entitling a voice in management and access to loans.[33] The organizers hoped that the new association would promote thrift within the community while providing a source of low-interest loans, freeing members from the dubious services of moneylenders.

In Bombay, official attitudes on caste credit societies were pragmatic. The Shamrao Vithal Society seemed to work well. One British official observed that caste was a good basis for organizations of this sort in Bombay city, "where it is difficult to discover any other

31. Cf. I. J. Catanach, *Rural Credit in Western India* (Berkeley, 1970); E. M. Hough, *The Cooperative Movement in India* (London, 1932). The full history of the development of cooperative institutions among the Saraswats will be reserved to a later monograph.

32. Registrar of Cooperative Societies, Bombay, *Report on the Working of the Cooperative Credit Society Act, . . . 1905–06*, p. 9; G. P. Murdeshwar, "Cooperation Among the Saraswats," *K. S.* 28 (April 1944) : 76–77.

33. Registrar of Cooperative Societies, Bombay, *Report, 1906–07*, pp. 4, 17; *First Annual Report of the Shamrao Vithal Cooperative Credit Society, 1906–07*, p. 2; *Twenty-fifth Annual Report of the Shamrao Vithal Cooperative Bank, Ltd.* [hereafter S. V. C. Bank] for the year ended March 31, 1931, pp. 2–3. Initial share capital was authorized at Rs. 100,000 divided into 4,000 shares of Rs. 25 each, payable in Rs. 2 installments.

nexus which ensures an equal degree of mutual acquaintance among the members."[34] In fact, the Saraswats' society proved to be a link beyond the caste members residing within the city. Membership steadily increased from 119 in 1907 to 667 in 1911, 1080 in 1916, 1656 in 1921, and 2012 in 1931. These figures included Bhanaps at virtually every place where the caste was represented throughout the Bombay Presidency.[35]

The reconstitution of the body as a cooperative bank in 1909 was one stimulus to further growth. Branches were opened at Karwar, Kumta, and Honavar in 1908, at Hubli in 1909, Sirsi in 1911, Dharwar in 1912, and Mangalore in 1915. Rural Saraswats now became directly involved in the bank's affairs. They also were enabled to utilize banking services otherwise unavailable in the mofussil. Although loans could be made only to members, and membership was restricted to the Saraswat *jāti*, interest-bearing deposits from nonmembers were welcomed. Deposits, which in the first year totaled Rs. 370, had reached Rs. 34,231 by 1911, Rs. 609,857 in 1921, and Rs. 1,189,249 by 1931.[36] The funds available for loans similarly increased. During 1919–20, Rs. 945,924 were loaned out to individuals as well as Rs. 22,835 to other cooperative societies.[37]

Categories of loans reflected the priorities of the membership. Short-term amounts under Rs. 21 and long-term loans limited to Rs. 200 for one year were initially offered. One exception was that a larger loan could be arranged to redeem a member's previous debts to usurers. Later the long-term loan could be as much as Rs. 2000 for up to four years. Cash credits were introduced in 1912 to facilitate commercial ventures. As a special benefit for rural members, loans for redemption of mortgaged properties were offered. Basic interest rates varied until 1921, depending upon the purpose for which the money was borrowed. Those loans given on personal security were at a basic rate of 9-3/8 percent, while those

34. R. W. Ewbank in *Report on the Working of Cooperative Societies, Bombay*, 1918–19 (Bombay, 1919), p. 11.

35. Based on S. V. C. Bank, *Annual Report* for years 1907–1931.

36. S. V. C. Bank, *Twenty-fifth Annual Report*, pp. 5–6. The activities of the branches were varied. The Karwar Branch had to pay high interest on deposits, while generating little interest on loans, but it proved a valuable source of deposits which were then used for loans for urban borrowers in Bombay. *K. S.* 4, no. 4 (October 1922) : 137.

37. *Report on the Working of Cooperative Societies*, 1919–20, p. 24.

which were secured by deposits or which were for educational, trade, or industrial purposes paid reduced interest of 7-13/16 per-cent. Thus the bank endeavored to encourage productive investments through which Saraswats might enter new fields of endeavor, escaping the numbing security of "service" occupations.[38]

Profits from the operation of the bank were dedicated to various charitable and corporate improvement activities within the caste. This had the effect of encouraging further organizations. Among institutions which received aid were the Shamraō Vithal Education Fund (after 1923 renamed the Saraswat Educational and Provident Cooperative Society); the Saraswat Poor Students' Fund, Mangalore; the Udipi Poor Students' Fund; the Kanara Saraswat Association's Medical Relief Fund and Building Fund; the Saraswat Educational Society's Fund for Ganapathi High School, Mangalore; the Kanara Saraswat Mahila Samaj; and at least fifteen others.

Most importantly, the cooperative bank served as a seedbed for a whole series of new special-purpose cooperative societies among Saraswats. The urban experience was applied in the mofussil. A producer's cooperative was formed in 1913 by the owners of the salt pans at Sanikatta near Kumta, the last place of salt manufacture in North Kanara, with the objective of protecting the owners against middlemen. Cooperative principles suffered somewhat, since the salt-pan owners did not permit actual workers to join, but rather pursued a course more akin to a syndicate or trust. Ultimately the group was reorganized as a marketing society. The techniques and organizing skills employed in this body of rural Saraswats were transferred, through personal caste ties of communication, from the metropolis and the office of the Registrar of Cooperative Societies. In both Kanaras, Bhanaps played major roles in both caste and public cooperative credit societies.[39] Their urban brethren were already experimenting with other cooperative innovations which might again serve the interests of the caste.

## *Cooperative Housing*

Saraswats created the first cooperative urban housing society in all of Asia. Shripad S. Talmaki had remained active in the Bombay co-

38. S. V. C. Bank, *Twenty-fifth Annual Report*, pp. 7–9.

39. *Report on the Working of Cooperative Societies*, 1916–17, p. 17; *ibid.*, 1920–21, p. 23; *ibid.*, 1930–31, p. 59.

operative movement. When he became aware of an opportunity for expanding cooperation in a new direction, he brought the cosmopolitan backers of the cooperative movement together with his caste fellows. He learned in 1914 that Sir Prabhashankar Pattani, another cooperation enthusiast, was prepared to financially back a pilot project in housing the following year. Talmaki thereupon pushed the Bombay Bhanaps to organize the Saraswat Cooperative Housing Society, Ltd. Its plan was to erect buildings on a plot of ground acquired from the Bombay City Improvement Trust in Gamdevi. Share capital was raised from prospective members, but it was Sir Prabhashankar's loan and a further loan from the Shamrao Vithal credit society that led to the project's realization.[40]

Housing in Bombay had been a perennial problem for most of its inhabitants. Nowhere was this more pronounced than among the Indian clerical middle classes, whose "white-collar" work brought salaries between Rs. 50 and Rs. 750 per month, though most earned between Rs. 75 and Rs. 225 monthly.[41] Although rising rents troubled family budgets, there was also an aggravated shortage in the city of rental accommodations which were judged by Saraswats and other middle-class Hindus to be "decent." Clean and well-maintained *chawls* and flats were by no means easily found. The Bombay Rent Act which came into effect in 1916 froze rents, but landlords then demanded extra cesses or *pagdi* and "key deposits."[42] The cooperative approach to housing offered escape from each of these difficulties which plagued middle-class householders.

The Gamdevi cooperative housing project was a tenant co-partnership. Five buildings were built, each with six tenements of three rooms plus kitchen, bath, and veranda. Membership was obtained by initial payment of Rs. 4000, of which at least one-third had to be given as down payment. Rentals for the flats were set

40. *Ibid*, 1914–15, p. 16; *ibid.*, 1915–16, pp. 18–19; Saraswat Cooperative Housing Society, Ltd., *Prospectus* (Bombay, 1915).

41. "Standard of Living of Indian Middle Classes in Bombay City," *Labour Gazette* (Bombay) 4 (December 1924) : 395: "Caste largely determines occupation and thereby income, and the number of individuals who in any generation rise to an income markedly above the normal are few. Hence it may be said that in India class strata are determined by caste, modified by income." This ignores another element—that the character of the job and its conditions was regularly a consideration.

42. *Report of the Rent Enquiry Committee* (Bombay, 1939) 1 : 36–37; *Labour Gazette* (Bombay) 4 (October 1924) : 159–168.

between Rs. 30 and Rs. 38 per month.[43] The advantages of new, clean, and spacious accommodations were enhanced by the favorable rents. A comparison of rentals in the surrounding D Ward of Bombay showed that during 1914–15, middle-class tenements in older buildings with "two or more" rooms rented on the average for Rs. 28/9/9 per month; by 1923–24 that average had risen to Rs. 35/15/9. in 1923–24 rentals of similar quarters in new buildings averaged Rs. 88/1/8.[44]

Not all Bhanaps could afford a down payment of Rs. 1334, and those who delayed joining in the hope of later forming another building society were frustrated by the rising costs of construction after the war. The success of the Gamdevi project nonetheless stimulated emulation. Several other caste societies were formed and built buildings, but they suffered the financial disadvantages of construction during a period of high capital costs. In 1924 some Saraswats who could not afford to invest in a building society tried a less expensive path to cooperation through formation of a "house-renting" society. They sought a preexisting *chawl* at a favourable guaranteed rent which they would then let out to members at cost, eliminating "most of the disadvantages and inconveniences of individuals renting from a landlord" and deriving "social amenities of a corporate life."[45] Other Saraswats took up the cooperative model. Fresh building societies were floated at the Bombay suburb of Santa Cruz and in Poona, Dharwar, and Bangalore. The scarcity of housing in Bombay, however, remained a constant preoccupation of the Indian middle class, including the Saraswats. Bhanap humor kept alive the story of a gentleman who during the monsoon stood on Apollo Bundar and saw another man struggling in the sea, obviously on the point of drowning. Instead of plunging in to the rescue, he took a taxi to the real estate office and, breathlessly dashing in, said, "I want to take Mr. Ramarao's flat. I know it is vacant as I have just seen him drown." "Very sorry," said the clerk, "you are too late to get the flat. The gentleman who pushed Mr. Ramarao in got here first."

The cooperative housing society at Gamdevi was the product of a pervasive economic need among Saraswats, coupled with skills

43. Hough, *Cooperative Movement*, pp. 193–194.

44. *Labour Gazette* (Bombay) 4 (October 1924) : 164–167.

45. *K. S.* 8, no. 4 (November 1924) : 17. Cf. comments of G. S. Ghurye, *Caste, Class and Occupation*, rev. ed. (Bombay, 1961), pp. 205–206.

and energies of several individual caste members who possessed special knowledge of and access to the cooperative movement. During the 1930s two more cooperative housing colonies were built by Bhanaps in the same Grant Road neighborhood. This broadened the base of participation within the caste. But even as the first tenants were moving into the Gamdevi buildings in 1916, the housing society was indirectly supporting a further integration of all Bhanaps in the city. Included in the society's buildings was a small hall which contained the quarters of the Shamrao Vithal Credit Society and another caste organization, the Kanara Saraswat Association. Thus institutions and residences of the caste focused upon Gamdevi and reinforced the already existing concentration of population in the Grant Road Station vicinity. Residential proximity did not guarantee that all Bhanaps developed close social ties. Kinship and friendships from home operated even to keep alive the old Badagi-Tenki distinctions among some of the migrants.[46] To overcome this fact and to enhance the ability of all Bhanaps to adjust and adapt to Bombay, a new caste association was developed.

### *The Kanara Saraswat Association*

When the Chitrapur Sangha did not revive, some of the Bombay Bhanaps organized informal social circles that would gather evenings and holidays for gossip and card playing. One of these groups took formal shape in 1911 as "The Friends' Social Club." Led by Balvalli Dattaram, Raghuvir Mugve, and Sheshgiri N. Kalbag, the club drew together a number of Bhanap newcomers whose families were still back in the Kanaras. Shripad S. Talmaki, the promoter of the Shamrao Vithal Cooperative Credit Society, had tried to organize a Saraswat Association about two years earlier. His club did not attract much support, and in 1911 he proposed a merger of the two groups. He suggested that the Friends' Social Club could be more than just a cards-and-gossip affair, doing service for the improvement of the Bhanap community. The merger of the two clubs was consummated in November 1911, creating the Kanara Saraswat Association.[47] S. N. Kalbag recalled

46. Interviews with R. N. Nayampalli, Feb. 8, 1971; R. A. Lajmi, March 18, 1971.

47. *K. S.* 25, no. 12 (December 1941) :378; *K. S.* 44 (November 1960) :289–291; Kanara Saraswat Association [hereafter K. S. A.], *First Annual Report* (1912), pp. 1–2.

that one immediate object was "bridging with silken ties of friendship the widening schism in the community consequent upon the then-prevalent *jāti bahishkar*" (excommunication arising from the *swami*'s dicta on sea-voyage and caste-unifications).[48] The choice of name was deliberate; no reference would be made to the Chitrapur *maṭha* or its *swami*. The association would be open to all members of the Saraswat caste, but membership would be defined not by religious institutional sanctions but by the pragmatic tests of kinship and consent.

The Kanara Saraswat Association (hereafter K. S. A.) was initially recruited predominantly among younger men of the community. Its managing committee attempted to attract support from older, more well-established gentlemen. The goal was:

> to secure the patronage of the more thoughtful and experienced members of the community necessary for the continued existence of the Association, the stability of which can only be ensured not simply by energy and enthusiasm of its members but as much by the generous response of those more favorably situated in life.[49]

Yet the majority of the 70 members at the end of the first year were young, and they were not terribly well placed in life. Only 9 were university graduates, and only 17 drew salaries over Rs. 100 per month. A monthly subscription of 8 *annas* (one-half rupee) was more than a mere trifle in most members' budgets.

In its early years the association's activities were almost exclusively confined to social gatherings and maintenance of a few magazine and newspaper subscriptions for a reading room. In 1912, at the urging of Talmaki, the K. S. A. conducted a census of the Saraswats in Bombay. This not only established the size of the community but revealed the costs and conditions of its housing and income. Talmaki used this data in winning official approval for the cooperative housing society in 1914.[50]

The census also portrayed a community in which 92% of its

48. *K. S.* 22, no. 12 (December 1938) : 2. The Badagi-Tenki hostilities complicated life in Bombay when arrangements for marriages had to be made. A Tenki father with a marriageable daughter had found no suitable matches. A friend suggested a boy from Honavar (i.e., a Badagi) who was working in Bombay. The father was irate and said he'd see her dead before married to a Badagi. His reason was that he thought Badagi families worked their women too hard and would be too old-fashioned in treatment of a new daughter-in-law. Interview with R. N. Nayampalli, Feb. 5 1971.

49. K. S. A., *First Annual Report*, p. 1.

50. K. S. A., *Third Annual Report* (1914), p. 3 remarks of B. W. Kissen.

wageearners were dependent upon "service." In 1913 the K. S. A. attempted to publicize the need for young Bhanaps to look to new occupations:

> Under present circumstances prevailing in our districts, it is mostly the poorer section of the community that sends out its youngsters to seek employment at a comparatively tender age, and as most of them come to Bombay in anticipation of a vast field here, we may expect the number of youngsters standing in need of pecuniary help to increase each year.[51]

Proposals were made for a philanthropic bureau to help poor new migrants: night classes in English composition and stenography, and a program of apprenticeships with tailors, cabinet-makers, and the like to broaden the economic options of the community. Apart from a small fund collected for charitable work, these plans bore no fruit. It seemed that the newcomers wanted the respectable if marginal rewards of service.

Young men of the caste were also encouraged to form a Students' Literary Society, which provided programs of lectures and debates. These were thought a useful help to inexperienced youth, who might thereby cultivate the self-confidence and verbal acuteness necessary for advancing in employment. Often the chosen topics, which were intended to be didactic, proved rather to be entertaining. Early topics included "Advantages and Disadvantages of Poverty," "The *Ramayana* as Epic and Allegory," "Sin Pays Its Own Penalty," and "Is Novel Reading Beneficial?" Lectures were not crowded, but social gatherings were. Over 700 Bhanaps turned out for a reception in honor of Sir Narayan Chandavarkar on the eve of his appointment as Dewan of Indore. It was on this occasion that the excommunicated reformer reaffirmed his warm feelings for his caste and their common heritage. The sentiment was returned with interest, for Chandavarkar was a recognized national figure from amongst their tiny caste. He spoke of identifying with them; they preferred being identified with him. Sir Narayan later accepted an honorary membership in the K. S. A., and his wife actively led the creation in 1917, of a Ladies Section, which later became the Saraswat Mahila Samaj.

The K. S. A. membership did not grow much after initial enthusiasms were expended. Its rented meeting rooms were thought to be neither convenient nor attractive. But with the opening of the

51. K. S. A., *Second Annual Report* (1913), pp. 8–9.

cooperative housing society at Gamdevi and the inclusion of a hall for K. S. A. use there, the organization began to attract members, and active participation in association activities increased.[52]

Talmaki's idea of a group which served the entire caste came closer to reality when a nonresident category of membership was created in 1917. The nonresident members could organize branches, and correspondents were sought wherever Bhanaps resided. The objective was "to provide means for bringing scattered members of the community into mutual touch so that the Association as *central unifying institution* may exert a unifying influence and help in bringing about communal solidarity."[53] Interest in the K. S. A. was further spurred by announcement of the publication of a caste magazine, *The Saraswat Quarterly*. It appeared between 1919 and 1921 without the regularity implicit in its title. The heavy costs of publication nearly bankrupted the K. S. A., but timely assistance from several individual Bhanaps permitted a resurrection in 1922. The journal was now renamed *Kanara Saraswat*. It was a quarterly until 1929; thereafter it was issued as a monthly.[54] The magazine was intended as a link between the increasingly dispersed Bhanaps for the transmission of caste news, births, deaths, and marriages, and the ventilation of current issues. The first editor, R. S. Padbidri, was an active and enthusiastic member of the Indian National Congress, but as the magazine was for all *jāti* brethren, it was thought best to keep politics from its pages.[55]

Because the articles and opinions of the magazine often favored some social reform, orthodox persons came to view the journal with suspicion. When challenged about their "neutrality," the editors replied; "A communal journal is the conscience of the community. It should not merely chronicle, it should forestall, educate, discriminate, organize, unite, and lead the community along the path of progress."[56] The editors and their critics really had

52. Based on K. S. A. *Annual Report* for years 1913–1917.

53. K. S. A., *Sixth Annual Report* (1917), p. 2.

54. The fact that several K. S. A. members, including Ganesh P. Murdeshwar, were promoting the All-India Saraswat Sabha at this time appears to have led some nonresident K. S. A. members to transfer to the other body and its quarterly. Ultimately the A. I. S. S. and its journal faded away, but when the K. S. A. magazine reappeared 1922, its new title, *Kanara Saraswat*, was chosen to clearly distinguish it from the other. *K. S.* 53 (October 1969) :298–299.

55. *Saraswat Quarterly* 1, no. 1 (April 1919) :1.

56. *K. S.* 6, no. 2 (April 1924) :7.

little need for worry. Many Bhanaps would share the sentiment expressed by one who said that when his *Kanara Saraswat* arrived, "I begin to read it like a Persian book, from the wrong end."[57] That is, he began with the obituaries, birth and wedding announcements, and notices of promotions and examination results, which were of primary interest to the dispersed caste.

When the Bhanap reader did turn to the front of his journal, he was presented with a wide array of articles on the caste's pressing needs. Articles examined topics such as the need for reductions in living expenses, adjustments in length and cost of rituals, educational innovations, and reports on new professions which young Saraswats might pursue. Textiles, chemistry, the merchant marine, and various *swadeshi* industries were carefully reviewed. "Service" was vigorously condemned. The journal argued that people in North and South Kanara "will do well not to send their sons to Bombay, because those days are gone when even a doll could get employment."[58] As the horizons of opportunity broadened, the journal carried reports of caste colonies in distant Calcutta, New Delhi, and Burma. Perhaps the most distant Bhanap was a young man who had gone to America to study dentistry. His plans changed, and the character of his new activities may be a sufficient word on Saraswat initiative. In 1929, another Bhanap student in America reported back to the magazine:

> Mr. Ganeshrao Padubidri came to this country over eight years ago and is now located in Chicago. He is known as Professor Rao, and in his Hindu Spiritual Temple, located right in the heart of Chicago, he gives spiritual solace to lacerated hearts and training in yoga. He does this for a modest sum of £ 20 which is payable in installments. He writes to me to say that he is doing well in this "business" and would like to see more Bhanaps with an adequate knowledge of Sanskrit, English, and our religion to take to it, as he thinks there is money in the proposition.[59]

### *Saraswat Associations in Other Cities*

In other urban centres where Bhanaps clustered, the patterns of association reflected the broader social and economic circumstances in which caste members lived. At Bangalore a social club, the Canara Progressive Union, had been founded in 1900 by a few migrant

57. S. R. S., "My Community," *K. S.* 20, no. 9 (September 1936) : 13–14.
58. *K. S.* 4, no. 1 (January 1922) : 23.
59. B. B. Mundkur, "A Letter from America," *K. S.* 12, no. 3 (January 1929) : 35.

Bhanaps employed in the Mysore State public service. In 1904, Dattatraya N. Sirur took over the managing agency of the Mysore Spinning Mills. Almost immediately the Saraswat population grew, for the mills' clerical offices soon filled with Bhanap "quill-drivers." This altered the pattern of Saraswat residence in Bangalore. While the government servants had lived throughout the city and adjoining cantonment, the mill employees clustered in the vicinity of their jobs in Malleshwaram.[60] That neighborhood became the site of a building for the social club, now renamed Canara Union. It was built in 1919 with the assistance of D. N. Sirur. Its premises contained a reading room, an area for games, and a hall for use in marriages and performance of *bhajans*.[61] Although the club did cooperate with the K. S. A. in Bombay, it retained its independent identity.

In Madras, by contrast, no Saraswat club was organized until 1932. The Bhanap population had grown after 1908 when the Madras and Southern Mahratta Railway's operating headquarters shifted from Hubli to Madras, but there was no move to establish another social club akin to the Nagarkar Library of the former town. A Saraswat Students' Club flourished briefly in the first decade of the century, but by its nature could not maintain a stable membership.[62] What did emerge in Madras was a byproduct of the GSB unification movement. In 1912, following a conference of that movement in Savantvadi, the conference president, Kalle Narayanrao, returned to Madras and set about creating a new Samyukta Gowda Saraswatha Sabha, which united members of all GSB sections including Saraswats. Besides Narayanrao, other sponsors were Rao Bahadur Savur Mangeshrao, Rao Bahadur Hattiangadi Narayanrao, and Rao Saheb G. A. Hoskote.[63] The main object was to ally Saraswats and other GSB in a purely social club. In 1920 a scholarship fund was added.

But in the same year some Madras Saraswats formed a small *bhajan mandal* for the annual celebration of Shri Krishna Jayanti and Shri Datta Jayanti. One of the founders was Shantaram M. Kumta. Unlike the eminent Madras Bhanaps who were prominent in education and government service, he had begun employ-

60. About 50% of the Bhanap population of Bangalore lived in Malleshwaram neighborhood in 1922. *K. S.* 4, no. 4 (October 1922) : 117–119.

61. *K. S.* 22, no. 10 (October 1938) : 15.

62. *The Hindu* (Madras), Jan. 12, 1909, p. 6.

63. *K. S.* 28 (April 1944) : 83–84; *Samyukta Gowda Saraswata Sabha, Madras, Silver Jubilee, 1937*, pp. 5–6.

ment at Bombay in the office of Killick, Nixon. Later he had moved to Hubli, joining the clerical staff of the Ubhayakar Brothers' cotton firm, who had transferred him to their Madras office. His family had been connected for many years with both Jayanti observances at the village of Mallapur near Kumta.[64] Although the K. S. A. correspondent in Madras stated that Saraswats there could derive more benefit by maintaining ties to the other GSB castes, the Saraswat *Bhajan Mandal* evolved into a separate Saraswat Association by 1932.[65] This did not mark any break with the GSB Sabha, but looked forward to the creation of a hall where *bhajans* and marriages could be performed within the Kilpauk neighborhood, where nearly half the Madras Saraswats lived.

In other cities where Saraswats had not yet become permanent residents, the patterns of association did not parallel those of Bombay. The Calcutta Bhanaps, whose slow and uneven growth of population has already been noted, attempted to form a local Saraswat association in 1922, but as members were transferred out of the city it proved to be ephemeral. A decade later, in 1932, the the Saraswat population was larger in size, but one Calcutta Bhanap reported back to Bombay that there was no need for a caste club. "Bhanaps here are so closely associated in their working as well as home life that a separate meeting place for the community seems altogether superfluous."[66] In keeping with their origins, many Calcutta Saraswats instead became enthusiastic participants in both the Maharashtra Mandal and the South Indian Association.

## *A New Caste Culture*

The publication of the *Kanara Saraswat* provided not only a link through which the "strategic intelligence" of the Bhanaps was transmitted, but also provided a vehicle for the articulation of a culture and identity which would preserve the caste in a changing world. Lectures in the K. S. A. hall on social reform could amount to little more than preaching to the converted. A journal could bring the message of reform even into the orthodox households of the mofussil. Articulating a caste culture was not unheard of among

64. Saraswat Association, Madras, *Souvenir*, April 9, 1967, and *Golden Jubilee Celebrations of Shri Krishna and Shri Datta Jayantis* (1970), p. 10.
65. *K. S.* 4, no. 2 (April 1922) :53–54.
66. *K. S.* 16, no. 1 (July 1932) :14.

Saraswats, since the Samyukta Gauda Sarasvata Brahmana Pariṣad movement had begun such an experiment in 1910, mobilizing support for a "progressive" caste culture for all GSB members.[67] That effort had been followed in 1917 by an All-India Saraswat Sabha which hoped to incorporate castes from Gujarat, Sind, and North India. Several of the leaders of the All-India group were also participants in the K. S. A. There was no apparent reason for exclusiveness, since they looked to both organizations as means for promoting the welfare and progress of their community.[68]

In unity there could be strength, but the separation of the Bhanaps from their GSB cousins had its own long legacy. Thoughtful Saraswat observers recognized that as a small caste they had tended to become ingrown even as they spread out across the map of India. Some argued that the flaw lay not in size but in language. Konkani, their mother-tongue, isolated them from the majority of their neighbors, whether Kannada- and Tulu-speakers in Karnataka, Tamil-speakers in Madras, Marathi- and Gujarati-speakers in Bombay, or Hindi-speakers in North India. S. R. Koppikar asserted that "Konkani as a mother tongue . . . checks free conversation in mixed company, and the shyness contracted on that account by our children continues late in life."[69] Cultivation of regional languages and of Hindi as a national language caught up Bhanap energies throughout South India during the 1920s. Yet the affection for Konkani and its place in Saraswat folklore and tradition was not overcome. It was, as the Bhanaps said, a thing that was "*amchi gelé*," "of our own." Nor did the well-developed sense of isolation erode:

> We become foreigners wherever we go. . . . Even in our own Kanara we are accustomed to this treatment, in spite of our long domicile there. There we became Kushasthalis, because Kanarese is not our mother tongue, and when we move out of it and settle, say, in Madras . . . we are treated as people of the west coast and have no *locus standi*; in the place of our adoption in Maharashtra we are Karwaris. . . . [We have] a North Indian name and a South Indian existence.[70]

67. Cf. Frank F. Conlon, "Caste by Association: The Gauda Sarasvata Brahmana Unification Movement," *Journal of Asian Studies* 33 (May 1974) : 351–365.
68. Interview with R. A. Lajmi, March 18, 1971.
69. *Sàraswat Quarterly* 2, no. 2 (January 1920) : 13.
70. "Our Mother Tongue," *K. S.* 11, no. 1 (April 1928) : 16–20. The assertion is inaccurate insofar as it is recalled that Bhanap competence with Kannada was the

While some insisted that Konkani had weakened the Saraswats' ability to participate in "national life," in fact many individuals of the caste made distinguished contributions in the Indian National Congress. R. S. Padbidri, Mrs. Umabai Kundapur, and "the uncrowned king of Kanara," Karnad Sadashivrao, were well-known examples.[71]

As in the earlier unification movement, the unspoken aim seemed to be the appropriation of individual achievements and identification of these with the caste. What was sought, though, was not simply the luxury of corporately basking in the reflected glory of individuals, but rather to identify the environment and characteristics attendant upon their achievements and to promote these among all Saraswats. If this appearance of corporate pursuit of individuality struck any Bhanaps at the time as contradictory, they did little to publicize their scepticism.

What was to be the very model of a very modern Saraswat? Probably the most systematic statement of reforms for the community emerged from a special caste conference which was held in the Bombay suburb of Santa Cruz during the Christmas holidays of 1926. Calls for a "Saraswat Conference" had been issued as early as 1919, but the general fiscal straits of the K. S. A. and the economic and political turmoil of the ensuing three years effectively put the meeting off into the future. The conference was planned for the entire caste; representatives from mofussil towns and other cities were invited.[72] Few attended, but preliminary meetings elsewhere to consider the proposed agenda did contribute some ideas. The conference would consider issues, pass resolutions, and create a "working committee" to popularize the resulting platform. The chairman of the reception committee, S. S. Talmaki, tersely justified the effort: "The age of the writers of the Shastras is long past, and that of public opinion has emerged, at any rate among the educated people."[73]

basis for successful employment in both Madras and Bombay; see Chapter 6 above. Cf. "Hindi in South Kanara," *K. S.* 13, no. 6 (December 1929) :9–10; "Hindustani for South Indian Saraswats," *K. S.* 12, no. 3 (January 1929) :20–22.

71. Bhagini Mandal, Hubli, *Umabai Kundapur* (1952); Karnad Sadashiv Rao Memorial Committee, *Apostle of Sacrifice : Deshbhakta Karnad Sadashiv Rao Memorial Volume* (Bombay: Popular Prakashan, 1971); "In Freedom's Struggle," *K. S.* 31 (October-November 1947) :529–532.

72. *K. S.* 10, no. 3 (January 1927) :34–50.

73. *Ibid.*, pp. 38–41.

The resolutions urged that age of marriage be no less than twenty-one for boys and sixteen for girls; that boys should not be married until able to support a family; and that extravagance in length and expense of weddings should be curtailed. Identification of causes of unemployment; advocacy of the abolition of untouchability; enlargement of the Saraswat Educational and Provident Cooperative Society; the practice of thrift; education of females; vocational education; and voluntary payment of dowry were each unanimously approved. A land-improvement cooperative was recommended to acquire fields in which Bhanaps could undertake scientific cultivation. The countryside was touched with a romantic aura which could be believed only by city dwellers. S. S. Talmaki drew a stark contrast with the evils of city life:

> Our people at one time led an almost exclusively rural life on the sea-coast of the Kanaras . . . where we owned landed properties and lived in dwellings surrounded by extensive compounds. This life in the open air . . . had a bracing effect on the health and constitution of our older generations. Contrasted to this, one can easily imagine the effect of the life now led by our people in congested towns in closely packed dwellings and pursuing sedentary occupations at office desks. But all this fades into insignificance when compared to the fate which has overtaken [those in Bombay] who are compelled to feed on adulterated foodstuffs . . . and live in pigeonholes which by courtesy are called *chawls*, and breathe the air surcharged with dust, smoke, humidity, and the poisoning gases emanating from the drains and sewers.[74]

The cry of "back to the soil" remained popular among the Bombay Bhanaps, but only as a cry. The city—adulterated food, poisonous gases, and all—remained the Saraswat mecca.

The president of the conference reiterated the need for all Saraswats to be more adaptable, to become one with an expanding Indian nation. The tone and content of the proceedings confirmed that in fact some, if not most, already had. The resolutions were turned over to the working committee and were little heard of again. Perhaps cynics could dismiss the conference as an empty show, but for its participants it seemed a benchmark in the evolution of a suitably progressive culture for their caste.[75]

The conference proceedings had included matters other than secular reforms. The president, S. R. Koppikar, stated that religion

74. *Ibid.*, pp. 8–9.

75. Fifteen years later, in 1942, a Chitrapur Saraswat Cultural Conference was convened by the next generation of students and recent graduates. Its impact will be examined in a subsequent study.

and spiritual concerns should not be ignored. What about the *maṭha* and the *swami*? These institutions were not altogether out of date. A *swami* could understand the needs and views of progressive men, who in turn would be sympathetic to him. The dispersal of Saraswats across the land had weakened old links which had operated in the Kanaras. Could the conference really reform the social condition of the caste without taking into account the main source of its spiritual inspiration? Koppikar added that even then the devotees of the *maṭha* did not consist "only of uneducated and backward villagers. You will find among them men of the highest education and a few who have finished it in Europe and have been repulsed by the material aspects of Western civilization." Could not the educated urban Saraswats reach out and help the still-young Anandashram Swami to develop "a modern outlook" through which he could still "guard and maintain Hindu culture"?[76]

The conference dutifully passed an initial resolution paying homage to Anandashram Swami and requesting the working committee to suggest ways and means to ensure full cooperation between the *maṭha* and its followers. Less than a month after these proceedings, in January 1927, the resolution was activated when the young *guru* journeyed north to study at Rishikesh and paused briefly at Bombay. He was accorded an enthusiastic reception by all, including the "reformers." One of them, the historian S. R. Sharma, commented that there was no fundamental contradiction between passing resolutions and worshipping the feet of one's *guru*: "If anyone sees in this any inconsistency, let him note the inconsistencies in his own life; let him watch the perpetual war between his heart and mind."[77]

Some who observed "this sudden and wonderful transformation" would echo the query of Sunderrao R. Dongerkery, who asked, "How far is it likely that the change will be lasting?" The question was not irrelevant. *Maṭha* and caste had been drifting apart for more than two generations. During the welcome of Anandashram Swami, more than a few Bombay householders found they were not even certain about the appropriate forms of doing homage to their *guru*. A brief visit by an appealing personality had certainly touched the hearts of many of the Bhanaps in the city. But the visit did not bring a sea-change; it only marked an opportunity for

76. *K. S.* 10, no. 3 (January 1927) : 21–22.
77. *K. S.* 10, no. 4 (April 1927) : 17.

one. The story of this opportunity and its development, Anandashram Swami's circumstances from 1915 to 1927, and the difficult tasks of the subsequent reconciliation and reconstruction will be examined in the following chapter.

The twentieth century brought to the Saraswats increasing urbanization and dependence upon urban occupations and standards. Bhanaps became more widely dispersed in towns and cities throughout India, but more and more of them were concentrated in a few urban centers, notably Bombay. There the corporate conditions of the caste's members induced them to organize voluntary associations for meeting pressing needs of the time and place. These techniques would later prove useful to Saraswats elsewhere. And as the Bombay Bhanaps faced the vexing split within the caste arising from excommunications, they embraced a concept of the caste defined by kin and culture rather than by adherence to the *maṭha*. It was a pragmatic solution to the circumstances of city life. But spiritual concerns were not put aside easily. In the process of developing a strong articulation of what a new Saraswat corporate culture should be, the Saraswats of Bombay encountered an unexpected force—the preparedness of the secular and progressive urban community to renew its ties of reverence to Shri Chitrapur *Matha* and its young *guru*, Anandashram Swami.

# 9

## RELIGION AND REFORM:

### *Reintegration of the Saraswat Jāti, 1915–1935*

THE ANCESTORS of the Saraswats had brought into being the ties of allegiance to their line of *gurus* and Shri Chitrapur *Maṭha* during the eighteenth century as a means of preserving their *dharma* and reinforcing the identity and status of their caste. As their descendants' material fortunes improved, the *maṭha* and its *swamis* also prospered. The *maṭha* became increasingly the central focus of spiritual guidance and social control of the caste during the nineteenth century. The process culminated in the 1869 *vantiga shasana*. That agreement, which marked the growing influence of government servants and lawyers in caste affairs, also, in effect, placed the greatest emphasis upon the subordination of local "tens" (*hattu samastaru*) to the *maṭha*, a relation symbolized by the increasing use of the new Sanskrit term *sabha* to identify these bodies. Pandurangashram Swami had acted upon the logic of the new arrangements to enhance and elaborate the ritual and secular activities and standing of the *maṭha*. In the process, his vision of the *dharma* of the Saraswats collided with an alternative, social-reform view held by a small number of educated, urban caste members.

The *swami* was acting upon a logical premise of orthodox duties and obligations. The reformers' logic was grounded in individualism. Most members of the caste could not comfortably accept either or both views without compromise. The resulting excommunications and alienation, coming at a period of increased Bhanap migration and dispersal to scattered towns and cities throughout India, threatened to tear apart the Saraswat social fabric. In the reign of

Pandurangashram Swami's *shishya*, Anandashram Swami, the relations of *matha* and caste deteriorated for a further decade, before a series of brief encounters between the young *guru* and urban leaders of the *jāti* provided a reconciliation which led to reorganization of Shri Chitrapur *Maṭha* and a reaffirmation of its place in the integration of the Saraswat Brahman caste.

Caste and *maṭha* had drifted apart during the troublesome controversies between 1890 and 1915. The malaise of alienation which clouded the closing years of Pandurangashram Swami's regime did not dissipate with his passing in 1915. Some Bhanap laity tried to mobilize support for the young Anandashram Swami, but found difficulty in overcoming the inertia that had developed within the *maṭha* and its establishment. On the basis of apparent inefficiencies in *maṭha* management, urban Saraswats could justify withholding their *vantiga*. This had the effect of plunging the institution into further debt and decay. Indifference toward the *maṭha* replaced hostility as a predominant attitude. Many caste members turned their attentions to their new caste cooperatives and associations and, the articulation of a modern Saraswat culture, and to the increasingly troublesome concerns of making ends meet.

Yet in the adversities of caste and *maṭha*, the tradition of devotion and allegiance could not so easily be discarded. S. R. Koppikar's dictum at the 1926 conference that the Bhanaps could not afford to ignore the spiritual life struck a responsive chord. A painful task of reconciliation and reconstruction was about to begin.

Pandurangashram Swami refused to name a *shishya* to succeed him, because he thought that too many disciples of the *maṭha* were no longer prepared to follow the *dharma* of their caste. The remaining devotees continued to assure him that they would be loyal and would support a successor if the *swami* would only name him. Pandurangashram Swami publicly prayed to Shri Bhavanishankar, the tutelary deity of the *maṭha*, that he would be kept firm in his resolve to adopt no *shishya*.[1] But, in the view of many disciples at least, Shri Bhavanishankar willed otherwise, for quite suddenly in June 1915 Pandurangashram Swami reversed himself and urgently concluded an act of *shishya svīkar* (adoption). He initiated Shantamurti, a twelve-year-old son of Haridas Ramachandra, a priest at the *maṭha*, and named him Anandashram. The ceremonies

1. R. S. C. M., Proceedings of the Mahasabha of Dec. 27–31, 1917, p. 2. [Translation assistance by Shri Padukone Prabhakarrao.]

were barely concluded when, on June 14, 1915, the old *guru* passed away.[2]

Twelve-year-old Anandashram Swami now faced the uncertain years of his minority without the guidance of a *guru*. Pandurangashram Swami had stipulated that until his successor had attained maturity the management of the *maṭha* would be vested in a representative of the Shukla Bhat family. Worship (*padapuja*) would be directed to the wooden sandals (*paduka*) of Pandurangashram Swami until the new *swami* felt himself adequately prepared to accept such homage. Anandashram Swami in the interim was to carry on his studies. Some Bhanaps worried that these arrangements placed the new *swami* in a position that was inferior to the *maṭha* staff. They suggested that a guardian be appointed by the Court of Wards. Such outside influence seemed objectionable, however. Saraswats of Karwar, perhaps the most consistent supporters of the *maṭha* during those troubled years, attempted instead to interpose a lay member of the caste in the *maṭha* management.[3] The staff's refusal to cooperate in this experiment frustrated its intentions. *Mahasabhas* were held in 1917 and 1922 to settle the management question and investigate the internal relations of the *maṭha* staff to the *swami*. Pious good intentions could not be easily translated into effective action. The drift continued.

The relationship of *maṭha* and caste in the post-1915 decade did not improve from their already deteriorated state. The effects of the *bahishkar* controversies were still felt. The bans remained unaltered, yet were not honored outside of a few rural villages. Where local *sabhas* still functioned, reports of erring Bhanaps would be reported to Shirali, and the usual prescriptions of *prayaschitta* were returned. The only change was that these orders were now sometimes sent by telegram.[4] In most places the local *sabhas* had practically ceased to function. The Mangalore *sabha* functioned, but with the support only of a minority of the town's Bhanap families. One of the town's inhabitants recalled. "It was as if the people had excommunicated the *maṭha*."[5]

2. *Times of India*, June 22, 1915, p. 5; G. S. Hattiangdi, *Fifty Years of Bliss*, pp. 6–11.

3. R. S. C. M., Proceedings of Mahasabha, 1917, pp. 3–7.

4. Such telegraphic orders were found among records of the Mangalore local *sabha* for 1920–21 in a cupboard at Shri Umamheshwar Temple, Mangalore, on Feb. 21, 1971.

5. Interview with Pandit Shivarao, Mangalore, Feb. 21, 1971.

The annual *vantiga* receipts fell from Rs. 10,834 in 1914–15 to Rs. 2,286 by 1917–18.[6] When Anandashram Swami made his first tour of North and South Kanara in 1921, the payments climbed dramatically to Rs. 14,580, but thereafter indifference toward payment became customary. Members of the growing urban segment of the caste discussed the possibility of reorienting the *maṭha* and offering the *swami* support in return for his assistance in the advancement of social reforms. A 1919 editorial in the *Saraswat Quarterly* justified renewed interest in the *matha* and its relation to the caste: "The supreme importance of this question is . . . if we could have the *maṭha* on our side in any attempts at social reform, we can achieve success far more speedily and smoothly than otherwise."[7] Such pragmatic secular speculation reflected a radical departure from an older generation's view, which G. S. Hattiangdi recalled in his grandmother's words: "Child, our swamis are Gods who speak."[8] Despite, or perhaps because of this, nothing substantive was done to put the *maṭha* and the *swami* on the side of reform.

This was in part due to the ambivalence felt by some city dwellers about rural religious institutions of their caste. As the Bhanap population had declined in Kanara, temple priests commenced visiting urban centres to canvass funds for renovations and other expenses. One Bombay Saraswat expressed a general sentiment:

> We in Bombay . . . are considered to be rich beyond the dreams of avarice of our relations . . . in the districts, and the result is that we are never allowed to be rich, much as we should like to be. [Ruralites] all flock to Bombay to gather a harvest of gold and take back with them what they can get.[9]

No one went away empty-handed, but Bombay residents expressed friendly curiosity as to whether or not the monies were thereafter properly expended.[10] So too with the *maṭha*. Rumors of mismanagement, factionalism among the staff, and even discourtesies toward Anandashram Swami were "disquieting." The *Kanara Saraswat* echoed rather than led public opinion when it stated: "It is high time a regular constitution is drawn up for the better management of the *maṭha*'s affairs."[11]

6. Hattiangdi, *Fifty Years of Bliss*, p. 15.
7. *Saraswat Quarterly* 1, no. 2 (July 1919) : 33–34.
8. G. S. Hattiangdi, *Pandurang, Pandurang*, p. 8.
9. *K. S.* 12, no. 4 (April 1929) : 19.
10. *K. S.* 11, no. 3 (January 1928) : 24–25.
11. *K. S.* 5, no. 1 (January 1923) : 43.

Anandashram Swami had to surmount another obstacle. The passing of Pandurangashram Swami had deprived him of his *guru.* The young *swami* had to acquire his education with the help of priests at the *maṭha* and visiting tutors, and, often, by self-instruction. The closed, factious atmosphere prevailing at Shirali did little to help Anandashram Swami's quest. On two occasions he gave up and left, wishing to pursue the truly unfettered life of a *sannaysin*, but both times he was induced to return.[12] Still dissatisified with his attainments, Anandashram Swami commenced his journey in January 1927 to study at Rishikesh with a north Indian brahman scholar, Krishnashrama, who had visited Shirali earlier. Anandashram Swami's pause at Bombay had a stunning impact upon the Saraswat community there. Ideas of putting the *maṭha* "on our side" were forgotten. The *Kanara Saraswat* editorial stated that it was "an occasion to us for the reaffirmation of the simple faith that comforted our fathers. . . . The Bombay Saraswats, one and all, were never before so stirred."[13] What had transpired to produce such an apparent reversal of thinking?

The intensity of the corporate and individual response to the *swami* might be viewed as a reflection of the changing conditions of the Saraswats in Bombay. Economic recession had brought uncertainties. Young men worried about finding employment. Older men worried about retrenchment. The golden lure of the city was badly tarnished. During this time, also, the Bombay Saraswat community began to include more persons of the older generation migrating from the Kanaras. As sons settled permanently in the city, they invited parents to give up the family home in the country and join them in Bombay. The presence of a member of an older, rural generation in an urban household could promote and maintain, or in some cases introduce, traditional religious practices and values.

As early as March 1922, a local *sabha* had met in Bombay and resolved to commence regular *vantiga* payments. It had mixed success, but revealed a new interest in the *maṭha*. At about the same time, another fund had been launched to create some memorial to the late Pandurangashram Swami. This was proposed to be used for construction of a temple for the caste in Bombay or its suburbs.[14]

12. Hattiangdi, *Fifty Years of Bliss*, p. 14.
13. *K. S.* 10, no. 3 (January 1927) : 1–10.
14. *K. S.* 4, no. 2 (April 1922) : 64.

While, again, no immediate progress was made in the project, it is clear that religious concerns were by no means foreign to the Bombay Bhanap. Just before the *swami*'s visit, the caste journal published an opinion that the *swami* should tour to spread awareness of religion, "bringing home to us the realization of God and the utility of the *maṭha* which . . . so need to be taught."

> As our people have migrated to distant places far away from our native land it is not humanly possible for His Holiness to arrange to visit each and every place where our community now resides. . . . The necessity of such contact cannot be overestimated, at least in these days of declining faith. At no time in the history of our community did we stand in greater need.[15]

It is unlikely that economic and demographic factors alone could explain the response of Bombay to Anandashram Swami in January 1927. Much had to do with the personality and character of the *swami* himself. Characterized by a serene temperament and a sensitive intellect, the young *guru* seemed to the harried householders of Bombay to be the embodiment of nonattachment and grace. He was seen to live a life in accord with *dharma* and tradition. To some he seemed a living validation of their ancestral religion. Later one disciple, a person known for blunt, direct communication devoid of rhetoric, said of his feelings toward Anandashram Swami:

> I would be failing in my duty if I did not openly state that I look upon him as a personification of true renunciation; of complete non-attachment to power and position; of equanimity in the midst of direst difficulities; of mercy, forgiveness, and peace.[16]

Another of Anandashram Swami's devotees, a member of one of the "social reform" families of Madras and Mangalore, wrote of a "spiritual force" which could not be known "except by its effects upon the psyche."

> He does not oppose, he does not argue, he does not resist. He is utterly silent, infinitely patient. He is content to state the truth about any problem, he is humble, willing to listen to anyone, to any suggestions. His love and utter self-effacement are disarming. How can anyone differ from one who understands you properly? To the 'learned,' the intellectually arrogant, he gives the impression of one who is constantly anxious to learn, and by this simple method frees them from their pride of knowledge.[17]

15. *K. S.* 10, no. 2 (October 1926) : 1–2.

16. H. Shankar Rau (ed.), *Shrimat Anandashram Ordination Jubilee Souvenir* (Bombay, 1941), p. 82.

17. Benegal Sanjivarao, "What I Have Learnt from Swami Anandashram," in Hattiangdi, *Fifty Years of Bliss*, pp. 205–206.

To acclaim such as this, Anandashram Swami would reply with characteristic restraint. On an occasion of a religious conference at Dharamsthala, South Kanara, the host had praised the qualities of the *swami*. To this, Anandashram Swami replied:

> We have noted the praise bestowed on us by Shriman Manjayya Heggade. It seems to us, however, that distance in this case has leant enchantment to the view. . . . The good men who think much of the minor virtues of others are very rare. We count Shriman Heggade as one of such good men. Though the words spoken about us by him may not be deserved, we take them as an indication of the high ideal which he has placed before himself in judging others. . . . And it will be our endeavour to cherish those ideas and follow those ideals in our career through life.[18]

The humility and dignity of the young *guru* moved many Bhanaps, rural and urban alike, to realization that in serving him they would add a new dimension to their own lives and personalities.

After departing Bombay for North India, Anandashram Swami made another visit that held implications for the future of the *maṭha*. During his stay in New Delhi he was the guest of Hattiangadi Shankar Rau, then holding the post of Deputy Controller of Currency for the Government of India. Not only was the host much attracted by the *swami*'s personality, he was troubled by the reports of the faltering condition of the *maṭha*. He resolved to turn his energies and skills to solution of the situation.[19] The stage was set for revitalizing Shri Chitrapur *Maṭha*.

The corporate groups of the Bombay Bhanaps also resolved to improve the *maṭha*'s condition. The Kanara Saraswat Association announced a prize contest for the best essays on "How to Improve the Status of the Chitrapur Math and Its Relations with the Community." The resulting essays were dominated by ideas of constitutionalism for the management of the *maṭha*, social-reform models for new active endeavors by the *maṭha*, and revalidation of a distinctive Bhanap religious culture by the *guru*. The winning entry, by L. S. Kàgal, argued that there was no need to fear the *maṭha* so long as it was an expression of an eternal ideal and not an instrument of spiritual autocracy: "Institutions are made for people and not people for institutions. . . . If the Chitrapur *maṭha* is to be the *maṭha* of the Saraswat people, it must have a character which

18. H. Shankar Rau, (ed.) *Anandashram Ordination Jubilee*, pp. 44–45.
19. Hattiangdi, *Fifty Years of Bliss*, pp. 20–21.

should fit it to be the *matha* of the Saraswat people."[20] All Bhanaps should be included among its devotees. The *matha* should be freed from "extreme puritanism." Kagal thought that the *swami* could "take us into that freer atmosphere of an expansive life capable of proper adjustment against the influences of time." The *swami* should be himself freed from the worries of *matha* administration, so that his spiritual leadership could grow. "He should be to the constitution of the *matha* as King George is to the constitution of Great Britain."[21]

Others underscored the historical heritage represented by the *matha*. "It came into being at a time of crisis in the life of the community. It served a great end at the time. It gave our community a status." "It has kept up the unity of the community against several disintegrating forces; it has given us the same sort of religious culture and a status in the eyes of other communities."[22] Regularity of management; tolerance, if not promotion, of reform; and preservation of religious culture all figured in the prescriptions of the urban Saraswats. What was still required was a means to step beyond the formation of public opinion to a course of positive action.

By early 1929 the leaders of the Kanara Saraswat Association in Bombay and associations in other towns and cities had developed a consensus in favor of convening a new *mahasabha*. A few individuals reviewed the record of such meetings under Pandurangashram Swami and wondered whether such a body could really achieve reform.[23] If the orthodox held power, or if the *swami* dominated the proceedings, as had occurred before, little would be accomplished. There was a strong sense that the *mahasabha* was to ratify social reforms supported by the 1926 Saraswat Conference. But who would be the members of this convention—adult males, women, those only who paid *vantiga*? There were no procedural guidelines. Nor was it certain that the venue should be necessarily at Shirali. More Bhanaps would find it easier to travel to Bombay.

No positive decisions were taken, however, until 1932, when several Karwar Saraswats met with Anandashram Swami to review the continued deterioration of the *matha* finances and buildings. A special committee of representatives from Bombay, Dharwar,

20. *K. S.* 11, no. 3 (January 1928) : 7–10.
21. *Ibid.*
22. *K. S.* 10, no. 5 [*sic* 11, no. 1] (July 1927) : 5; *K. S.* 12, no. 1 (July 1928) : 19–23.
23. *K. S.* 12, no. 4 (April 1929) : 38–39.

Madras, and Bangalore joined Kanara men at Shirali to resolve the problem. They settled on creation of an executive officer for the *maṭha* responsible to a supervising committee to be appointed from among the laity. It was resolved that every member of the community should pay not less than one percent of his annual income as *vantiga*, and that a reconstruction fund should be started to meet the crushing burden of debts incurred during the previous twenty years—the annual interest costs alone were Rs. 5,000.[24]

After the special meeting, the representatives returned to their towns and cities to kindle broader support for the reforms. A newly reconstituted Bombay local *sabha* assumed the responsibility for collecting and holding the reconstruction fund until the new management could commence. It was agreed that a *mahasabha* would be convened that December in Shirali. New procedures envisioned the *swami* taking no direct part in the deliberations, but instead giving an opening address and later receiving the resolutions. Also, for the first time, the number of delegates to be selected was delimited; 87 delegate positions were apportioned to various centers of Bhanap population, according to their size. This was made possible by the just-completed caste census conducted for the Kanara Saraswat Association by Hattiangadi Shankar Rau.[25]

When the delegates gathered at the *maṭha* in December 1932, Anandashram Swami welcomed them and set the agenda for the meetings. They were to consider revision of the rules against foreign travel and participation in the GSB unification movement; develop improved means of religious instruction to assure the caste an adequate supply of trained priests; revise the procedures for *vantiga* collection; revise constitutions of the local *sabhas* and *mahasabha*; and, finally, establish a standing committee to act upon *mahasabha* resolutions as sanctioned by the *maṭha*.[26] The delegates quickly gave form to those proposals. Restrictions on foreign travel and on participation in the unification movement were removed. Religious instruction was encouraged. A standing committee was authorized. The *vantiga* minimum was reduced to one percent. H. Shankar

24. *Proceedings of the Committee Summoned by His Holiness Swami Shri Anandashram of Chitrapur Math, Shirali, for the purpose of making suggestions with regard to the future administration of math affairs and the improvement of the financial condition of the math* (Kumta, 1932), p. 12.

25. *Ibid.*, pp. 13–15.

26. *K. S.* 17, no. 1 (January 1933), "Mahasabha Supplement" :6–7.

Rau observed that, on the basis of his census data on incomes, that percentage, if honored, would produce an annual revenue of Rs. 54,000. The special *maṭha* reconstruction fund was authorized, and local *sabhas* were designated for every village or town with one hundered or more Saraswat residents. Membership and procedures and duties were formally defined, and regular procedures for *mahasabhas* were recorded.[27]

Anandashram Swami accepted the resolutions fully, explaining though that in the matter of foreign travel he could not say that it was permitted, but that it would be treated as any minor sin to be absolved by a nominal *prayaschitta*. In the aftermath of the *mahasabha*, a few urban Bhanaps wondered if all that had been "secured was the privilege to pay." But this overlooked the main purpose—"to bridge the ever-widening gulf between the Math and its followers."[28] H. Shankar Rau, elected president of the standing committee, commenced a sustained program of tours and publicity on behalf of the *maṭha* and the reconstruction fund. The flow of *vantiga* began to increase, jumping from Rs. 8,399 in 1931–32 to Rs. 24,039 the following year, to which was added a further Rs. 28,595 collected for the reconstruction fund.[29] When asked by some why the Saraswats should take interest in such an out-of-date institution as Shri Chitrapur *Maṭha*, H. Shankar Rau responded:

> Quite frankly, I cannot hope to satisfy those who think that the Maṭh is not needed. I can only hope that experience will make them wiser. It is essentially a matter of faith, and I must leave it at that.[30]

The overwhelming majority of the Bhanaps accepted that view and renewed ties to the institution. In some ways the allegiance to the *maṭha* was now akin to the principles of voluntary association which had already worked so well in the secular life of the community.

The divisions within the community which had remained since the social-reform controversies at the beginning of the century no longer had any basis. The caste began in earnest to publicly erase the distinctions. Perhaps the most poignant and emotional scene occurred at Mangalore where, for the first time in over thirty years,

27. *Ibid.*, pp. 17–19.
28. *K. S.* 17, no. 2 (February 1933) : 13, 1.
29. Hattiangdi, *Fifty Years of Bliss*, p. 32.
30. H. Shankar Rau, "*Maṭha* Affairs: Questions and Answers," *K. S.* 17, no. 2 (February 1933) : 7. Cf. Kilpadi Guru Dutt, *Chitrapur Saraswat Retrospect* (Bangalore, 1955), pp. 270–295, for a more complicated and elaborate "profession of faith."

a *gramabhiksha*—dinner for all caste members of the town—was held on February 12, 1933, during a visit of Anandashram Swami. All Saraswats ate together in the ritually solid line (*pankti*). Nayampalli Subbarao sat beside Anandashram Swami himself. The long ambivalence and inconvenience of excommunication had ended. All were truly "of our own."[31]

By extending their loyalty, cooperation, and fiscal support to Shri Chitrapur *Maṭha*, urban Saraswats, led be the Bombay residents, modernized the institution's internal arrangements. In so doing they placed emphasis upon the *swami*'s role as a spiritual guide rather than as a social controller. Anandashram Swami was freed, as he desired, to continue study and spiritual development, although he frequently put these aside to visit and bless his disciples. The *maṭha* reconstruction fund reached the goal of Rs. 100,000 in five years of intense canvassing. All debts were discharged. With that the standing committee began a program of soliciting funds as permanent "*vantiga* capital," the interest on which would cover costs of maintaining the institution and rituals.[32] Almost every Bhanap fāmily was now linked to the *maṭha* through contributions. With the stabilization of *maṭha* finances, some funds could be dedicated to various projects of social and economic amelioration. *Maṭha* and caste were again integrated.

Nearly fifteen years had transpired since the young *guru* Anandashram Swami had appeared in Bombay. By all accounts indifference and hostility had melted in an instant. But it had taken decade and a half to act upon the good intentions of freeing the *swami* for spiritual endeavor. Without the corporate abilities which the caste members had already developed, along with the steady work of several outstanding individuals, the effort might have been in vain.

31. *K. S.* 17, no. 2 (February 1933) :15–16.
32. Hattiangdi, *Fifty Years of Bliss*, pp. 42–44.

# EPILOGUE

It is hoped that Chitrapur Saraswat Brahmans themselves will find this historical narrative of the career of their caste to be of interest. The story might well be a source of legitimate pride, for it is in many ways a chronicle of a progressive and adaptive community whose ancestors often made great sacrifices to accommodate changing circumstances. On the other hand, it would be understandable that some findings which do not match with Bhanap popular tradition might be greeted with skepticism. In history, unlike science, the same exercise repeated by another will not necessarily yield the same results. Another scholar, with access to the same evidence I used, might produce a quite different narrative. What appears here reflects my interest in the corporate identity of the Saraswats and how it—and they—were changed and affected change during the past two and a half centuries.

Other readers without personal ties to the Saraswat traditions may take the study in other lights. It is both a history of a caste and an illustration of some varieties of the social and economic changes produced in India by British rule. Those changes have been presented as they were experienced by one fairly well-defined group of people and wherever possible, as those people perceived them. As such the book may provide insights into the way members of a caste could adapt to new conditions while endeavoring to preserve and strengthen their social unit. It also attempts to present evidence against the view that India's "traditional" society and culture were static and changeless. Making allowances for the particular circumstances of the Saraswats in social status and geographical locale, one must still observe that their boundaries, internal institutions, and occupations were the subjects of almost continuous alteration and adaptation, even in times which Saraswats themselves have regarded as periods of hidebound traditionalism.

The importance of external forces cannot be overlooked. British colonial administrative policies and practices were a major element.

Decisions to employ local men in district administration, to transfer North Kanara to Bombay, or to not build a railroad to Karwar, all created opportunities and problems for Saraswats. In each instance the new opportunities tended to be exploited by those in the more disadvantageous situations—the "southerners" in the early nineteenth century, the "northerners" after 1862, or the struggling clerical workers of Bombay after the 1890s. The stereotypical images of earlier golden ages when every government office in Kanara was a Bhanap–haven appear to have grown with time's passing. As Shrimat Anandashram Swami said in another context, "Distance lends enchantment to the view." Nevertheless, government service did provide new openings for some Saraswats who mastered the new techniques and language of the emerging bureaucracy. Learning the new knowledge did not turn Saraswats away from their religious and social traditions. Rather, it is clear that they contributed their skills and a portion of their wealth for the betterment of Shri Chitrapur *maṭha* and its *swamis*.

This was to be expected, for the *maṭha* and *swamis* were the reaction of the caste's elders who had committed themselves and their descendents to the guidance and control of a new *guruparampara*. It was a spiritual link which served to confirm the caste's brahmanical status—an important consideration for an immigrant community. At the same time, it provided a mode of communication and social control among the Saraswat settlements scattered up and down the west coast of Kanara. The subsequent growth and elaboration of the *maṭha* and the caste temples during the nineteenth century reveal the constructive potencies of orthodoxy during a period of Indian history when most historians have concentrated upon a few widely visible critics and reformers of a modern persuasion.

Mention of reform brings the story forward into the intense internal controversies over sea-voyage and widow-marriage which seemed to threaten the survival of both caste and *maṭha* in the late nineteenth century. Discussions of social reform in India have tended to focus upon intellectual issues of the ideas of reform. This approach, while certainly valid, yields little explanation of the traumas and trials which reform-minded Indians and their opponents endured. In the Saraswat *jāti*'s experience, the sea-voyage controversy was magnified because Shrimat Pandurangashram Swami, the caste's *guru* from 1864 to 1915, was himself attempting to reform and revitalize his flock's religious and social life in precisely the opposite direction from the reformers. He promoted a purer brahmanical standard of behavior just as Narayan Chandavarkar was exploring the potentialities of modern rationalism. Ideological disputes were unhealthy for a human community; clearly most Bhanaps were anxious for compromise. The alienation of the *maṭha* from the growing segment of urban laity was as much a reflection of the relatively limited resources of the early Saraswat migrants as it was a result of their independence of mind and spirit produced by breathing the free air of a modern metropolis.

Looking at the social context and social costs of reform, one is struck by the difficulties faced by all but a very few well-to-do families, and even those families would be dependent upon the *jāti* when marriages had to be arranged. The overall decline of support for the *maṭha* reflects the turning away of the urban Bhanaps to new concerns and enterprises. Until the maturity of Shrimat Anandashram Swami, there would be no mechanism by which the *maṭha* could be reconciled with the ever more widely dispersed community which had pushed beyond the confines of the home districts.

The urbanization of the Saraswats may be seen to reveal a diverse set of motivations and patterns. Migration for education, as from Mangalore to Madras, or in employment, as from Kumta to Hubli, will be familiar enough. But it is unexpected that the growth of the colony in Bombay would be as much the product of economic or educational failure as of success. The strangeness of the metropolis was combatted by residential clustering which eventually produced the most substantial concentration of Bhanaps at any time in the caste's history. This was confirmed by the emergence of voluntary associations: a cooperative bank, social club, and housing society, which were predicated upon caste membership. In light of the excommunications and alienation surrounding the reform controversies, the urban Saraswats postulated a caste identity based not upon the purity of ritual standing but upon the "natural identity" of being born a Saraswat. By the 1920s the initiative within the caste had clearly shifted to its urban segment. Yet, influenced by stressful conditions, relocated elders, and the compelling personality of Anandashram Swami, and given a lead by several skilled and energetic individuals, the Saraswats renewed and revitalized their allegiance and support for Shri Chitrapur *Maṭha*. It was not the end of the story, but a prelude to a new epoch.

# GLOSSARY

Where correct transliteration of Indian language terms varies from the forms used in the text of this book, transliteration is given in parentheses.

*Adil Shahi* : A Muslim dynasty, centered on Bijapur, which succeeded the Bahmani Sultanate in the Western Deccan, A. D. 1489–1686.

*advaita* : the doctrine of monism teaching that there is an integral, undivided underlying principle encompassing all reality.

*agamokta-vidhi* : a tradition of routines and rituals as prescribed in an *āgama*, or manual of ritual.

*agraharam* (agrahāram) : a village donated by a king as a settlement for brahmans, the produce of its lands dedicated to their maintenance and the perpetuation of their services free of assessment.

*amil*, *amildar* : a collector of revenue for the government.

*amin* (amīn) : an officer in charge of police or revenue affairs of a taluka; a *sadr amin* was a judicial officer.

*anna* (āna) : a sixteenth part of a rupee, but also refers to fractional parts of other objects.

*Arya Samaj* (Ārya Samāj) : a Hindu reform association founded in 1875 by Swami Dayananda Saraswati, who sought to purify Hinduism of social evils and to restore it to the traditions of the Veda. While most influential in North India, there were small clusters of Arya Samaj members throughout India.

*Ashadha* (āśāḍha) : the lunar month of the Hindu calender corresponding approximately to June-July.

*badagi* (baḍagī) : "northerner," a nickname for members of Saraswat families whose villages were in the north of Kanara, of uncertain date. Cf. *tenki*.

*bahishkar* (bahiṣkāra) : expulsion from caste, excommunication.

*Bants*, *Bunts* : a large land-holding and cultivating caste of South Kaṇara; most are Hindu, but some profess Jainism; a majority speak Tulu, but some use Kannada. They appear to be descendants of a formerly dominant military class, and are noted for their legal traditions of matrilineal succession.

*Baramahal* : a portion of Salem district, annexed by the East India Company in 1792; site of the establishment of *ryotwari* land-tenure system.

*barghare* : lit., "twelve houses," an informal expression used among GSB of Bombay city in the nineteenth century to identify influential families whose ancestors had been early settlers in the city.

*bhajan* : ạdoration or worship; hymn sung in praise of a god. A *bhajan mandal* (maṇḍala) is a group or association which gathers to perform *bhajans*.

*Bhanap* : a nickname of uncertain origin by which Chitrapur Saraswat Brahmans often refer to themselves and their caste.

*bhat* (bhaṭ) : a brahman, often one who lives upon charity.

*Bhavani-Shankar* : the tutelary deity of Shri Chitrapur *Maṭha*.

*Billava* : a Tulu-speaking caste of toddy-drawers in South Kanara; of low ritual status.

*Brahman* : (brāhmaṇa) : traditionally the sacerdotal class of Hindu society, the ritually highest *varna* (q.v.); a *jāti* of that status, or member thereof.

*Brahmo Samaj* : a Hindu theistic religious and social reform group founded in 1828 by Raja Ram Mohan Roy; very influential among Bengali middle classes, but chapters of the organization were spread throughout India.

*Canara* : see *Kanara*.

*chalgeni* : in the land system of Kanara, a temporary tenancy-at-will for a short period, usually one year; chalgeni tenants, *chalgenigars*, had no rights in the soil. Cf. *mulgeni*.

*chaturmas* (cāturmāsya) : the four-month period in the Hindu calendar from Ashadh, Shukla 10. to Karttika, Shukla 10 (approx. July-October), during which *sannyasins* may stay in one place, it being the rainy season; a time of retreat or of sustained visits with devotees by *swamis* of Shri Chitrapur *Maṭha*.

*Chowpati* : a beach in Bombay city at the head of Back Bay, adjacent to Girgaum and Malabar Hill; for many years a favorite Sunday and holiday recreational spot and site of many public meetings.

*chawl* (chāl) : a type of housing in Bombay usually consisting of a series of one- or two-room tenements connected by a verandah or internal passage. The term may be derived from the idea of the passage connecting all tenements with a stair and, usually, a sanitary block.

*cutcherry* (kacheri): a court or office where government business is conducted.

*dahajana* (dāhajana): ten men, an alternative term for *hattu samastaru*; a body of elders of a caste within a village.

*daftar*: an official record, account, or files; a *daftardar* was a record-keeper.

*dakshina* (dakṣiṇa): money, presents given to brahmans or students on ceremonial occasions. Also means the south.

*darshan* (darśana): sight, seeing; the deliberate beholding of an auspicious person or object thought to infuse the beholder with the virtues of the person or object.

*dastak*: see *tastik*.

*Datta*, *Dattatreya* (Dattātreya): a three-headed deity much revered in Maharashtra; his birthday (*Datta Jayanti*) was widely observed by Saraswat families.

*dayadi* (dāyadi): a kinsman, descendants from the same ancestry.

*Deshastha* (deśaṣṭha): lit., "resident of the country"; the name of a large caste cluster of brahmans in Maharashtra or their descendants in South India; there they were often associated with government service in the nineteenth century.

*dharma*: moral duty or obligation.

*dharmashastra* (dharmaśāstra): science of *dharma*; a code or body of Hindu law.

*dharmshala* (dharmśāla): a pious ediface, a pilgrim rest house usually built as a charitable act. In South India it is often termed a *choultry*.

*dhoti* (dhotī): an Indian male lower garment worn wrapped around the body, the end being then passed between the legs and tucked in at the waist.

*diwan*, *dewan* (dīvān): under the British, the chief Indian officer of a government office or establishment; a chief minister of an Indian state; *Dewan Bahadur* was a rank of honor conferred by the British Indian government usually upon retired government servants and other men prominent in public affairs (other than nationalist politics).

*double daftar*: an East India Company practice of keeping district accounts in two languages by two sets of employees as a check upon corruption.

*ekadashi* (ekādaśī): the eleventh day of the bright or dark half of each lunar month in the Hindu calendar—a time particularly important to Vishnu and his devotees.

*Gamdevi*: a neighborhood of Bombay immediately north of Chowpati; site of first Saraswat cooperative housing project.

*Ganesha*, *Shri Ganesha* (Ganeśa): the elephant-headed god of auspicious occasions.

*Gangavali*: a river which rises in Dharwar district and flows about 85 miles southwest into the Arabian Sea near Gokarn; traditionally described as the border between Haiga and Konkan; known also as the Bedti river.

*gaonkar* (gā̃vkara): village founder, families with special landed rights in Goa.

*Gaud* (gauḍa): traditional name for region of central Bengal; the term is also applied as general name for the northern divisions of brahmans.

*gavdo*: in Goa, a non-brahman priest of village and local deities.

*ghat* (ghāṭ): lit. step, passage; a mountain range dividing regions, especially applied to the western escarpment of the Deccan plateau.

*Girgaum*: a village with extensive coconut gardens which evolved during the nineteenth century into a densely settled neighborhood of Bombay city, occupied predominantly by high-caste Maharashtra Hindus and Christians.

*gomastah* (gumāśta): an agent, clerk, appointee; in the Madras Presidency, the term designated a subordinate accountant in the revenue department.

*gotra*: family, clan, descent, mythical lineage; traditional sections into which brahmans were divided according to descent from ancient sages. The system has been altered and elaborated to the point of contradiction, but at least one element remains— it is inappropriate for one to marry another from within the same *gotra*, even though of a different family.

*gṛhastha*: a householder; head of family; second stage of ideal Hindu life.

*guru* (gurū): a teacher, spiritual preceptor.

*guruparampara* (gurūparaṃparā): a regular succession of *gurus*, a spiritual lineage.

*Haidar Ali*: a Muslim military adventurer (A. D. 1721–1782) who seized power in a Hindu state centering on Mysore and then launched a successful military expansion to create by 1765 a strong power which vied with the British for dominance in South India.

*hattu samastaru* : lit. "ten all," ten combined; a deliberative body of caste elders in a village, equivalent to the more commonly known phrase *panchayat*.

*Holi* (hoḷī) : a major Hindu festival during the month of Phalguna (Feb.–Mar.); an occasion for sanctioned departure from social proprieties by shouting of obscenities, hurling of filth, sprinkling colored water, and generally boisterous behavior.

*huzur* (huzūr) : the presence, the royal presence; the presence of a superior authority such as judge or collector, or abstractly, the state. The term was also used in Madras to denominate ranks in subordinate offices.

*inam* (inām) : land free of revenue demand, the resources having been granted for services or favors.

*ishtadevata* (iṣṭadevāta) : lit., "loved, favored deity"; a tutelary deity of a person or household.

*jagadguru* : lit., "world teacher"; title assumed by eminent Hindu spiritual preceptors.

*jāti* : kind, sort, species, class, usually referring to the endogamous commensal unit called caste or subcaste. (Cf. Introduction.)

*jāti bahishkar* (bahiṣkāra) : expulsion from caste, excommunication.

*jāti dharma* : duties appropriate to members of a particular *jāti*.

*Kadamba* : a royal family or clan which came to power in the South-Western Deccan in the third century A. D. and dominated the area in the fourth to sixth centuries.

*Kalbadevi* : a neighborhood and main road in Bombay named for a temple of Kalka- or Kalbadevi. The area extends from Dhobi Talao northward to Pydhoni.

*kaliyuga* : the age of Kali, the final era of cosmic and moral decay.

*Kanara* : the name given the west coast of India between Goa and Malabar, perhaps derived from the language, Kannada, or a corruption of Karnataka; the term was used by the Portuguese, who referred to its inhabitants as *Canarims*. As a district of the Madras Presidency, it was divided as North Kanara and South Kanara in 1799–1805; the northern portion, except Kundapur taluka, was transferred to the Bombay Presidency in 1862. The districts are now part of Karnataka state.

*Kandevadi* : a neighborhood of Bombay between the Girgaum (now Jaganath Shankarsett) Road and Girgaum Back (now Vithalbhai Patel) Road.

*Kannada* : a major Dravidian language.

*Karhada* (karhāḍā): a caste of brahmans of Maharashtra predominantly residing in the Western Deccan and southern Konkan regions.

*karkun* (kārkūn): a clerk; an official rank in Bombay Presidency government service.

*karma*: lit., "action"; Hindu law of moral causation in which actions have consequences in this life and the next; deeds in former lives produce merit or demerit in this life.

*karnam* (karaṇam): a village accountant.

*Karnataka*: traditional name of Kannada-speaking region of India.

*Kashi yatra*: pilgrimage to Kashi (Benares).

*khanaval* (khāṇavala) : an eating-house.

*Khetwadi*: a neighborhood of Bombay city to the north and east of Girgaum.

*Konkan*: the western littoral of peninsular India, variously bounded, but usually defined as the land between the Gulf of Cambay and either Goa or the Gangavali River, between the Arabian Sea and the Western Ghats. *Konkani*, of the Konkan, may refer to persons of the region, the region's language, or its speakers.

*Krishna jayanti* (kṛṣṇa jayañtī): festival of Krishna's anniversary.

*Kshatriya*: (kṣatriya): second division of Hindu society ascribed warrior role.

*kshetra* (kṣetra): lit., "a field"; a pure or sacred spot suitable for pilgrimage.

*kuladevata* (kuladevatā): family god, the tutelary deity of a lineage; an important element in the religious heritage of the Saraswats.

*kulkarni* (kuḷkarṇī) : a revenue accountant.

*kut, koot, kuttam* (kuttam): lit., "assemblage"; a tumultuous assemblage, as applied to the disturbances in Kanara in 1831 when cultivators refused to accept assessments of land revenue.

*laukika*: secular, public; of or pertaining to brahmans who pursue secular rather than sacred (*vaidika*) vocations.

*Lingayat* (lingāyata) : [see *Virashaiva*].

*Lohar Chal*: a street and neighborhood of Bombay in the vicinity between the former Crawford Market and Kalbadevi.

*maharahotseva* (māhārahotseva): a car festival; a Hindu holiday in which a sacred image is taken from its shrine in a large wooden "car" (*ratha*) for a brief ride.

*Maharashtra Mandal* (mahārāṣṭra maṇḍala): Maharashtra circle, a term often used by informal associations of Marathi-speakers residing outside Maharashtra in some locality, e.g. Calcutta, New Delhi, London, Toronto.

*mahasabha* (mahāsabhā): lit., "great assembly"; applied to extraordinary meetings of representatives of the disciples of Shri Chitrapur *Maṭha*.

*mahasamadhi* (mahāsamạdhi): lit., "great mediation, absorption"; respectful term describing cessation of physical life of the gurus of Shri Chitrapur *Maṭha*.

*malnad* (malnād): the above-ghat country of western Mysore plateau.

*mamlatdar* (māmlatdār): officer holding authority and collecting revenue of a taluka or district; a term used in Maharashtra and extended by British practice throughout the Bombay Presidency.

*mantra* (mañtra): a sacred verse from Hindu scriptures or specially composed; of little value when learned from a book, it is highly potent when heard from the voice of one's guru.

*maṭha*: the seat of a spiritual authority or guru; a monastery.

*Mimamsa* (mīmāṃsā): one of the six orthodox systems of Hindu philosophy.

*mleccha*: generic term for barbarians or foreigners—those speaking a foreign language and not subject to the usual Hindu institutions. The inelegance of the word matches the presumed sloth of foreign speech, and may be compared with the origin of the Greek source for "barbarian.")

*mofussil*: in East India Company usage, the "provinces" as distinguished from the "Presidency," but generally referring to rural as opposed to urban.

*moksha* (mokṣa): release from continuing rebirth, salvation.

*moyen zabitah*: the sanctioned establishment or work force of a government office.

*Mugbhat*: a neighborhood in Bombay city adjacent to Girgaum.

*mulgeni*: in the land system of Kanara, permanent tenants with inalienable rights of cultivation and invariable rents. The holders (*mulgenigar*s) could mortgage, but not sell, their rights.

*mulki*: of a country or province, referring here to a public-service qualifying exam.

*Munro, Thomas*: one of the most prominent British officers to serve in South India; associated with the development of *ryotwari* tenure, he was first collector of Kanara in 1799–1800, later Governor of Madras; lived 1761–1827.

*munshi* (munśī) : a writer or secretary in government or private offices; Europeans often applied the term to teachers of Indian languages.

*munsif*, *moonsiff* (munsīf): an Indian civil judge.

*mutsidi*, *mootsidi* (mutasaddī): a writer, clerk; supervisor.

*nadkarni* (nādakarṇī): a revenue officer of pre-British Kanara, often a hereditary position.

*naib* (nāyab): a deputy; a deputy officer, e.g., *naib sheristedar*.

*nayaka*, *naik*, *naique* (nāyaka): chief; a ruler or warrior; title used by several royal lineages of small states succeeding the Vijayanagar empire.

*nazar* : presents, offerings; payment made to a superior for a boon or office.

*Nyaya Shastra* (nyāya śastra) : brahmanical texts on logic and analysis.

*padapuja* (padapūjā) : worship of the feet; a customary form of reverence to the *swami* of Shri Chitrapur *Maṭha* by his devotees.

*paduka* (pādukā) : a wooden shoe or slipper, most often wooden clogs; in Hindu religious life, the *paduka* of saints and *swami*s are objects of veneration.

*pagdi* (pagaḍī): tribute, an extra charge—usually illegal—exacted by landlords from tenants.

*pagoda* : of uncertain derivation, identifying temples, but used here to name certain coins circulating in South India; *bahaduri pagoda*s were gold coins of Haidar Ali, valued fractionally less than the East India Company's Madras "Star" *pagoda*s; on conversion to the standard rupee in 1818 the coins were reckoned at about Rs. 3.5.

*panchayat* (pañcāyata): five, a generic term for a group of elders either of a caste or village with deliberative authority over caste or village affairs.

*pandit* (paṇḍita): a learned brahman.

*pankti* (pañkti): a line, a row of people sitting down at a meal in ritual unity; *pankti bhojana* was dinner served in accord with orthodox prescription that all caste fellows sit in one line.

*paricita nav* (paricita nāv) : familiar name; nickname.

*parishad* (pariṣad): an assembly or congress.

*patel*, *patil* (pāṭil) : a village head; the right to the office was called the *patelki*.

*Pathan*: although complexly subdivided by tribe and clan, the inhabitants of the Northwest Frontier Province who migrated to other parts of India were known by this generic term; in Bombay they were often migratory workers who also offered high interest loans and were generally feared as persons who could combine strength with violence.

*Pathare Prabhu* : a caste of Bombay city, one of the earliest settled there and early participants in opportunities of British rule; *prabhu* came in English usage to signify an Indian clerk during the early nineteenth century.

*pora* : child, with diminutive imputation of "brat" or "whelp."

*Prarthana Samaj* (prārthanā samāj): "prayer society"; a theistic Hindu reform association founded in Bombay in 1867 on the lines of the Brahmo Samaj.

*prayaschitta* (prāyaścitta): penance; rite of purification, as upon return from a foreign land.

*purohit* (purohita): family priest; the brahman who conducts all ceremonials and sacrifices of a household or family.

*Rao Bahadur*, *Rao Saheb* (rāv bahādūr, rāv sāheb): like *Dewan Bahadur*, these were honorary ranks bestowed by the British Indian government upon its Indian subjects.

*ratha* : a chariot or car; a large wooden cart employed in certain festivals at some Hindu temples in which the image of the temple deity is paraded.

*Ṛg veda* : the first and oldest of the four Vedas or collections of sacred knowledge of the Indo-Aryans.

*riyasa* (rāyasa) : a letter from a superior; a proclamation from a guru.

*ryot* (rāiyat) : a subject; in agriculture, a cultivator.

*ryotvari* (rāiyatvari): a revenue system wherein government makes an annual agreement with each individual landholder (not necessarily the actual cultivator, as is often imagined) to settle the taxes.

*sabha* (sabhā): an assembly; a meeting.

*sadavarta* (sadāvartta): a daily distribution of food to brahmans and/or mendicants, usually in fulfillment of a religious vow.

*saheb lok* : a colloquial Indian expression identifying the British, i.e., the people who are all "sahebs," masters.

*Sahyadri Khanda* (sahyādri khaṇḍa) : a portion of the *Skanda Purana* purporting to present traditional histories of castes and holy places of western India.

*samadhi* (samādhi) : meditation, absorption; also a memorial ediface erected over the burial place of a saint or *swami*.

*samparkam* : contact; connection by touching; social intercourse.

*samsthana* : (saṃsthāna) : a royal city or a place of a god, a temple.

*sangha* : meeting; association.

*sannyasin* (sannyāsīn) : one who has cast off all worldly possessions and affections; a "twice-born" Hindu in the fourth, final stage of religious life; a wandering mendicant.

*sari* (sāḍī) : unsewn garment worn by Indian women.

*sayar kamavisdar* (sāir kamāvīsdāra) : a subordinate officer in district administration in charge of non-land revenues; a supervisor of excise collections.

*seva* : service, attention, worship; adoration of a holy image.

*shakala* (śakala) : the first of the two branches of the *Ṛg veda*.

*shanbhog* (śanabhoga) : a village clerk or accountant who kept registers of cultivation, assessment, and revenue collection; also used to identify any writer or clerk.

*Shankaracharya* (śaṃkarācārya) : celebrated medieval Hindu teacher (c. A. D. 788–838) of Vedanta; the term was applied during the nineteenth century to *swami*s presiding over the *maṭha*s he founded, and other such preceptors.

*shasana* (śāsana) : a grant, decree, charter.

*shastra* (śāstra) : scripture, science; especially pertaining to Hindu law.

*shatkarma* (ṣaṭkarma) : the six duties appropriate to brahmans: procuring sacrifice, study of *veda*, alms-giving, conducting sacrifice, teaching *veda*, accepting donations; brahmans entitled to perform all six were *shatkarmi*, contrasted with those who could do only the first three, *trikarmi*.

*shendi* (śeṇḍī) : the tuft or lock of hair left on the top of the head of Hindu males, especially among brahmans.

*Shenvi* (śeṇavī) : name applied to some Gaud Saraswat Brahmans in Maharashtra; of uncertain derivation and the subject of controversial interpretation, it was in Goa employed as an honorific for teachers or learned men.

*sheristedar* (śiristedāra) : chief secretary to the District Collector, hence the highest-ranking Indian in Madras district administration.

*shishya* (śiṣya) : a pupil disciple; term affixed to a disciple chosen by a *swami* to be his successor.

*shishya svikar* (śiṣya svīkāra) : the act of adoption of a disciple; the affirmation of a chosen successor by a *swami*.

*Shrimat* (śrīmat): an honorific title signifying an exhalted and excellent personage.

*shruti* (śruti): lit., "that which was heard," used for early Vedic literature.

*Skanda Purana*: one of the eighteen major puranas, but peculiar in its heterogeneity: there is no agreed text throughout India; it is known better in a wide variety of fragments (*khaṇḍa*s, *māhātmya*s) associated with specific regions and localities.

*smarta*: one who follows the *smṛti*, or codes of law; among South Indian brahmans, many are designated *smarta* because they are neither sectarian Vaishnavas nor Shaivites, honoring both deities along with Parvati, Ganesha, and Surya; in principle, followers of *advaita vedanta* philosophy.

*sutra* (sūtra): lit., "a thread"; aphorisms summarizing religious and philosophical doctrines; treatises condensing knowledge.

*swadeshi* (svadeśī): of one's own country; indigenous, as applied to goods and services produced by Indians without use of foreign components, especially in patriotic boycotts of British goods.

*swami* (svāmī): lord, master; title applied to a deity, spiritual preceptor or other holy person.

*tahsildar* (tahṣīldāra): chief Indian revenue officer of a district subdivision called *tehsil* in North India, *taluka* in South India.

*taluka* (tālukā): subdivision of a district.

*tastik*, *tasdik* (taṣdik): attestation; a fixed amount or scale of expenditure in support of temples and religious endowments by government.

*tenki*: lit., "southerner;" a nickname for members of Saraswat families in the southern portions of Kanara. Cf. *badagi*.

*Tipu Sultan*: the son of Haidar Ali and ruler of Mysore from 1782 until his death at Seringapatam at the close of the Fourth Anglo-Mysore War; lived c. 1750–1799.

*umedvar* (umedvār): a volunteer, a person securing employment by initially doing volunteer work in an office.

*upanayan* (upanayana): initiation ceremony for young men of "twice-born" *varna*s, symbolized by putting on of sacred thread.

*Upasana Sabha* (upāsanā sabhā): a theistic association founded in Mangalore parallel to the Brahmo Samaj, later becoming a branch of that body.

*vaidika*: relating to *veda*s, a brahman who follows sacred ritual as a vocation.

*vangad* (vāñgaḍa): extended lineages; family lines or clans identified as devotees of particular deities in Goa.

*vantiga* (vāṇṭeka): lit., "share"; a tithe, a sum paid by devotees to Shri Chitrapur *Maṭha.*

*varaha* (varāha): the boar avatar of Vishnu; here referring to its image on certain pre-British coins; after the coins ceased circulating, the term remained an expression of value roughly equal to four rupees.

*varg* : in Kanara, an account of property, but the term came to mean the estate itself; its hereditary proprietor was a *vargdar.*

*varna* (varṇa): lit., "color"; the fourfold hierarchic social and ritual classification into which Hindu society in India was traditionally arranged and described.

*veda*: lit., "knowledge"; the earliest scriptures of brahmanical religion.

*vidya* (vidyā): wisdom, knowledge.

*vihara* (vihāra): Jain or Buddhist monastery.

*vinayoga* (vināyoga): used here in the sense of certain rituals.

*Virashaiva* (vīraśaiva) [or *Lingayat*]: a devotional sect of Karnataka dating from the twelfth century A. D., strictly revering Shiva.

*xenin* : a Portuguese version of *shenvi*, used in Goa to denominate teachers.

*zamindar* (zamīndāra) : a landholder; although in many parts of India this term described a particular form of land tenure and proprietorship, it was also employed simply as a label of persons who were landholders of some standing.

*Zamorin* : the title for many centuries of the Hindu ruler of Calicut and surrounding territory; the term is a European corruption of a Malayalam modification of a Sanskrit term meaning the sea, a reflection of Calicut's importance in maritime commerce.

# BIBLIOGRAPHY

## CONTENTS



## *I. UNPUBLISHED SOURCES*

### OFFICIAL RECORDS

*Maharashtra State Archives, Secretariat Record Office, Bombay*

Proceedings of Bombay Government:
- Educational
- General
- Judicial
- Revenue

*India Office Records, India Office Library, London*

- Board's Collections
- Bombay Civil Establishments
- Bombay General Proceedings
- Bombay Revenue Proceedings
- Madras Board of Revenue Proceedings
- Madras Civil Establishments
- Madras, History of Services of Gazetted and Other Officers
- Madras Revenue Proceedings
- Personal Records
- Reports on Mofussil Municipalities
- Reports on Native Newspapers

*Madras Record Office, Madras*

Proceedings of Madras Government:
- Board of Revenue
- Educational
- Revenue

Miscellaneous Records of the Board of Revenue
Printed Selections from the Records of the Collector of South Canara

MISCELLANEOUS MATERIALS, PRIVATE PAPERS, ETC.

*Bombay*

Papers of Narayan Dabholkar, in possession of Shri L. S. Dabholkar, Queens Road, Bombay 1

Census enumeration registers, Kanara Saraswat Association Talmakiwadi, Tardeo Road, Bombay 7

Papers relating to Suit No. 43 in Bombay High Court, Original Side, 1896, in possession of the Trustees of the Temples, Charitable Institutions, and Funds of the Goud Saraswat Brahman Community of Bombay, Bhuleshwar, Bombay 2

*Cochin*

Papers on historical subjects of Shri N. Purushottham Mallaya, Konkani Bhasha Prachar Sabha, Cochin 2

"Marathaka-Pachcha or the Glory of the Emerald Idol," unpub. ms. in possession of Shri V. R. Kilikar, Mattancheri, Cochin 2

*London, India Office Library*

Ms. Mackenzie Collection: Translations of Vernacular Tracts

Mss. Eur. C 167, T. W. Venn, "Pirates and Picaroons: The Pax-Britannica on the Bombay Coast," 1959.

*Mangalore*

"History of the Basel Mission Churches in India," typed-ms. by R. Scheurmeir, 1964, in possession of the Reverend B. A. Furtado, Kanara Theological College, Balmatta, Mangalore

Bundle of papers relating to Mangalore local *sabha* of Shri Chitrapur *Maṭha*, Shri Umamaheshwar Temple, Mangalore

*Poona*

Papers of Rao Bahadur S. S. Talmaki, in possession of Shri R. V. Nadkarni, Prabhat Road, Poona 4

*Shirali, North Kanara district*

Records of Shri Chitrapur *Matha*

Manuscript Notes on Shri Chitrapur *Maṭha* prepared by Sujir Sundarrao, 1964

## *II. PUBLISHED SOURCES*

NEWSPAPERS AND PERIODICALS

*All-India Saraswat Quarterly*, Bombay

*Indian Social Reformer*, Madras, Bombay

*Bombay Gazette*
*Bombay Guardian*
*Bombay Witness*
*Canarese Informer*
*Citrāpura Ravikiran* (*Chitrapur Sunbeam*), Bombay
*Hindu*, Madras
*Illustrated Canarese Journal*, Mangalore
*Indu Prakash*, Bombay
*Kanara Saraswat*, Bombay
*Labour Gazette*, Bombay
*Mahārāṣṭra Sārasvata*, Bombay
*Native Öpinion*, Bombay
*Saraswat Quarterly*, Bombay
*Śarāda*, Bombay
*Subhoda Patrika*, Bombay
*Vividhajñānavistara*, Bombay

OFFICIAL PUBLICATIONS

*Census reports* :

*Census of the Island of Bombay taken Feb. 2, 1864*, by A. H. Leith (Bombay, 1864)

Census of India 1871/2: *Report on the Census of the Madras Presidency*, 2 vols., by W. R. Cornish (Madras, 1874)

Census of India 1871/2: *Census Statement of Population of 1871 in Each Village of the South Canara District arranged according to area, caste, and occupation* (Madras, 1874)

Census of India 1871/2: *Census of the Bombay Presidency* taken on Feb. 21, *1872*, 3 parts (Bombay, 1875)

Census of India 1881 : *Operations and Results in the Presidency of Bombay including Sind*, by J. A. Baines, 2 vols. (Bombay, 1882)

Census of India 1881 : *Census of City and Island of Bombay*, by T. S. Weir (Bombay, 1883)

Census of India 1881: *Operations and Results in the Madras Presidency*, by Lewis McIver, 2 vols. (Madras, 1883)

Census of India 1891, vol. 7 : *Bombay and Its Feudatories*, by W. W. Drew, 2 parts (Bombay, 1892)

Census of India 1891, vols. 13–15 : *Madras* : *Report on the Census*, by H. A. Stuart, 3 vols. (Madras, 1893)

Census of India 1901, vol. 9: *Bombay*, by R. E. Enthoven, 3 parts (Bombay, 1901)

Census of India 1901, vol. 10 : *Bombay Town and Island*, by R. E. Enthoven and S. M. Edwardes, 3 parts (Bombay, 1901)

Census of India 1901, vol. 15 : *Madras*, by W. Francis, 3 parts (Madras, 1902)

Census of India 1911, vol. 7: *Bombay*, by P. J. Mead and G. Laird Macgregor, 2 parts (Bombay, 1912)

Census of India 1911, vol. 8 : *Bombay* (*Town and Island*), by P. J. Mead and G. Laird Macgregor (Bombay, 1912)

Census of India 1911, vol. 12 : *Madras*, by J. Chartres Molony, 3 parts (Madras, 1912)

Census of India 1921, vol. 8: *Bombay Presidency*, by L. J. Sedgwick, 2 parts (Bombay, 1922)

Census of India 1921, vol. 9: *Cities of the Bombay Presidency*, by L. J. Sedgwick, 2 parts (Bombay, 1922)

Census of India 1921, vol. 13: *Madras*, by G. T. Boag, 4 parts (Madras, 1922)

Census of India 1931, vol. 8 :*Bombay Presidency*, by A. H. Dracup and H. T. Sorley, 4 parts (Bombay, 1933)

Census of India 1931, vol. 9: *Cities of the Bombay Presidency*, by H. T. Sorley, 2 parts (Bombay, 1933)

Census of India 1931, vol. 14: *Madras*, by M. W. N. Yeatts, 3 parts (Madras, 1933)

*Gazetteers and Manuals*

*Gazetteer of the Baroda State*, Govindbhai Desai and A. R. Clarke (comps.), 2 vols. (Bombay, 1923)

*The Gazetteer of Bombay City and Island*, S. M. Edwardes (comp.), 3 vols. (Bombay, 1909)

*Gazetteer of the Bombay Presidency*, James M. Campbell (ed.), 27 vols. (Bombay, 1877–1901)

Vol. 9: *Gujarat Population*, 2 parts (1899–1901)
Vol. 10: *Ratnagiri and Sawantwadi* (1880)
Vol. 11: *Kolaba and Janjira* (1883)
Vol. 13: *Thana*, 2 parts (1882)
Vol. 15: *Kanara* (North), 2 parts (1883)
Vol. 16: *Nasik* (1883)
Vol. 18: *Poona*, 3 parts (1885)
Vol. 19: *Satara* (1885)
Vol. 20: *Sholapur* (1885)
Vol. 21: *Belgaum* (1884)
Vol. 22: *Dharwar* (1884)
Vol. 24: *Kolhapur* (1886)
Vol. 26: *Materials . . . Bombay Town and Island*, 3 parts (1893–94)

*Cochin State Manual*, C. Achyuta Menon (ed.) (Ernakulam, 1911)

*Imperial Gazetteer of India*, new ed., 26 vols. (Oxford, 1908–09)

*Imperial Gazetteer of India*: *Provincial Series*: *Bombay Presidency*, 2 vols. (Calcutta, 1909)

*Indore State Gazetteer*, L. C. Dhariwal (comp.), rev. and enlarged ed., 3 vols. (Indore, 1931).

*Madras District Manuals*: *South Canara*, vol. 1, J. Sturrock (comp.) (Madras, 1894)

*Madras District Manuals* : *South Canara*, vol. 2, Harold A. Stuart (comp.) (Madras, 1895)

*Madras District Gazetteers* :*Statistical Appendix, together with a supplement to the two District Manuals for South Kanara District*, K. N. Krishnaswami Ayyar and J. F. Hall (comps.) (Madras, 1938)

*Selections from Government Records*

*Selections from the Records of Bombay Government* [SRBG] New Series: No. 10: *Memoir on the Sawunt Waree State* by W. Courtney and Major

J. W. Auld and R. Hughes Thomas (ed.), *Statistical Report on the Portuguese Settlements in India*, (1855)
No. 158: *Correspondence relative to the Revenue Survey and Assessment of the Karwar Taluka of the Kanara Collectorate* (1883)
No. 163: *Papers relative to the Revised Rates of Assessment of the Kumta and Ankola Talukas of North Kanara* (1883)
No. 169: *Papers relating to the Original Survey Settlement of 40 Villages of the Honavar Taluka of the Kanara Collectorate* (1885)
No. 173: *Papers relating to Proposals for the Survey Settlement into 21 Villages of the Sirsi Taluka of the Kanara Collectorate* (1885)
No. 210: *Papers relating to the Introduction of Revised Rates of Assessment into 55 villages of the Honavar Taluka of the Kanara Collectorate* (1887)
No. 553: *Papers relating to Second Revised Survey Settlement of Karwar Taluka, Kanara District* (1913)
No. 554: *Papers relating to First Revision Settlement of Honavar Taluka of the Kanara Collectorate* (1913)

*Selections from the Educational Records of the Government of India*, vol. 1 (Delhi, 1960)

*Selections from the Records of the Madras Government* [SRMG]:
Dutch Records No. 2: *Memoir written in the year 1781* A. D. *by Adriaan Moens, Extraordinary Member of the Batavia Council, Governor and Director of the Malabar Coast, Canara and Vingurla, for his successor* (1908)
Dutch Records No. 13: *The Dutch in Malabar, being a translation of selections nos. 1 and 2 with introduction and notes*, by A. Galletti, A. J. Van Der Burg, and P. Groot (1911)
"New Series" (Second Series):
No. 17: *Report on Public Instruction in Madras, 1854–55*
No. 35: *Report on Public Instruction in Madras, 1855–56*
No. 69: *Report on Public Instruction in Madras, 1859–60*
No. 76: *Report on Public Instruction in Madras, 1862–63*
No. 87: *Report on Public Instruction in the Madras Presidency for 1864–65*
No. 87-B: *Report on Public Instruction in the Madras Presidency for 1865-66*
"New Series" (Third Series):
No. 5: *Report on Public Instruction in the Madras Presidency for 1866–67*
No. 11: *Report on Public Instruction in Madras Presidency for 1867–68*
No. 15-A: *Report on Public Instruction in the Madras Presidency for 1868–69*
No. 23: *Report on Public Instruction in the Madras Presidency for 1869–70*
No. 28: *Report on Public Instruction in the Madras Presidency for 1870–71*
No. 35: *Report on Public Instruction in the Madras Presidency for 1871–72*
No. 38: *Report on Public Instruction in the Madras Presidency for 1872–73*
No. 41: *Report on Public Instruction in the Madras Presidency for 1873–74*
No. 51: *Report on Public Instruction in the Madras Presidency for 1874–75*
No. 58: *Report on Public Instruction in the Madras Presidency for 1875–76*

*Miscellaneous publications, reports*

Bombay, Educational Dept., *Directory of the Bombay Educational Department* (annual), 1867–71, 1892–1919.

———, *Directory of Vernacular Teachers Holding Certificates*, with an appendix of untrained headmasters in the Kanarese districts of the Southern Division, 22nd issue (Dharwar, 1908)

Bombay, Labour Office, *Report of an Enquiry into Middle-Class Unemployment in the Bombay Presidency* (Bombay, 1927)

———, *Report on an Enquiry into Middle-Class Family Budgets in Bombay City* (Bombay, 1928)

Bombay, Registrar of Cooperative Societies, *Report of the Working of the Co-operative Credit Society Act*, (1905–1912)

———, *Report on the Working of Cooperative Societies*, 1912–1936.

Bombay, *Report of the Rent Enquiry Committee*, vol. 1, (1939)

India, Education Commission, *Report [and Evidence] of the Bombay Provincial Committee*, 2 vols. (Calcutta, 1884)

———, *Report by the Madras Provincial Committee, with evidence taken before the committee and memorials addressed to the Education Commission* (Calcutta, 1884)

India, Public Service Commission. *Proceedings*, vols. 4 and 5 (Calcutta, 1887)

[India] Great Britain, Royal Commission on Public Service in India, *Report*, vol. 6: *Minutes of Evidence Taken in the Bombay Presidency* (London, 1913)

Madras, *Manual of the Administration of the Madras Presidency, in illustration of the Records of government and the Yearly Administration Reports* Charles Maclean (ed.), 3 vols. (1885–93)

Madras, Medical Board Office, *Report on the Medical Topography and Statistics of the Provinces of Malabar and Canara* (1844)

PRIVATE INSTITUTIONS: SERIAL PUBLICATIONS

Basel German Evangelical Mission [Basel Mission], *Annual Reports*, 1841–1899

Kanara Saraswat Association, *Annual Reports*, 1912–1944

Samyukta Gauḍa Sārasvata Brāhmaṇa Pariṣad, *Reports* [title varies], 1910–1935

Saraswat Philanthropic Bureau, *Reports*, 1914–1916

Shamrao Vithal Cooperative Bank, *Annual Reports*, 1909–1932

Shri Umamaheshwar Temple, Mangalore, *Umamaheshvara Devasthana Varadi*, Shaka 1803–1830 (Kannada) [Umamaheshwar Temple, Report, 1881–1909] (1910)

ARTICLES, BOOKS, PAMPHLETS, AND THESES:

*A. Subba Rao Pai: Reminiscences by One Who Knew Him* (Mangalore, 1946)

*Ad-hoc Committee for Enquiring into the Present Condition of Temples and Shrines of Saraswath Community* (Shirali: Shri Chitrapur *Maṭh*, 1966)

Alexander, P. C., *The Dutch in Malabar* (Annamalainagar: Annamalai University, 1946)

Anantha Krishna Iyer, L. K., *The Cochin Tribes and Castes*, 2 vols. (Madras: Government of Cochin, 1909–1912)

Arbuthnot, Alexander, *Major General Sir Thomas Munro: Selections from His Minutes*, 2 vols. (London: C. P. Paul, 1881)

Archeological Survey of India, *Revised List of Antiquarian Remains in the Bombay Presidency*, vol. 8, (Bombay: Government Central Press, 1897)

Arur, Umabai, *Śricitrāpuraguruparamparācaritra* (Marathi) [Deeds of the Line of Gurus of Chitrapur], rev. ed. (Bombay: Popular Book Depot, 1965)

Āthalye, Viṣṇu Vāsudeva, *Karhāḍe Brāhmaṇāñcā Ithihāsa* (Marathi) [History of Karhada Brahmans] (Poona: Sitabai Karandikar, Shaka 1869 [A. D. 1947])

Baden-Powell, B. H., "The Villages of Goa in the Early Sixteenth Century," *Journal of the Royal Asiatic Society of Great Britain and Ireland*, 1900, pp. 261–291

Badley, B. H., *Indian Missionary Directory and Memorial Volume*, rev. ed. (Lucknow: Methodist Episcopal Church Press, 1881)

Bailey, F. G., *Caste and the Economic Frontier* (Manchester: Manchester University Press, 1957)

———, "Closed Social Stratification in India," *Archives Européenes de Sociologie* 4 (1963): 107–124

Ballhatchet, Kenneth, *Social Policy and Social Change in Western India, 1817–1830* (London: Oxford University Press, 1957)

Basel Mission, *A Retrospect of the Work Done by the Basel Mission for the Educational, Material, and Social Progress of South Canara* (Mangalore, 1907)

Berreman, Gerald D., "Structure and Function of Caste Systems," in George De Vos and Hiroshi Wagatsuma, *Japan's Invisible Race* (Berkeley and Los Angeles: University of California Press, 1972), pp. 277–307

Béteille, Andre, "A Note on the Referents of Caste," *Archives Européenes de Sociologie* 5 (1964): 130–134

Bhardwaj, Surinder M., *Hindu Places of Pilgrimage in India: A Study in Cultural Geography* (Berkeley and Los Angeles: University of California Press, 1973)

Bhat, K. S. Haridasa (ed.), *Mangalore: A Survey of the Place and Its People* (Manipal, S. K.: Syndicate Bank, n.d. [c. 1958])

Borradaile, Harry, *Borradaile's Gujarat Caste Rules*, published from the original answers of the castes with the sanction of Her Imperial Majesty's High Court of Judicature of Bombay, 2 vols. (Bombay: Sir Manguldass Nathoobhoy, 1884–87)

Boxer, Charles Ralph, *Race Relations in the Portuguese Colonial Empire: 1415–1815* (Oxford: Oxford University Press, 1963)

Braganca Pereira, A. B. de, *Etnografia da India Portuguesa* 2 vols. (Bastora: Tipografia Rangel, 1940)

Brown, F. C., *Letters to and from the Government of Madras relative to the Disturbances in Canara in April, 1837* (London, 1838)

Buchanan, Francis [Hamilton], *A Journey from Madras through the countries of Mysore, Canara, and Malabar*, 3 vols. (London, 1807)

Canara High School, Mangalore, *Diamond Jubilee Souvenir* (Mangalore, 1951)

Catanach, Ian J., *Rural Credit in Western India* (Berkeley and Los Angeles: University of California Press, 1970)

Chandavarkar, Ganesh L., *Dattatraya Narayan Sirur* (n.p., 1950)

———, *A Wrestling Soul* (Bombay: Popular Book Depot, 1955)

Chandavarkar, Narayan Ganesh, *The Speeches and Writings of Sir Narayan G. Chandavarkar*, L. V. Kaikini, ed. (Bombay: Kashinath Raghunath Mitra for Manoranjak Grantha Prasarak Mandali, 1911)

Charpentier, Jarl, "Parashu-rama: The Main Outlines of His Legend," pp. 9–16 in *Mahamahopadyaya [S.] Kuppuswami Sastri Commemoration Volume* (Madras, n.d.)

Chavan, V. P., *Vaishnavism of the Gowd Saraswat Brahmins, etc., and a few Konkani Folklore Tales* (Bombay: Ramchandra Govind & Son, 1928)

Chitrapura Sangha, *Chitrapura Panachanga* (Kannada) [Chitapur Almanac] (Bombay: Chitrapura Sangha, 1896)

Conlon, Frank F., "Caste by Association: The Gauḍa Sārasvata Brāhmaṇa Unification Movement," *Journal of Asian Studies* 33 (May 1974): 351–366.

Connemora, Lord, *Minutes of the Seventh Tour of H. E. Lord Connemora, Governor of Madras* (Madras, 1888)

Cunha Rivara, J. H. da, *Archivo Portuguez Oriental*, 6 vols. in 11 parts (Nova Goa: Imprensa Nacional, 1863–75)

Cunningham, Alexander, *Ancient Geography of India*, rev. ed. (Calcutta, 1924)

Dadachanji, Faredun K. (comp.), *List of Hindu Charities in Bombay* (Bombay, 1919)

Danvers, Frederick C., *The Portuguese in India*, 2 vols. (London: W. H. Allen, 1894)

Das Gupta, Ashin, *Malabar in Asian Trade: 1740–1800.* (Cambridge: Cambridge University Press, 1967)

Davis, Kingsley, *The Population of India and Pakistan.* (Princeton: Princeton University Press, 1951)

Day, Francis, *The Land of the Permauls or Cochin, Its Past and Its Present.* (Madras: Gantz Brothers, 1863)

D'Costa, Anthony, *The Christianisation of the Goa Island, 1510–1567* (Bombay: author, 1965)

Della Valle, Pietro, *The Travels of Pietro Della Valle in India* ["from the old English translation of 1664 by G. Havens"], Edward Grey (ed.), 2 vols. London: Hakluyt Society Publication ,, 2nd series, nos. 84–85, 1892)

Dhareshwar, Sadashiv, *Proceedings of the Committee summoned by His Holiness Shri Swami Anandashram of Chitrapur Math, Shirali, for the purpose of making suggestions with regard to the future administration of the maṭha*. (Kumta, N. K., 1932)

Dobbin, Christine, *Urban Leadership in Western India : Politics and Communities in Bombay City, 1840–1885* (London: Oxford University Press, 1973)

Dongerkery, Kamala S., *On the Wings of Time* (Bombay: Bharatiya Vidya Bhavan, 1968)

Dongerkery, Sundar R., *History of the University of Bombay* (Bombay: University of Bombay, 1957)

Dowson, John, *A Classical Dictionary of Hindu Mythology and Religion, Geography, History and Literature*, 10th ed. (London: Kegan Paul, Trench, Trubner & Co., 1961)

Dubāśī, Vāmana Mangeśa, *Gauḍa Sārasvata Brāhmaṇa Jñātīcī Kamgiri* (Marathi *Mahārāṣṭra Sārasvata* Bombay, 1918 [originally published in *Mahārāṣṭra Sārasvata* 2 (1918) :36–61])

Dubois, Abbe J. A., *Hindu Manners, Customs and Ceremonies*, 3rd ed. (Oxford: Clarendon Press, 1906)

Dumont, Louis, *Homo Hierarchicus : The Caste System and Its Implications*, trans. Mark Sainsbury (London: Weidenfeld & Nicholson, 1970)

Edwardes, S. M., *The Rise of Bombay : A Retrospect* [reprinted from vol. 10 of Census of India, 1901] (Bombay, 1902)

Enthoven, R. E., *Tribes and Castes of Bombay*, 3 vols. (Bombay: Government Central Press, 1920–22)

Farquhar, J. N., *An Outline of the Religious Literature of India* (Oxford, 1920)

Fawcett, Sir Charles, *The First Century of British Justice in India* (Oxford: Clarendon Press, 1934)

Fonseca, Jose Nicolau da, *An Historical and Archaeological Sketch of the City of Goa, preceded by a short statistical account of the Territory of Goa* (Bombay: Education Society's Press, 1878)

Forbes, James, *Oriental Memoirs : A Narrative of Seventeen Years Residence in India*, 2nd ed., 2 vols. (London, 1834)

Forrest, G. W., *Cities of India* (Westminster: Archibald Constable, 1903)

Fox, Richard G., "Resiliency and Change in the Indian Caste System: The Umar of U. P.," *Journal of Asian Studies* 26 (1967): 575–587

Fryer, John, *A New Account of East India and Persia, being Nine Years' Travels, 1672–1681*, William Crooke, ed. 2 vols. (London: Hakluyt Society Publications, 2nd series, nos. 19 and 20, 1909–12)

Frykenberg, Robert E., "Traditional Processes of Power in South India," *Indian Economic and Social History Review* 1 (1963): 122–142

———, *Guntur District, 1788–1848: A History of Local Influence and Central Authority in South India* (Oxford: Clarendon Press, 1965)

——— (ed.) *Land Control and Social Structure in Indian History* (Madison: University of Wisconsin Press, 1969)

Ganapathi High School Diamond Jubilee Committee, *Diamond Jubilee Souvenir, Ganapathi High School, Mangalore, 1870–1930* (Mangalore, 1930)

Gereon, P., "Die Konkani-Brahminen an der Malaburkuste," *Anthropos* 32 (1937): 435–439.

Germano da Silva Correia, Alberto C., *Les Mahrattes de l'Inde Portugaise* (Bastora: Imprimarie Rangel, 1934)

Gerson da Cunha, J., *The Origin of Bombay*: *Journal of the Bombay Branch of Royal Asiatic Society, extra number* (Bombay, 1900)

——— (ed.), *The Sahyadri-khanda of the Skanda Purna* (Bombay, 1877)

Ghurye, G. S., *Caste and Race in India* 5th ed. (Bombay: Popular Prakashan, 1961)

———, *Caste, Class and Occupation*, rev. ed. (Bombay: Popular Prakashan, 1961)

Gleig, G. R., *The Life of Major General Sir Thomas Munro*, 3 vols. (London, 1830)

Gode, P. K., "The Antiquity of the Caste Name 'Senavi,'" *Journal of the University of Bombay*, 6 (May 1937): 152–155

Gould, Harold A., "The Adaptive Functions of Caste in Contemporary Indian Society," *Asian Survey* 3 (1963): 427–438.

*Gowd Saraswath Brahman Seva Sangh, Mangalore, Silver Jubilee Souvenir* (Mangalore, 1964)

Grant Duff, J. C., *History of the Mahrattas* rev. ed., 2 vols. (London: Oxford University Press, 1921)

[Grant Duff, Mountstuart Elphinstone], *Minutes by His Excellency the Right Hon. The Governor—1884 and 1886* (Madras, 1886)

[———], *Tour Minutes [1882–83] by the Right Honorable M. E. Grant-Duff, Governor of Madras*, vol. 8 (Madras, n.d.)

Guha, B. S., "Racial Affinities of the Peoples of India," pp. xxix-xxx, in *Census of India, 1931*, volume 1: *India*, part 3: *Ethnographical* (Calcutta, 1933)

Gulvadi, Annaji Rao, *Rohini* (Kannada) (Calicut, 1906) [collection of short stories]

Gulvadi, Venkat Rao, *Indira Bai or the Triumph of Truth and Virtue*, Trans. M. E. Couchman (Mangalore, 1903)

Gulvane, Vāmana Rāmacañdra, *Brāhmaṇa Sabhecī Gelī Saṭha Varṣe* (Marathi) [The Past Sixty Years of the Brahman Sabha] (Bombay: Brahman Sabha, 1949)

Gumperz, Ellen McDonald, "English Education and Social Change in Late Nineteenth-Century Bombay, 1858–1898" (unpub. Ph. D. diss. University of California, Berkeley, 1965)

Gune, Vithal T., *Ancient Shrines of Goa: A Pictorial Survey* (Panjim, 1965)

Guñjīkar, Rāmachañdra Bhikāji, *Sārasvatīmaṇḍala athavā Mahārāṣtra Deśātīla Brāhmaṇājātīce Varnan* (Marathi) [Sarasvata Mandala, or A Description of the Brahman Castes in the Maharashtra Country] (Bombay, 1884)

Guru Dutt, K.—see K[ilpadi] Gurudutt [Sundar]

Harnetty, Peter, "Indian and British Commercial Enterprise: The Case of the Manchester Cotton Company, 1860–1864," *Indian Economic and Social History Review* 3 (1966): 396–421.

Harrison, Selig S., *India : The Most Dangerous Decades* (Princeton : Princeton University Press, 1960)

H[attiangadi] Shankar Rau [Ramarao], *The Chitrapur Saraswat Directory, 1933* (Bombay: author, 1933)

———, *A Chitrapur Saraswat Miscellany* (Bombay: author, 1938)

——— (ed.) *The Shrimat Anandashram Ordination Jubilee Souvenir* (Bombay: editor, 1941)

Hattiangdi, Gopal S., *Fifty Years of Bliss* (Bombay: author, 1965)

———, *Pandurang, Pandurang* (Bombay: author, 1965)

Heimsath, Charles H., *Indian Nationalism and Hindu Social Reform* (Princeton : Princeton University Press, 1964)

Heras, Henry, "Pre-Portuguese Remains in Portuguese India," *Journal of Bombay Historical Society* 4 (1931) : 24–43.

*History of Higher Education in South India*, 2 vols. (Madras: University of Madras, 1957)

Hough, Eleanor, M., *The Co-operative Movement in India* (London: P. S. King, 1932)

Inden, Ronald, *Marriage and Rank in Bengali Culture* (Berkeley and Los Angeles: University of California Press, 1976)

Irschick, Eugene F., *Politics and Social Conflict in South India : The Non-Brahman Movement and Tamil Separatism, 1916–1929* (Berkeley and Los Angeles: University of California Press, 1969)

Jambhekar, Ganesh G:, *Memoirs and Writings of Acharya Bal Gangadhar Shastri Jambhekar (1812–1846) : Pioneer of the Renaissance in Western India and Father of Modern Maharashtra*, 3 vols. (Poona, 1950)

Jayakar, Mukund R., *The History of the Pathare Prabhu Social Samaj, 1888–1913* (Bombay, 1913)

Kalelkar, Govinda Mangeśa, *Mumbaī Ilākhyāñtīla jāti* (Marathi) [Castes in the Bombay Province] (Bombay: A. A. Moramkar, 1928)

Kanara Saraswat Association, *Census of Kanara Saraswats in Bombay, 1912* (Bombay: Kanara Saraswat Association, 1912)

———, *The Kanara Saraswat Association Golden Jubilee Souvenir* (Bombay, n.d. [1961])

———, *Triennial Directory of the Kanara Saraswat Association* (Bombay, 1920)

———, Census Working Committee, *The Chitrapur Saraswat 1956 Census Report and Directory* (Bombay: Kanara Saraswat Association, 1956)

———, ———, *Chitrapur Saraswat 1971 Census Report and Directory* (Bombay: Kanara Saraswat Association, 1972)

———, ———, *Portrait of a Community : Chitrapur Saraswat Census Report* (Bombay : Popular Prakashan, 1972)

Kane, P. V., *History of Dharmaśastra*, 5 vols. (Poona: Bhandarkar Oriental Research Institute, 1930–1962)

Karāṇḍe Śāstrī, Rāmacañdra Vāmana Nayaka, *Kaivalyapura Maṭhācā Sañkṣipta Itihāsa* (Marathi) [Brief History of Kavle Math] (Mhapsa [Goa], Shaka 1832 [A. D. 1910].)

Karnad Sadashiv Rao Memorial Committee, *Apostle of Sacrifice: Deshbhakta Karnad Sadashiv Rao Memorial Volume* (Bombay: Popular Prakashan, 1971)

Karnataki, Śrīnivāsa Nārāyaṇa, *Gurūvarya Dokṭara Sār Rāmakṛṣṇa Gopaḷa Bhandarkar yāñce caritra* (Marathi) [Learned Doctor Sir Ramkrishna Gopal Bhandarkar: A Biography] (Poona, n.d.)

Karve, Irawati, *Hindu Society: An Interpretation* (Poona: Deccan College, 1961)

———, *Kinship Organization in India* (Poona: Deccan College, 1953)

———, and Vishnu Mahadeo Dandekar, *Anthropometric Measurements of Maharashtra* (Poona: Deccan College, 1951)

Karwar Municipality, *Karwar Municipality Centenary Souvenir* (Karwar, 1964)

Katre, Sumitra Mangesh, *The Formation of Konkani* (Poona: Deccan College, 1966)

Keni Śāstrī, Lakṣmana Nārāyaṇa, *Śrī Daśaprakārana* (Marathi) [Honorable Ten Chapters] (Bombay: Shaka 1793 [A. D. 1872])

Ketkar, Shridhar V., *The History of Caste in India*, 2 vols. (Ithaca, N. Y.: Taylor & Carpenter; London: Luzac, 1909–1911) [Vol. 2 title: *An Essay on Hinduism: Its Formation and Future*]

Khanolkar, G. D., "Gauḍasārasvata Brāhmana he mulāñe Bangalīc," *Vividhajñānavistāra* 57 (February 1926): 70–72 (Marathi [The G. S. B. were originally of Bengal]

Khare, Ganesh H., "The Archives of the Vaishnava Matha of Sarasvata Brahmans at Partagali,' *Indian Historical Records Commission: Proceedings* 28 (1951): 50–55.

Khare, R. S., *The Changing Brahmans: Associations and Elites among the Kanya Kubjas of North India* (Chicago: University of Chicago Press, 1970)

K[ilpadi] Guru Dutt Sundar, *Chitrapur Saraswat Retrospect* (Bangalore, 1955)

———, *Hindu Culture: Essays and Addresses* (Bombay: author, 1951)

Koppīkar, Shankara Nārāyaṇa, and Rāmamohan Ve. Koppīkar, *Bailuru Śrī Lakṣminārāyaṇa Devara hāgū ā devara bhajakarāda Koppīkar Kuṭumbada Itihāsa* [History of Bailur Shri Lakshminarayan Temple and Its Devotees, the Koppikar family] (Udipi: authors, 1932)

Kosambi, Damodar Dharmanand, "Development of the Gotra System," pp. 215–224 in *P. K. Gode Commemoration Volume*, part 2 (Poona, 1960)

———, *An Introduction to the Study of Indian History* (Bombay: Popular Book Depot, 1956)

———, *Myth and Reality: Studies in the Formation of Indian Culture* (Bombay: Popular Prakashan, 1962)

Kudva, V. N., *History of the Dakshinatya Saraswats* (Madras: Gowda Saraswat Sabha, 1972)

Leach, Edmund R. (ed.) *Aspects of Caste in South India, Ceylon and Northwest Pakistan* (Cambridge: Cambridge University Press, 1962)

Linschoten, John Huyghen van, *Discourse of Voyages into ye East and West Indies*, 2 vols. London: Hakluyt Society Publications, old series, nos. 70–71, 1885)

Lushington, F., *Comparative Tables of Provincial Establishments, Madras, for 1857* (Madras, 1858)

Maclean, Charles—see under Official Publications, Madras

Maclean, James Mackenzie, *A Guide to Bombay: Historical, Statistical and Descriptive*, 29th ed. (Bombay, 1905)

Madgā̃vkar, Goviñda Nārāyaṇa, *Mumbaĩce Varṇan* (Marathi) [Description of Bombay] (Bombay, 1863) [Has English title page, "Bombay Past and Present"]

Mahratta Education Fund, Madras, *South Indian Maharashtrians: (Cultural and Economic Studies)* (Madras: Mahratta Education Fund, 1937)

Malabari, Behramji M., *Bombay in the Making (1661–1726)* (London: T. Fisher Unwin, 1910)

Mandelbaum, David G., *Society in India*, 2 vols. (Berkeley and Los Angeles: University of California Press, 1970)

*Mangalore Almanac for 1854* (Mangalore, 1853)

*Mangalore Almanac for 1855* (Mangalore, 1854)

Mangalore Municipality, *Centenary Celebration Souvenir, Mangalore Municipality, 1866–1966* (Mangalore, n.d. [1967])

Marriott, McKim, and Ronald B.Inden, "Caste Systems," *Encyclopedia Britannica*, 15th ed., "Macropaedia" 3:982–991.

Marshall, Thomas, *Statistical Reports of Pergunnahs in the Southern Maratha Country* (Bombay, 1822)

Marx, Karl, and Friedrich Engels, *The First Indian War of Independence* (Moscow, 1959)

Mayer, Adrian C., *Caste and Kinship in Central India* (Berkeley and Los Angeles: University of California Press, 1960)

McCormack, William, "Lingayats as a Sect," *Journal of the Royal Anthropological Institute* 93 (1963):59–71.

Menon, K. P. Padmanabha, *A History of Kerala, written in the form of notes on Visscher's letters from Malabar*, T. K. Krishna Menon, ed., 2 vols. (Ernakulam: Cochin Government Press, 1924–29)

Michael, L. W., *The History of the Municipal Corporation of the City of Bombay* (Bombay, 1902)

Minayeff, Ivan P., *Travels and Diaries of India and Burma*, trans. H. Sanyal (Calcutta, n.d.)

Misra, B. B., *The Indian Middle Classes: Their Growth in Modern Times* (London: Oxford University Press, 1961)

Moegling, Hermann, *Twelve Letters* (Mangalore, 1859)

Molesworth, J. T., *A Dictionary: Marathi and English*, 2nd ed. (Bombay, 1857)

Moraes, George Mark, *The Kadamba Kula: A History of Ancient and Medieval Karnataka* (Bombay: B. X. Furtado, 1931)

———, *Mangalore: A Historical Sketch* (Bombay: Indian Historical Research Institute, 1927)

Mullens, Joseph, *Missions in South India Visited and Described* (London, 1854)

Nāḍkarṇī, Ānand, *Kadrekar-Nāḍkarṇī kulavrattāñt* (Marathi) [Kadre Nadkarni Family History] (Bombay: P. S. Nadkarni, 1965)

———, *Karvara* (Marathi) (Karwar: author, 1951)

Nanundayya, H. V., and L. K. Ananthakrishna Iyer (eds.), *The Mysore Tribes and Castes*, 4 vols. (Mysore: Government of Mysore, 1935)

Narasimha Pauranika [of Bhatkal] and Kumta Nārāyaṇacharya, *Śrīguruparāmparāmritama* (Marathi) [The Nectar of the Immortal Succession of Gurus] (Khanapur, Belgaum District, 1904)

Nilakanta Sastri, K. A., *Development of Religion in South India* (Bombay: Orient Longmans, 1963)

———, *A History of South India*, 2nd ed. (Bombay, 1958)

Pai, M. Govinda, "Nama Hiryaranu Kuritu" (Kannada) [Regarding Our Ancestors], pp. 63–85 in *Gowd Saraswath Brahman Seva Sangh, Mangalore, Silver Jubilee Souvenir* (Mangalore, 1964)

Panchanadikar, K. M., and J. M. Panchanadikar, "Process of Social Change in India Under the Colonial and Decolonial Era—An Analysis of Changing Rural-Urban Complex," *Sociological Bulletin* 14, no. 2 (September 1965) :9–26.

Panchapakesa Ayyer, A. S., *Twenty-Five Years a Civilian* (Madras, 1962)

Pandurangashram Swami, *Vidhavodhvāhacikīṣumatabhanjanam* (Kannada) [The breaking into pieces of the opinion of one who wants to do widow marriage] (Bombay: Shaka 1810 [A. D. 1888])

Paruḷekar, Gaṇeśa Mukunda, *Śrī Kuḍaldeśkara kīva Dakṣinetila Adya Gauḍa Brāhmaṇa* (Marathi) [Kudaldeshkars, or The Original Gaud Brahmans in the South] (Bombay, 1915)

Pathare Prabhu Social Samaj, *A Report of the Census of the Pathare Prabhu Community*, taken under the auspices of the Pathare Prabhu Social Samaj on Dec. 5, 1914 (Bombay, 1916)

Patterson, Maureen L. P., "Changing Patterns of Occupations among Chitpavan Brahmans," *Indian Economic and Social History Review* 7 (1970) :375–396.

———, "Chitpavan Brahman Family Histories: Sources for a Study of Social Structure and Social Change in Maharashtra," pp. 397–411 in M. Singer and B. S. Cohn (eds.), *Structure and Change in Indian Society* (Chicago: Aldine, 1968)

Pearson, Michael N., "Wealth and Power: Indian Groups in the Portuguese Indian Economy," *South Asia* 3 (August 1973) :36–44.

Pharoah and Company (pubs.), *A Gazetteer of Southern India* (Madras: Pharoah and Company, 1855)

Pickett, J. Waskom, *Christian Mass Movements in India* (New York, 1933)

Pingulkara, Viṭhṭhala Purūṣottama, *Sāvantvāḍi Saṁsthanacā Itihāsa* [History of Savantvadi State] (Bombay, 1911)

Pisurlēkar [Pissurlencar], Pāṇḍuranga Sadāśiva (ed., *Śrī Śāntādurga Catuśatābdī Mahotsava Grañtha* (Marathi) [Shri Shantadurga Fourth Centenary Commemoration Book] (Bombay, 1966)

Pissurlencar, Panduranga S. S., *Agentes da Diplomacia Portuguesa na India* (*Hindus, mucalmanos, judeus, e parses*) (Bastora: Tipografia Rangel, 1952)

———, *Goa Pré-Portuguesa atraves dos Escritores Lusitanos dos Seculos XVI e XVII* (Bastora: Tipografia Rangel, 1962)

———, *Portugueses e Marathas*, 6 vols. (Nova Goa, Bastora, 1926–40)

Prabhakar, Sharada [Amembal], "*Anna*" : *The Life Story of Devarao Shivaram Ubhayakar* (Bombay: Popular Book Depot, 1960)

Prabhu, M. N. (pub.), *Sārasvata Samāja* : *Koṇkani Brāhmaṇarendare Yaru*? (Kannada) [Saraswat Community: Who Are the Konkani Brahmans?] (Mangalore: M. N. Prabhu, 1938)

Priolkar, Anant Kakba, *The Goa Inquisition, Being a Quatercentenary Commemoration Study of the Inquisition in India* (Bombay: author, 1961)

Punāḷekara, Rāmacañdra Namdēva, *Bārdeśkara Gauḍa Sārasvata Brāhmaṇācā Itihāsa va Jantrī* (Marathi) [Bardeshkar GSB History and Census] (Bombay, 1939)

Raghavan, V. "Methods of Popular Religious Instruction in South India," pp. 503–514 in *The Cultural Heritage of India*, rev. ed., vol. 4 (Calcutta, 1956)

Raghunathji, K., *The Hindu Temples of Bombay* (Bombay: author, 1900)

Rājādhyakṣa, Narahara Vyankaji, *Śindeśāhīca Kharā Itihāsa athvā Bakṣībahādar Mujāphara Daula Jivājī Ballāl urf Jivabādādā Kerkar Bahādar Phattejanga yañce caritra* . . . (Marathi) [True History of the Sindhias, or the biography of Jivaji Ballal alias Jivabadada Kerkar] (Bombay, 1907)

Renou, Louis, *Religions of Ancient India* (New York: Schocken, 1968)

Richter, G., *Manual of Coorg* : *A Gazetteer of the Natural Features of the Country and the Social and Political Condition of Its Inhabitants* (Mangalore, 1870)

Richter, Julius, *A History of Missions in India*, trans. Sydney H. Moore (Edinburgh: Oliphant, Anderson & Ferrier, 1908)

Rudolph, Lloyd I., and Susanne H. Rudolph, "The Political Role of India's Caste Associations," *Pacific Affairs* 28 (1955) :235–253

Saldanha, C. F., *A Short History of Goa* ([Nova] Goa: Imprensa Nacional, 1957)

Saldanha, Jerome Antony, *The Indian Caste*, vol. 1: *Konkani or Goan Castes* (Sirsi, N. K., 1904)

———, "Savantwadi Castes and Village Communities," *Journal of the Anthropological Society of Bombay* 8 (1909) :498–520

Saletore, Bhaskar Anand, *Ancient Karnataka*, vol. 1: *History of Tulava* (Poona: Oriental Book Agency, 1936)

Sankalia, Hasmukh D., *Studies in the Historical & Cultural Geography and Ethnography of Gujarat* . . . (Poona: Deccan College, 1949)

*Saraswat Association, Madras, Souvenir, April 9, 1967* (Madras, 1967)

Saraswat Association, Madras, *Golden Jubilee Celebrations of Shri Krishna and Shri Datta Jayantis* (Madras, 1970)

Sardesai, Govind S., *New History of the Marathas*, 3 vols. (Bombay: Phoenix, 1946–48)

Sarkar, U. C., *Epochs in Hindu Legal History* (Hoshiarpur, 1958)

Śarma, Maṭhāstha Gaṇeśa Rāmacañdra, *Mañgaḷūra yethe 1907/08 salī bharleli Gauḍasārasvata Brāhmana Pariṣad va ticī vistrita hakigata.* (Marathi) [The 1907–08 meetings of the Gaud Saraswat Brahman Parishad in Mangalore and their amplified report] (Khanapur, Belgaum District, 1909)

———, *Sārasvata Bhūṣaṇa* (Marathi) [An Ornament to the Saraswats] (Bombay: Popular Book Depot, 1950)

———, *Sārasvata Ratnamala* (Marathi) [A Necklace of Saraswat Gems], vol. 1 (Belgaum, 1910)

Sastri, Sivanath, *History of the Brahmo Samaj*, 2 vols. (Calcutta, 1911–12)

Seal, Anil, *The Emergence of Indian Nationalism: Competition and Collaboration in the Later Nineteenth Century* (Cambridge: Cambridge University Press, 1968)

Śeḷdekara, Viṣṇu Rañgājī, *Gomantakāñtīla Gauḍa Sārasvata Brāhmaṇa aṇi tyāñce Kuladeva* (Marathi) [The GSB in Goa and their Family Deities] (Bombay: author, 1938)

———, and Mukuñda Sadāśiva Śeḷdekara, *Gomantakāñtīla Kaivalyapura [Kavle] yethīla Śrī Śāntadurgā Saṃsthānacā Sañkṣipta Itihāsa.* (Marathi) [A Brief History of Shri Shantadurga Temple at Kavle in Goa] 2nd ed. (Bombay: authors, 1935)

Shankar Rau, H.—see H [attiangadi] Shankar Rau Ramarao

Singer, Milton, and Bernard S. Cohn (eds.) *Structure and Change in Indian Society* (Chicago: Aldine, 1968)

Sohanī, Rāmacañdra Narahara, *Gauḍasārasvata Brāhmaṇāñcā Itihāsa* (Marathi) [GSB History] (Khanapur, Belgaum District, 1937)

Somappa, H., *A Brief History of the Mangalore Brahmo Samaj, 1870–1970* (Mangalore, n.d. [c. 1970])

Spate, O. H. K., and A. T. A. Learmonth, *India and Pakistan: A general and Regional Geography*, 3rd ed. (New York: Barnes & Noble, 1967)

Srinivas, M. N., *Caste in Modern India and Other Essays* (Bombay: Asia Publishing House, 1962)

———, et al, "Caste: A Trend Report and Bibliography," *Current Sociology* 8 (1959): 135–183.

Srinivasachari, C. S., *History of the City of Madras* (Madras, 1939)

Steele, Arthur, *The Law and Custom of Hindoo Castes within the Dekhun Provinces subject to the Presidency of Bombay, chiefly affecting civil suits* (London: W. H. Allen, 1868 ["A New Edition," reprint of 1827 ed.])

Stein, Burton, "Integration of the Agrarian System of South India," pp. 175–216 in R. E. Frykenbrg (ed.), *Land Control and Social Structure in Indian History* (Madison; University of Wisconsin Press, 1969)

———, "Social Mobility and Meḍieval South Indian Hindu Sects," pp. 78–94 in James Silverberg (ed.), *Social Mobility in the Caste System in India: An Interdisciplinary Symposium* [*Comparative Studies in Society and History: Supplement III*] (The Hague: Mouton, 1968)

Swaminathan, K. D., *The Nayakas of Ikkeri* (Madras: P. Varadachary, 1957)

Talmaki, S[hripad] S., *Saraswat Families*, 3 vols. (Bombay: author, Kanara Saraswat Association, 1935–50)

Thurston, Edgar, *Castes and Tribes of Southern India*, 7 vols. (Madras, 1909)

Trilokekar, S. N. M., *The Pathare Prabhu Social Club Golden Jubilee Souvenir* (Bombay, 1938)

Tripathi, Dwijendranath, "Opportunism of Free Trade—The Sadasheogarh Harbour Project, 1855–1865," *Indian Economic and Social History Review* 5 (1968): 389–406.

U[dyavar] Ananda Rao, *A Life Sketch of Karnick Devapah, Head Sheristedar, Canara District* (Cocanada: author, 1915)

———, *Life Sketch of Udyavar Ananda Rau* (Mangalore: author, 1934)

U[grankar] V[enkatrao] L., *A Brief Biographical Sketch of Shamrao Vithal Kaikini, J. P.: A Saraswat Patriot and Philanthropist* (Bombay, 1911)

Vagḷe, Śrīpāda Vyāñkateśa (pub.), *Konkanakyāna urf Dakṣinatya Sārasvata Brāhamaṇakhyāna* (Marathi) (Bombay: S. V. Vagle, Shaka 1831 [A. D. 1909])

Vaidya, Dvarkanāṭha Goviñda, *Nārāyaṇa Ganeśa Cañdavarkar* (Marathi) [a biography] (Bombay: Karnataka Publishing House, 1937)

[Varde-Vālāvalīkār, Vāmanrao Rāghunātha] Śaṇaī Gõyabāba, *Góyakārāñcī Gõyābhāyalī Vasṇūka* [Konkani] [The Habitation of Goans Outside Goa], vol. 1 (Bombay: Gomantak Press, 1928)

———, *Kāhi Marāṭhi Lekha* (Marathi) [Some Marathi Writings], part 1 (Bombay: author, 1945)

Venkataraman, K. R., *The Throne of Transcendental Wisdom: Sri Sankaracharya's Sarada Pitha in Srngeri*, 2nd ed. (Madras: Akhila Bharata Samkara Seva Samiti, 1967)

Venn, T. W., *Mangalore* ([Cochin], 1945)

Weber, Max, *The Religion of India: The Sociology of Hinduism and Buddhism*, trans. H. H. Gerth and Don Martindale (Glencoe, Ill.: Free Press, 1958)

*The West Coast Directory*, 1920 (Calicut, n.d.)

Wilks, Mark, *Historical Sketches of the South of India*, 2 vols. Mysore, 1930)

Wilson, Horace Hayman, *A Glossary of Judicial and Revenue Terms and of Useful Words*, rev. ed. (Calcutta: Eastern Law Book House, 1940)

Wilson, John, *Indian Caste*, 2 vols. (Bombay: Times of India, 1877)

Xavier, Filipe Nery, *Bosquejo Historico das Communidades das Aldeas das Concelhas Ilhas, Salcete a Bardez*, 2nd ed., 3 vols. (Bastora: Tipografia Rangel, 1903–07)

Zachariah, K. C., *Migrants in Greater Bombay* (Bombay: Asia Publishing House, 1968)

# INDEX